Remembering and Forgetting Early Childhood

This book brings together the scholarship that contributes diverse new perspectives on childhood amnesia – the scarcity of memories for very early life events.

The topics of the studies reported in the book range from memories of infants and young children for recent and distant life events, to mother–child conversations about memories for extended lifetime periods, and to retrospective recollections of early childhood in adolescents and adults. The methodological approaches are diverse and theoretical insights rich. The findings together show that childhood amnesia is a complex and malleable phenomenon and that the waning of childhood amnesia and the development of autobiographical memory are shaped by a variety of interactive social and cognitive factors.

This book will facilitate discussion and deepen an understanding of the dynamics that influence the accessibility, content, accuracy, and phenomenological qualities of memories from early childhood. This book was originally published as a special issue of *Memory*.

Qi Wang is Professor of Human Development at Cornell University. Her research examines individual and cultural mechanisms underlying autobiographical memory. She is the author of *The Autobiographical Self in Time and Culture*.

Sami Gülgöz is Professor of Psychology at Koç University. His past work includes topics varying from text processing to personality. In the last decade, he has concentrated on memory in everyday life, primarily autobiographical memory.

Remembering and Forgetting Early Childhood

***Edited by*
Qi Wang and Sami Gülgöz**

LONDON AND NEW YORK

First published 2020
by Routledge
2 Park Square, Milton Park, Abingdon, Oxon, OX14 4RN

and by Routledge
52 Vanderbilt Avenue, New York, NY 10017

Routledge is an imprint of the Taylor & Francis Group, an informa business

© 2020 Taylor & Francis

Chapter 1 © 2018 Ineke Wessel, Theresa Schweig and Rafaële J. C. Huntjens. Originally published as Open Access.

With the exception of Chapter 1, no part of this book may be reprinted or reproduced or utilised in any form or by any electronic, mechanical, or other means, now known or hereafter invented, including photocopying and recording, or in any information storage or retrieval system, without permission in writing from the publishers. For details on the rights for Chapter 1, please see the chapter's Open Access footnote.

Trademark notice: Product or corporate names may be trademarks or registered trademarks, and are used only for identification and explanation without intent to infringe.

British Library Cataloguing in Publication Data
A catalogue record for this book is available from the British Library

ISBN13: 978-0-367-46630-5

Typeset in Myriad Pro
by Newgen Publishing UK

Publisher's Note
The publisher accepts responsibility for any inconsistencies that may have arisen during the conversion of this book from journal articles to book chapters, namely the inclusion of journal terminology.

Disclaimer
Every effort has been made to contact copyright holders for their permission to reprint material in this book. The publishers would be grateful to hear from any copyright holder who is not here acknowledged and will undertake to rectify any errors or omissions in future editions of this book.

Contents

Citation Information	vi
Notes on Contributors	viii
Introduction: New perspectives on childhood amnesia *Qi Wang and Sami Gülgöz*	1
1 Manipulating the reported age in earliest memories *Ineke Wessel, Theresa Schweig and Rafaële J. C. Huntjens*	6
2 Looking at the past through a telescope: adults postdated their earliest childhood memories *Qi Wang, Carole Peterson, Angel Khuu, Carissa P. Reid, Kayleigh L. Maxwell and Julia M. Vincent*	19
3 Consistency of adults' earliest memories across two years *Berivan Ece, Burcu Demiray and Sami Gülgöz*	28
4 Thirty-five-month-old children have spontaneous memories despite change of context for retrieval *Trine Sonne, Osman S. Kingo, Dorthe Berntsen and Peter Krøjgaard*	38
5 What happened in kindergarten? Mother-child conversations about life story chapters *Michelle D. Leichtman, Kristina L. Steiner, Kaitlin A. Camilleri, David B. Pillemer and Dorthe Kirkegaard Thomsen*	49
6 Predictors of age-related and individual variability in autobiographical memory in childhood *Patricia J. Bauer and Marina Larkina*	63
7 Origins of adolescents' earliest memories *Elaine Reese and Sarah-Jane Robertson*	79
8 Recollection improves with age: children's and adults' accounts of their childhood experiences *Karen Tustin and Harlene Hayne*	92
9 The relationship between sociocultural factors and autobiographical memories from childhood: the role of formal schooling *Manuel L. de la Mata, Andrés Santamaría, Eva Mª Trigo, Mercedes Cubero, Samuel Arias-Sánchez, Radka Antalíková, Tia G.B. Hansen and Marcia L. Ruiz*	103
10 Unravelling the nature of early (autobiographical) memory *Mark L. Howe*	115
Index	122

Citation Information

The chapters in this book were originally published in *Memory*, volume 27, issue 1 (2019). When citing this material, please use the original page numbering for each article, as follows:

Introduction: New perspectives on childhood amnesia
Qi Wang and Sami Gülgöz
Memory, volume 27, issue 1 (2019), pp. 1–5

Chapter 1
Manipulating the reported age in earliest memories
Ineke Wessel, Theresa Schweig and Rafaële J. C. Huntjens
Memory, volume 27, issue 1 (2019), pp. 6–18

Chapter 2
Looking at the past through a telescope: adults postdated their earliest childhood memories
Qi Wang, Carole Peterson, Angel Khuu, Carissa P. Reid, Kayleigh L. Maxwell and Julia M. Vincent
Memory, volume 27, issue 1 (2019), pp. 19–27

Chapter 3
Consistency of adults' earliest memories across two years
Berivan Ece, Burcu Demiray and Sami Gülgöz
Memory, volume 27, issue 1 (2019), pp. 28–37

Chapter 4
Thirty-five-month-old children have spontaneous memories despite change of context for retrieval
Trine Sonne, Osman S. Kingo, Dorthe Berntsen and Peter Krøjgaard
Memory, volume 27, issue 1 (2019), pp. 38–48

Chapter 5
What happened in kindergarten? Mother-child conversations about life story chapters
Michelle D. Leichtman, Kristina L. Steiner, Kaitlin A. Camilleri, David B. Pillemer and Dorthe Kirkegaard Thomsen
Memory, volume 27, issue 1 (2019), pp. 49–62

Chapter 6
Predictors of age-related and individual variability in autobiographical memory in childhood
Patricia J. Bauer and Marina Larkina
Memory, volume 27, issue 1 (2019), pp. 63–78

Chapter 7
Origins of adolescents' earliest memories
Elaine Reese and Sarah-Jane Robertson
Memory, volume 27, issue 1 (2019), pp. 79–91

Chapter 8
Recollection improves with age: children's and adults' accounts of their childhood experiences
Karen Tustin and Harlene Hayne
Memory, volume 27, issue 1 (2019), pp. 92–102

Chapter 9
The relationship between sociocultural factors and autobiographical memories from childhood: the role of formal schooling
Manuel L. de la Mata, Andrés Santamaría, Eva Mª Trigo, Mercedes Cubero, Samuel Arias-Sánchez, Radka Antalíková, Tia G.B. Hansen and Marcia L. Ruiz
Memory, volume 27, issue 1 (2019), pp. 103–114

Chapter 10
Unravelling the nature of early (autobiographical) memory
Mark L. Howe
Memory, volume 27, issue 1 (2019), pp. 115–121

For any permission-related enquiries please visit:
www.tandfonline.com/page/help/permissions

Notes on Contributors

Radka Antalíková, Department of Communication and Psychology, Aalborg University, Aalborg, Denmark

Samuel Arias-Sánchez, Department of Experimental Psychology, University of Seville, Seville, Spain

Patricia J. Bauer, Department of Psychology, Emory University, Atlanta, GA, USA

Dorthe Berntsen, Center on Autobiographical Memory Research, Department of Psychology and Behavioral Sciences, Aarhus University, Aarhus C, Denmark

Kaitlin A. Camilleri, Department of Psychology, University of New Hampshire, Durham, USA

Mercedes Cubero, Department of Experimental Psychology, University of Seville, Seville, Spain

Burcu Demiray, Department of Psychology, University of Zurich, Zürich, Switzerland

Berivan Ece, Department of Psychology, Faculty of Economics, Administrative and Social Sciences, MEF University, Istanbul, Turkey

Sami Gülgöz, Department of Psychology, Koç University, Istanbul, Turkey

Tia G.B. Hansen, Department of Communication and Psychology, Aalborg University, Aalborg, Denmark

Harlene Hayne, Psychology Department, University of Otago, Dunedin, New Zealand

Mark L. Howe, Department of Psychology, City, University of London, London, UK

Rafaële J. C. Huntjens, Clinical Psychology and Experimental Psychopathology, University of Groningen, Groningen, Netherlands

Angel Khuu, Department of Human Development, Cornell University, Ithaca, NY, USA

Dorthe Kirkegaard Thomsen, Department of Psychology and Behavioural Sciences, CON AMORE, Aarhus University, Aarhus C, Denmark

Peter Krøjgaard, Center on Autobiographical Memory Research, Department of Psychology and Behavioral Sciences, Aarhus University, Aarhus C, Denmark

Osman S. Kingo, Center on Autobiographical Memory Research, Department of Psychology and Behavioral Sciences, Aarhus University, Aarhus C, Denmark

Marina Larkina, Department of Psychology, Emory University, Atlanta, GA, USA

Michelle D. Leichtman, Department of Psychology, University of New Hampshire, Durham, USA

Manuel L. de la Mata, Department of Experimental Psychology, University of Seville, Seville, Spain

Kayleigh L. Maxwell, Department of Psychology, Memorial University of Newfoundland, Newfoundland, Canada

Carole Peterson, Department of Psychology, Memorial University of Newfoundland, Newfoundland, Canada

David B. Pillemer, Department of Psychology, University of New Hampshire, Durham, USA

Carissa P. Reid, Department of Psychology, Memorial University of Newfoundland, Newfoundland, Canada

Elaine Reese, Psychology Department, University of Otago, Dunedin, New Zealand

Sarah-Jane Robertson, Psychology Department, University of Otago, Dunedin, New Zealand

Marcia L. Ruiz, Multidisciplinary Academic Unit of Sciences, Education and Humanities, Autonomous University of Tamaulipas, Victoria, Mexico

Andrés Santamaría, Department of Experimental Psychology, University of Seville, Seville, Spain

Theresa Schweig, Clinical Psychology and Experimental Psychopathology, University of Groningen, Groningen, Netherlands

Trine Sonne, Center on Autobiographical Memory Research, Department of Psychology and Behavioral Sciences, Aarhus University, Aarhus C, Denmark

Kristina L. Steiner, Department of Psychology, University of New Hampshire, Durham, USA

Eva Mª Trigo, Department of Experimental Psychology, University of Seville, Seville, Spain

Karen Tustin, Psychology Department, University of Otago, Dunedin, New Zealand

Julia M. Vincent, Department of Psychology, Memorial University of Newfoundland, Newfoundland, Canada

Qi Wang, Department of Human Development, Cornell University, Ithaca, NY, USA

Ineke Wessel, Clinical Psychology and Experimental Psychopathology, University of Groningen, Groningen, Netherlands

Introduction: New perspectives on childhood amnesia

Qi Wang and Sami Gülgöz

ABSTRACT
This special issue brings together the scholarship that contributes diverse new perspectives on childhood amnesia – the scarcity of memories for very early life events. The topics of the studies reported in the special issue range from memories of infants and young children for recent and distant life events, to mother–child conversations about memories for extended lifetime periods, and to retrospective recollections of early childhood in adolescents and adults. The methodological approaches are diverse and theoretical insights rich. The findings together show that childhood amnesia is a complex and malleable phenomenon and that the waning of childhood amnesia and the development of autobiographical memory are shaped by a variety of interactive social and cognitive factors. This collective body of work will facilitate discussion and deepen our understanding of the dynamics that influence the accessibility, content, accuracy, and phenomenological qualities of memories from early childhood.

This special issue of Memory is devoted to research that brings together new perspectives on childhood memory. Since the time Freud (1905/1953) noted the phenomenon of childhood amnesia – the scarcity of memories for very early life events – the fascination with childhood memory has persisted both in popular culture and among memory researchers. In the general public, there is considerable interest in the "mystery of why you can't remember being a baby" (http://www.bbc.com/future/story/20160726-the-mystery-of-why-you-cant-remember-being-a-baby). In psychology and related fields, numerous studies have been done and theories developed to account for the neurological, cognitive, linguistic, social, and cultural mechanisms underlying the paucity of early memories and the flourishing of memory from late preschool years onward (e.g., Bauer, 2015; Hayne, 2004; Howe, 2003; Josselyn & Frankland, 2012; Nelson & Fivush, 2004; Pillemer & White, 1989; Reese, 2009; Rubin, 2000; Wang, 2013).

More recently, there have been some exciting new findings that provide important extensions and empirical evidence to what has already been known about this intriguing phenomenon, while others pose questions and challenges to existing theories and shed critical lights on the forgetting and retention of early memories (e.g., Akhtar, Justice, Morrison, & Conway, 2018; Kingo, Bohn, & Krøjgaard, 2013; Reese, Jack, & White, 2010; Wang & Peterson, 2014). This special issue brings together the scholarship that contributes diverse new perspectives, with the aim to facilitate discussion and deepen our understanding of the dynamics that influence the accessibility, content, accuracy, and phenomenological qualities of memories from early childhood. The contributions reflect two general themes.

First, earliest childhood memories are vulnerable to reconstruction and errors

Although the idea that memory is subject to reconstruction in line with individuals' current goals and general knowledge is not new (Bartlett, 1932), only until recent decades have researchers started to examine the veracity of early childhood memories. Previous studies that attempted to verify participants' memories with parents or other adults who were present at the time of the events have concluded that earliest childhood memories of both children and adults are generally accurate in content and age estimates (Bauer, Burch, Scholin, & Güler, 2007; Bruce, Dolan, & Phillips-Grant, 2000; Howes, Siegel, & Brown, 1993; Jack, MacDonald, Reese, & Hayne, 2009; Peterson, Wang, & Hou, 2009). However, with new methodological and analytical approaches, more recent studies have provided evidence that earliest childhood memories are highly malleable and that the age at earliest memory can shift across contexts and time (e.g., Kingo et al., 2013; Wang & Peterson, 2014, 2016).

Several studies in the special issue have examined the estimated age of adults' earliest childhood memories. Working with two large samples of young adults, Wessel, Schweig, and Huntjens found that the retrieval and dating of earliest childhood memories were highly sensitive to contextual factors such as whether the instructions allowed sketchy memories, consistent with other recent findings (e.g., Kingo et al., 2013). In study 1, participants who read examples of earliest memories from around age 2 prior to the memory task recalled earlier first memories and were more likely to guess their age when dating their memories, compared with those who read memory examples from around age 6. Similarly, in study 2, participants who were reminded of personal or public information from their first three years of life recalled earlier first memories than those who were not reminded of any information from an early life-time period. These findings demonstrate that earliest childhood memories are not fixed but malleable. Notably, because the manipulation was done prior to the recall and dating of earliest childhood memories, participants in the early or experimental condition might have recalled memories from an earlier time period or simply dated their memories at an earlier age. Thus, whether the contextual factors facilitate memory retrieval or interfere with memory dating or both remains an open question.

Wang, Peterson and colleagues examined the accuracy of memory dating by verifying young adult participants' age estimates of their earliest childhood memories with independent age estimates collected from the participants' parents. Their findings are consistent with what they have previously observed among children (Wang & Peterson, 2014, 2016; Wang, Peterson, & Hou, 2010). For the memories that parents dated as happening before 48 months, young adults dated significantly later by approximately 12 months (Study 1) and 6 months (Study 2). Adjusting for the telescoping error of postdating memories resulted in an age of earliest memories at 2.5 years, one year earlier than what is commonly believed at 3.5 years. Wang, Peterson and colleagues called the attention of memory researchers that when verifying the dating accuracy of early childhood memories, it is important to take into account the age at encoding. Pooling all memories together by comparing the *mean* age estimate provided by participants against the *mean* age estimate provided by parents or participants themselves previously can lead to the false conclusion that there are no systematic dating errors in early childhood memories (e.g., Bauer et al., 2007; Bruce et al., 2000; Eacott & Crawley, 1998; Howes et al., 1993; Jack et al., 2009).

Ece, Demiray, and Gülgöz provided direct evidence for the importance of considering the age at coding to detect memory dating errors. They tested young adults' earliest childhood memories at two time points, where participants reported their earliest memories, estimated ages, and rated their recollections on memory qualities with a two-year interval. They found that the *mean* age estimates of earliest memories from the two time points were almost identical, consistent with prior studies using a similar analytical approach (e.g., Bauer et al., 20072007; Bruce et al., 2000; Eacott & Crawley, 1998; Howes et al., 1993 Jack et al., 2009). However, when examining the memories on the basis of a 48-month cutoff point, Ece and colleagues found that participants predated their "later" memories for 9.36 months and postdated their "earlier" memories for 3.72 months at time 2 (although the postdating effect was nonsignificant). Furthermore, almost half of the participants (44%) at time 2 recalled a different earliest childhood memory from time 1, which demonstrates again that earliest childhood memories are not fixed but malleable. The rated qualities of earliest memories (e.g., emotional intensity, personal importance) showed high levels of consistency across the two time points, which suggests stable individual characteristics in childhood recollections. Together, these studies point to the necessity to investigate the mechanisms underlying memory dating and how they interact with the context and the processes of remembering.

Modern societies intervene the developmental process by educating the children and thus influencing their development in many respects, including social, cognitive, and linguistic development (Burger, 2010; Cole, 1992). It is therefore pertinent to investigate how literacy and education impact memory processes. The study by de la Mata, Santamaria, Trigo, Cubero, Arias, Antalikova, Hansen, and Ruiz examined the changes associated with the educational levels of adults in the content of memories for early childhood. Across three levels of education – just literate, basic education, and university degree – the researchers compared memory qualities and the autonomous orientation, self-orientation, and individual versus social orientation. They observed both quantitative and qualitative differences in the memories, whereby university graduates reported more voluminous and specific memories than did the other two groups and also reported memories that were more self-focused and individually oriented. These results provide a glimpse of the probable influence of education not only in terms of how and how well childhood events are remembered but also in terms of the role of the self in the construction of autobiographical memory.

Second, developmental research is critical for our understanding of the mechanisms underlying childhood amnesia

Childhood amnesia appears to be an emerging phenomenon. Although adults exhibit limited abilities to retrieve memories from their early childhood, young children, including toddlers, are capable of recalling information about their past experiences following delays of days, months, and even years (e.g., Bauer, 2015; Hayne, Gross, McNamee, Fitzgibbon, & Tustin, 2011; Jack, Simcock, & Hayne, 2012; Reese, 2009). Yet many of the early memories become inaccessible or "forgotten" as children grow older such that by late adolescence, children exhibit childhood amnesia to a similar extent or magnitude as adults do (see Bauer, 2015, for a review). What happened to those very early memories? Can they be accessed under certain conditions? For the memories that survive, what are the factors that make it possible? And what are the cognitive and social origins for the memories that flourish following the childhood amnesia period? These questions key to childhood amnesia need to be answered through developmental research. Several articles in the special issue illuminate on new methods and approaches to studying the complex process of autobiographical memory development across childhood.

Extending the wealth of developmental research showing the amazing abilities of even very young children to remember past experiences following extended delays (e.g., Bauer, 2015; Hayne et al., 2011; Jack et al., 2012; Reese, 2009), the study by Sonne, Kingo, Berntsen, and Krøjgaard investigated the influence of contextual cues on children's memory for a previously experienced event. Rather than asking young children to recall and talk about their past experiences, a method commonly used in memory research, Sonne and colleagues examined spontaneous verbal memories triggered by contextual cues, which is less cognitively demanding and may thus better reflect young children's memory competence. A group of 35-month old children visited the lab and engaged in some fun activities. One week later the children revisited the lab, with half of them being sent to the same room as the first visit and the other half to a visually distinct new room, as a manipulation of the contextual cues. The children spontaneously talked about the activities they experienced a week before. However, the spontaneous memories were not significantly reduced by the children's returning to a new room, which suggests that the change of room might not be sufficiently salient to the children. The researchers offered several explanations of their findings in relation to childhood amnesia.

Research on childhood memory, and autobiographical memory more generally, has focused on episodic memory for specific, one-moment-in-time events. Yet, in challenging the privileged statues of episodic memory in memory theories and research, there has been increasing evidence that other forms of memory, such as vicarious memory for experiences of other people and general memory for routine or repeated events, can be just as important for individuals' sense of self, connection with important others, and well-being (Peterson, Baker-Ward, & Grovenstein, 2016; Pillemer, Steiner, Kuwabara, Thomsen, & Svob, 2015; Steiner, Pillemer, & Thomsen, 2017; Wang, 2013). In two studies, Leichtman, Steiner, Camilleri, Pillemer, and Thomsen examined life chapter memories – memory for extended lifetime periods – and the socialisation through mother–child conversations. Mothers were asked to discuss with their kindergarten children extended periods in the children's lives (study 1), or with their school-aged children the kindergarten year versus a specific episode (study 2). The researchers found that the life-chapter conversations largely focused on general information (e.g., people, locations, activities) and repeated events; and that the mothers' memory questions and yes/no questions during a conversation were effective to elicit memory responses from children. In addition, individual differences in maternal conversational style and child contribution were consistent across different types of conversations. This work represents a significant extension to research on the contribution of family narrative practices to memory development (Nelson & Fivush, 2004; Reese et al., 2010; Wang, 2013). It calls for more research on general memory and the role such memory plays in childhood amnesia.

Other than asking the question of why we forget memories from the earliest years of life, Bauer and Larkina asked the question of why we remember memories from the late preschool years onward. They conducted a 3-year cohort-sequential study, following samples of 4-year-olds, 6-year-olds, and 8-year-olds to observe age-related changes in autobiographical memory over a 3-year period. In addition to children's memory reports, they measured at each time point a variety of potential correlates, including language skills, maternal narrative style, domain-general cognitive abilities (speed of processing, working memory, sustained attention), and memory-specific abilities (non-autobiographical story recall, deliberate and strategic remembering and metamemory, source memory). The researchers found that the children's memories became increasingly lengthy, complete, and coherent. Non-autobiographical story recall and other memory-specific as well as domain-general cognitive abilities predicted memory growth, whereas language skills and maternal narrative style did not when the other predictors were taken into consideration. This study provides valuable data and insights into the correlates of the flourishing of memories following the childhood amnesia period by including domain-general cognitive variables that may underlie specific skills.

Reese and Robertson's impressive longitudinal study traced the development of childhood amnesia from age 1.5 years through adolescence. The researchers included a battery of measures at the early childhood phase, including self-awareness, attachment security, nonverbal and verbal memory, language and narrative skills, theory of mind, and maternal narrative style. The earliest memories were measured at ages 12 and 16 years. The researchers found that childhood amnesia continued to develop during adolescence such that the age of earliest memory was shifting to older ages over the 4-year period, from 40 months at age 12 to 52 months at age 16. Maternal narrative style emerged to be the single most important predictor for individual differences in the age of earliest memory, whereby higher levels of maternal elaborative reminiscing in early childhood were uniquely associated with earlier first memories at both adolescent ages. At age 16, this association was further moderated by children's self-awareness early on, such as higher levels of elaborative reminiscing were associated with earlier first memories only in adolescents who had lower levels of self-awareness as toddlers. These findings support integrated theories that view the demise of early memories as a result of a complex interplay among a variety of neural-cognitive-social-linguistic factors.

Bridging the first and second themes, the cross-sectional study by Tustin and Hayne examined the malleability of the content of early childhood memories by taking into account both age at encoding and age at retrieval. The researchers interviewed adults for childhood memories and interviewed children and young adolescents about recent events. The age at encoding could therefore be matched by, for example, asking both adults and 5-year-old children to recall events from when they were age 5. Although adults would have been expected to report less information about the events given that their retention interval was substantially longer than that of the children (more than a decade versus less than a month), Tustin and Hayne found that adults in fact reported more event details than did children. Adults also reported the same amount of information regardless of whether the events took place in their childhood or recently. The researchers suggested that adults' retrospective reports of childhood events might include not just what they originally encoded as children, but also information from other sources such as family stories, photos and videos, as well as inferences based on personal knowledge. Thus, retrospective studies with adults may have overestimated the content of early childhood memories. These findings demonstrate that studying children's memory can provide critical insights about adults' childhood memory. They further have important implications for memory theories and real-life settings (e.g., in the court).

Take home messages

The studies reported in this special issue suggest that childhood amnesia is a complex and malleable phenomenon and that some of the common beliefs about childhood amnesia, such as those pertaining to the age of earliest memory and the content of early childhood memories, need to be revisited (Ece, Demiray, & Gülgöz, 2019; Tustin & Hayne, 2019; Wang et al., 2019; Wessel, Schweig, & Huntjens, 2019). If the "onset" of childhood amnesia is indeed as elusive as the studies have shown, then theories built around a fixed age of earliest memory, namely 3.5 years, beg for reflection and revision. The context of remembering and the individual differences clearly influence the ages of these memories, the estimations of the dates, or both. Interestingly, in the studies by Reese and Robertson (2019) and Tustin and Hayne (2019), the content and age estimates of the memories reported by participating children and adults, when presented to parents for verification, were judged by parents as largely accurate. These findings differ from those of studies when *independent* recall and dating information was obtained from parents (Wang et al., 2010, 2019) or participants themselves at different time points (Ece et al., 2019; Wang & Peterson, 2014, 2016). The methodological differences should be addressed in future research in evaluating memory accuracy and the dating processes. It is evident in Ece et al. (2019) that in some cases, even if the memories reported as earliest memories are consistent across time, the ages attributed to these memories may change, suggesting different processes for remembering and dating. Therefore, it is necessary that future research addresses the influences of contexts of remembering and individual differences both and independently on the processes of remembering and dating.

Moreover, the studies in the special issue reveal that a variety of social and cognitive factors influence the nature of childhood memories in children and adults (e.g., de la Mata et al., 2019; Sonne, Kingo, Berntsen, & Krøjgaard, 2019). They further suggest that social and cognitive factors may interact in determining whether the characteristics of early childhood memories are associated with particular environmental and individual variables. For example, maternal reminiscing style may emerge as a strong predictor for memory development (Leichtman, Steiner, Pillemer, Camilleri, & Thomsen, 2019; Reese & Robertson, 2019) except when other cognitive variables were included in the prediction formula (Bauer & Larkina, 2019). More large scale and longitudinal studies are called for to examine multiple factors and their interactions in shaping memory development throughout childhood and adolescence and the retrospective recollections of early childhood in adults. Such studies may require team science and multilevel approaches and will contribute to the theoretical understanding of childhood amnesia.

Disclosure statement

No potential conflict of interest was reported by the authors.

References

Akhtar, S., Justice, L. V., Morrison, C. M., & Conway, M. A. (2018). Fictional first memories. *Psychological Science*, 1–8. doi:10.1177/0956797618778831

Bartlett, F. C. (1932). *Remembering: A study in experimental and social psychology*. Cambridge: Cambridge University Press.

Bauer, P. J. (2015). A complementary processes account of the development of childhood amnesia and a personal past. *Psychological Review*, 122(2), 204–231. doi:10.1037/a0038939.

Bauer, P. J., Burch, M. M., Scholin, S. E., & Güler, O. E. (2007). Using cue words to investigate the distribution of autobiographical memories in childhood. *Psychological Science*, 18, 910–916. doi:10.1111/j.1467-9280.2007.01999

Bauer, P. J., & Larkina, M. (2019). Predictors of age-related and individual variability in autobiographical memory in childhood. *Memory*. doi:10.1080/09658211.2017.1381267

Bruce, D., Dolan, A., & Phillips-Grant, K. (2000). On the transition from childhood amnesia to the recall of personal memories. *Psychological Science*, 11, 360–364. doi:10.1111/1467-9280.00271

Burger, K. (2010). How does early childhood care and education affect cognitive development? An international review of the effects of early interventions for children from different social backgrounds. *Early Childhood Research Quarterly*, 25, 140–165. doi.org/10.1016/j.ecresq.2009.11.001.

Cole, M. (1992). Cognitive development and formal schooling: The evidence from cross-cultural research. In L. C. Moll (Ed.), *Vygotsky and education: Instructional implications and applications of sociohistorical psychology* (pp. 89–110). Cambridge, UK: Cambridge University Press.

De la Mata, M. L., Santamaría, A., Trigo, E. M., Cubero, M., Aria, S., Antalíková, R., … Ruiz, M. L. (2019). The relationship between sociocultural factors and autobiographical memories from childhood:

The role of formal schooling. *Memory*. doi:10.1080/09658211.2018.1515316

Eacott, M. J., & Crawley, R. A. (1998). The offset of childhood amnesia: Memory for events that occurred before age 3. *Journal of Experimental Psychology: General, 127*, 22–33.

Ece, B., Demiray, B., & Gülgöz, S. (2019). Consistency of adults' earliest memories across two years. *Memory*. doi:10.1080/09658211.2018.1458321

Freud, S. (1905/1953). Childhood and concealing memories. In A. A. Brill (Trans & Ed.), *The basic writings of sigmund freud* (pp. 62–68). New York, NY: The Modern Library.

Hayne, H. (2004). Infant memory development: Implications for childhood amnesia. *Developmental Review, 24*, 33–73.

Hayne, H., Gross, J., McNamee, S., Fitzgibbon, O., & Tustin, K. (2011). Episodic memory and episodic foresight in 3- and 5-year-old children. *Cognitive Development, 26*, 343–355. doi:10.1016/j.cogdev.2011.09.006.

Howe, M. L. (2003). Memories from the cradle. *Current Directions in Psychological Science, 12*, 62–65.

Howes, M., Siegel, M., & Brown, F. (1993). Early childhood memories: Accuracy and affect. *Cognition, 47*, 95–119.

Jack, F., MacDonald, S., Reese, E., & Hayne, H. (2009). Maternal reminiscing style during early childhood predicts the age of adolescents' earliest memories. *Child Development, 80*, 496–505. doi:10.1111/j.1467-8624.2009.01274.x

Jack, F., Simcock, G., & Hayne, H. (2012). Magic memories: Young children's verbal recall after a 6-year delay. *Child Development, 83*(1), 159–172.

Josselyn, S. A., & Frankland, P. W. (2012). Infantile amnesia: A neurogenic hypothesis. *Learning & Memory, 19*, 423–433. doi:10.1101/lm.021311.110.

Kingo, O. S., Bohn, A., & Krøjgaard, P. (2013). Warm-up questions on early childhood memories affect the reported age of earliest memories in late adolescence. *Memory (Hove, England), 21*, 280–284. doi:10.1080/09658211.2012.729598

Leichtman, M. D., Steiner, K. L., Pillemer, D. B., Camilleri, K. A., & Thomsen, D. K. (2019). What happened in Kindergarten? Mother-child conversations about life story chapters. *Memory*. doi:10.1080/09658211.2018.1483515

Nelson, K., & Fivush, R. (2004). The emergence of autobiographical memory: A social cultural developmental theory. *Psychological Review, 111*, 486–511. doi:10.1037/0033-295X.111.2.486

Peterson, C., Baker-Ward, L., & Grovenstein, T. N. (2016). Childhood remembered: Reports of both unique and repeated events. *Memory (Hove, England), 24*, 240–256. doi:10.1080/09658211.2014.1001991.

Peterson, C., Wang, Q., & Hou, Y. (2009). "When I was little": Childhood recollections in Chinese and European Canadian grade school children. *Child Development, 80*(2), 506–518. doi:10.1111/j.1467-8624.2009.01275.x.

Pillemer, D. B., Steiner, K. L., Kuwabara, K. J., Thomsen, D. K., & Svob, C. (2015). Vicarious memories. *Consciousness and Cognition: An International Journal, 36*, 233–245. doi:10.1016/j.concog.2015.06.010.

Pillemer, D. B., & White, S. H. (1989). Childhood events recalled by children and adults. In H. W. Reese (Ed.), *Advances in child development and behavior* (Vol. 21, pp. 297–340). New York, NY: Academic Press.

Reese, E. (2009). The development of autobiographical memory: Origins and consequences. *Advances in Child Development and Behavior, 37*, 145–200. doi:10.1016/S0065-2407(09)03704-5.

Reese, E., Jack, F., & White, N. (2010). Origins of adolescents' autobiographical memories. *Cognitive Development, 25*, 352–367.

Reese, E., & Robertson, S.-J. (2019). Origins of adolescents' earliest memories. *Memory*. doi:10.1080/09658211.2018.1512631

Rubin, D. C. (2000). The distribution of early childhood memories. *Memory (Hove, England), 8*, 265–269.

Sonne, T., Kingo, O. S., Berntsen, D., & Krøjgaard, P. (2019). Thirty-five-month-old children have spontaneous memories despite change of context for retrieval. *Memory*. doi:10.1080/09658211.2017.1363243

Steiner, K. L., Pillemer, D. B., & Thomsen, D. K. (2017). Life story chapters, specific memories, and conceptions of the self. *Applied Cognitive Psychology, 31*, 478–487.

Tustin, K., & Hayne, H. (2019). Recollection improves with age: Children's and adults' accounts of their childhood. *Memory*. doi:10.1080/09658211.2018.1432661

Wang, Q. (2013). *The autobiographical self in time and culture*. New York, NY: Oxford University Press. doi:10.1093/acprof:oso/9780199737833.001.0001

Wang, Q., & Peterson, C. (2014). Your earliest memory may be earlier than you think: Prospective studies of children's dating of earliest childhood memories. *Developmental Psychology, 50*, 1680–1686.

Wang, Q., & Peterson, C. (2016). The fate of childhood memories: Children postdated their earliest memories as they grew older. *Frontiers in Psychology: Cognition, 6*, 2038. doi:10.3389/fpsyg.2015.02038.

Wang, Q., Peterson, C., & Hou, Y. (2010). Children dating childhood memories. *Memory (Hove, England), 18*(7), 754–762.

Wang, Q., Peterson, C., Khuu, A., Reid, C. P., Maxwell, K. L., & Vincent, J. M. (2019). Looking at the past through a telescope: Adults postdated their earliest childhood memories. *Memory*. doi:10.1080/09658211.2017.1414268

Wessel, I., Schweig, T., & Huntjens, R. J. C. (2019). Manipulating the reported age in earliest memories. *Memory*. doi:10.1080/09658211.2017.1396345

Manipulating the reported age in earliest memories

Ineke Wessel, Theresa Schweig and Rafaële J. C. Huntjens

ABSTRACT
Previous work suggests that the estimated age in adults' earliest autobiographical memories depends on age information implied by the experimental context [e.g., Kingo, O. S., Bohn, A., & Krøjgaard, P. (2013). Warm-up questions on early childhood memories affect the reported age of earliest memories in late adolescence. *Memory, 21*(2), 280–284. doi:10.1080/09658211.2012.729598] and that the age in decontextualised snippets of memory is younger than in more complete accounts (i.e., event memories [Bruce, D., Wilcox-O'Hearn, L. A., Robinson, J. A., Phillips-Grant, K., Francis, L., & Smith, M. C. (2005). Fragment memories mark the end of childhood amnesia. *Memory & Cognition, 33*(4), 567–576. doi:10.3758/BF03195324]). We examined the malleability of the estimated age in undergraduates' earliest memories and its relation with memory quality. In Study 1 ($n = 141$), vignettes referring to events happening at age 2 rendered earlier reported ages than examples referring to age 6. Exploratory analyses suggested that event memories were more sensitive to the age manipulation than memories representing a single, isolated scene (i.e., snapshots). In Study 2 ($n = 162$), asking self-relevant and public-event knowledge questions about participants' preschool years prior to retrieval yielded comparable average estimated ages. Both types of semantic knowledge questions rendered earlier memories than a no-age control task. Overall, the reported age in snapshots was younger than in event memories. However, age-differences between memory types across conditions were not statistically significant. Together, the results add to the growing literature indicating that the average age in earliest memories is not as fixed as previously thought.

Infantile or childhood amnesia is the phenomenon that adults have very few to no memories from their first years of life (see for overviews, Bauer, 2014; Pillemer, 1998; Rubin, 2000). Overall, a large body of research suggests that the grand average of the age reported in first memories is 3.5 years across multiple studies (Tustin & Hayne, 2010).

There is some evidence, however, that the age in earliest memories is not carved in stone. To begin with, Wang and Peterson (2014) interviewed children in various age groups (ranging from 4 to 13 years old) about their earliest memory twice, with a delay of 1–2 years between interviews. On the second interview, the same event was, on average, dated 5–7 months later. The results of a subsequent study (Wang & Peterson, 2016) assessing a subgroup of the children 8 years after the initial interview, suggested that the younger children (4–5 years old at baseline) continued to postdate the same memories. The memories were dated as having occurred more than a year later than at initial recall. Thus, dating earliest memories may fall prey to a spontaneous postdating bias (i.e., forward telescoping, Janssen, Chessa, & Murre, 2006). Furthermore, the age in earliest memories may be affected by experimental manipulations. Kingo, Bohn, and Krøjgaard (2013) examined the effects of "warm-up" retrieval. That is, prior to retrieving their very first memory, participants were instructed to recall events from when they were either 3 or 6 years old. This procedure rendered earlier first memories in the age 3 group than in the age 6 group. Likewise, Peterson, Kaasa, and Loftus (2009) found that participants who had overheard confederates talking about very early experiences reported earliest memories in which they were younger than participants who had not been exposed to social influence. In addition, Malinoski and Lynn (1999) reported that at the start of their study, 11% of their participants reported earliest memories from before the age of 2. Yet, at some time during an extensive probing procedure, 78% of the participants reported memories of such a young age.

Together, these results indicate that the age in earliest memories is malleable. This fits with the general notion that dating memories is a reconstructive activity (Friedman, 1993; Janssen et al., 2006). Unlike digital photos, memories do not contain a time-stamp (Arbuthnott & Brown, 2009).

CONTACT Ineke Wessel j.p.wessel@rug.nl Clinical Psychology and Experimental Psychopathology, University of Groningen, Grote Kruisstraat 2-1, 9712 TS Groningen, Netherlands

© 2018 The Author(s). Published by Informa UK Limited, trading as Taylor & Francis Group
This is an Open Access article distributed under the terms of the Creative Commons Attribution-NonCommercial-NoDerivatives License (http://creativecommons.org/licenses/by-nc-nd/4.0/), which permits non-commercial re-use, distribution, and reproduction in any medium, provided the original work is properly cited, and is not altered, transformed, or built upon in any way.

Sometimes a specific date is part of the factual knowledge (i.e., semantic memory) that is activated together with the recollective re-experiencing (i.e., episodic memory) of a particular event, such as one's wedding day. More often, however, the "when" of a recalled event is inferred from characteristics of the memory representation (e.g., clarity, familiarity, ease of accessibility) or from context information (e.g., the distance of the retrieved event relative to a landmark event; Arbuthnott & Brown, 2009; Janssen et al., 2006). This may of course, easily result in errors (Peterson et al., 2009). Yet, the studies on dating malleability raise the intriguing possibility that earliest memories could be of an earlier age than is generally assumed in the literature on infantile amnesia (Wang & Peterson, 2014, 2016). For example, compared to the grand average of 3.5 years (Tustin & Hayne, 2010), younger average ages were obtained in the experiments reported by Kingo et al. (2013; $M = 2.7$ years in the complete age 3 group) and Peterson et al. (2009; $M = 2.99$ years in the confederate group). Perhaps the age information provided by the study context (e.g., 3 vs. 6 years old) primes participants to search for a memory within a particular life-time period (e.g., "when I was in Kindergarten" vs. "when I was in primary school"). This fits with evidence suggesting that using cues is important for obtaining relatively early memories. Tustin and Hayne (2010) used idiosyncratic timelines displaying photos of the participants at various ages ranging from new-born to current age in an ascending order. Roughly 40% of participating children (up to 12–13 years old) recalled events from before age 2, compared to 4% of adults. Jack and Hayne (2010) found that even adults can come up with memories from under age 2 when a timeline is combined with exhaustive interviewing.

Why would extensive cueing bring about earlier memories than merely asking participants for their earliest memory? The instruction to retrieve an earliest memory likely invites a strategic search in memory (i.e., generative retrieval, Conway, 2005). However, in itself such a general instruction contains few cues, and it is up to the rememberer to generate them. In general, retrieval success depends on the extent to which retrieval cues match some aspect of the memory representation (Tulving & Thomson, 1973). A detailed episodic representation will have a higher probability of being recalled, especially when it is connected to various bits of factual knowledge (i.e., semantic memory), simply because multiple types of cues will match. However, compared to later memories, early memories are impoverished in that they contain fewer narrative categories (e.g., who, where; Bauer & Larkina, 2014; West & Bauer, 1999) and that they have fewer connections with factual knowledge (Howe, 2013; Pillemer, 1998). In addition, factual knowledge may be absent or organised differently in children than adults (Conway, 2005; Howe, 2013), resulting in reduced ways of accessing early representations with further development. Thus, for older children and adults, general "describe-your-earliest-memory" instructions would elicit too few cues that overlap with too few elements in early representations for retrieval to be successful. Extensive cueing would provide more specific cues matching these sketchy memories (Pillemer, 1998). That does not mean that all early experiences could be accessed if only the right trigger were available. Early, sketchy memories are thought to have a high probability of getting lost because retrieval opportunities are limited due to a lack of narrative organisation (e.g., Bauer, 2014; Bauer & Larkina, 2014).

Nevertheless, some sketchy early memories may survive and turn up in a memory search in adulthood. Mullen (1994) observed that 12–15% of adults' earliest memories retrieved under general instructions were images rather than events. Interestingly, the age in these image memories was younger than in the event memories. Bruce et al. (2005, experiment 2) took this a step further and instructed their participants to report their earliest fragment memories as well as their earliest event memories. Fragment memories were defined as "noncontextualized, stand-alone snippets of the past that are recollections of sensory experiences (images of a visual, auditory, olfactory, or other sensory nature), behaviors or actions, or feelings or emotions" (Bruce et al., 2005, p. 568). An event memory was defined as a story with a beginning and end. The results suggested that earliest fragment memories were of a younger age than earliest event memories. In addition, the memory types differed on a number of dimensions. For example, compared to event memories, fragments were rated as less vivid, less often rehearsed, evoking less intense feelings at the time and rendering less confidence about age estimates (Bruce et al., 2005, experiment 2; Bruce, Phillips-Grant, Wilcox-O'Hearn, Robinson, & Francis, 2007).

The findings regarding memory fragments may have methodological implications for studies on earliest memories. Next to having a lower chance of retrieval due to relatively few appropriate cues, sketchy early memories may not be recognised as memories. That is, characteristics such as vagueness may cause rejection of a fragment as a suitable memory candidate. If so, the fragment will not be reported. Tustin and Hayne (2010) suggested that this may explain their finding that children reported younger earliest memories than adults. Perhaps adults set a higher bar and only report detailed memories, whereas children may accept more sketchy fragments as memories. In line with this, a study instructing adult participants to only report memories that they were certain to remember yielded relatively late memories (i.e., older than age 6 on average; Wells, Morrison, & Conway, 2014).

We present two studies that further examined the malleability of age in earliest memories, taking the possibility that memory fragments are underreported into account. Specifically, prior to instructing participants to retrieve their earliest memory, we explicitly informed them that early memories may be sketchy, and presented them with examples of both fragment and event memories. In this way, we aimed at lowering the bar for reporting sketchy memories. Study 1 addressed the possibility that including information about age in experimental instructions would affect the average age reported for earliest memories (cf. Kingo et al., 2013; Peterson et al., 2009). The instructions contained vignettes referring to either an early or a late age (around 2 years vs. 6 years). We expected younger average ages in the early than the late condition. In addition, if fragment memories are from an earlier age, we expected to find more fragment memories in the early condition than in the late condition. To briefly preview the results, we found no fragment memories in a strict sense (i.e., disconnected pieces of memory). We had adapted Bruce et al.'s (2005) coding scheme to include snapshot memories, i.e., mental pictures without a temporal sequence. We therefore explored whether the early condition would report more snapshot memories than the late condition. Alternatively, the late age group was expected to report more event memories containing an elaborate, narrative structure. Furthermore, we explored the strategies that people used to date their memory and whether the different instructions would affect age estimates in fragment and event memories differently.

Study 1

Method

Participants

$N = 141$ undergraduate students (34% male) participated in exchange for course credit. Their mean age was 20.4 years (SD = 1.62, range 17–28). They were enrolled in an international (English-language) bachelor programme of psychology of a Dutch university. The majority was West-European, i.e., German (75.9%), Dutch (6.4%) or British (2.1%). The remaining 15.6% of the sample had various other backgrounds. The participants were assigned to either an early ($n = 74$) or a late ($n = 67$) condition. Participants in these conditions did not differ with respect to current age, gender and West-European nationality (see Table 1). The study was approved by the departmental ethics committee.

Material

The questionnaire was constructed in English, using Qualtrics software (Version October, 2014) and consisted of the following sections.

Earliest memory and age manipulation. Participants reported their earliest memory after reading three examples of earliest memories (inspired by Peterson et al., 2009) that contained age information. Critically, the early condition read vignettes from around age 2, and the late condition from around age 6. In addition, because in general participants may be unsure whether decontextualised fragments would count as "memories", we attempted to facilitate the reporting of fragment memories in two ways. First, the examples contained an event memory (i.e., a second vs. a sixth birthday party), a fragment memory (i.e., taking first steps vs. learning to ride a bicycle) and a description containing characteristics of both memory types (i.e., a fight with a sibling). Second, the actual instructions specifically mentioned the possibility of fragment memories (i.e., lacking continuity, background information and details). Participants were also instructed to report an experience that they could actually remember and not one that they merely knew that had happened to them.

Age estimation, confidence and strategies. After describing their memory, participants estimated their age in the memory by using separate drop-down menus for the year and the month (e.g., 4 years; 6 months). In addition, they indicated how confident they were in both estimates using slider scales ranging from 0 (= *not at all sure*) to 100 (= *100% sure*). Participants indicated how they came up with their age estimates by choosing one of three options (i.e., "I just knew"; "I used a strategy" and "It was a wild guess"). If participants indicated that they just knew or that they used a strategy, they were asked to describe how they arrived at their estimate as detailed as possible.

Memory characteristics. Memory characteristics (adapted from the AMCQ, Boyacioglu & Akfirat, 2015; and Bruce et al., 2005) were assessed with 66 items using 7-point Likert scales (1 = *Totally disagree*–7 = *Totally agree*). Originally, the AMCQ has 63 items distributed over 14 subscales (ranging from 3 to 5 items per subscale). We omitted one item (*I can remember the district in which the event took place*) because it does not apply to the Netherlands. The AMCQ dimensions capture the characteristics probed by Bruce et al. (2005), except for continuity and uniqueness. Therefore, we added two items about the extent to which participants recalled things that took place immediately before and after the reported event (Continuity, Cronbach's $a = .69$) and two items about whether the memory reflected a one-time experience (Cronbach's $a = .81$). Reliability analyses of the AMCQ showed poor alphas for two subscales (Time and Place details, Cronbach's $a = .32$; Emotional Distancing, Cronbach's $a = .17$), so these subscales were not used in the analyses. For the other subscales, alpha's were fair to excellent (Vividness, Cronbach's $a = .84$; Belief in Accuracy, Cronbach's $a = .77$; Sensory Details, Cronbach's $a = .71$; Sharing, Cronbach's $a = .88$; Observer Perspective, Cronbach's $a = .81$; Field Perspective, Cronbach's $a = .84$; Narrative Coherence, Cronbach's $a = .63$; Valence, Cronbach's $a = .96$; Emotional Intensity, Cronbach's $a = .87$; Preoccupation with Emotion, Cronbach's $a = .87$). For two subscales, poor Cronbach's alphas improved after removing one item with low item-total correlations (Accessibility Cronbach's $a = .86$; Recollection Cronbach's $a = .76$).[1] We used these adjusted subscales.

Fragmentation. We constructed two items to measure subjective sense of memory fragmentation. First, we provided descriptions of fragment and event memories. Two slider scales (range 0 = "strongly disagree"–100 = "strongly

Table 1. Demographic variables, belief in memory from age 2 and under, age in earliest memory, memory type and strategies in the early and late conditions in Study 1.

	Condition		Test statistic	Effect Size
	Early ($n = 74$)	Late ($n = 67$)		
Current age, years (M, SD)	20.2 (1.34)	20.5 (1.87)	$t(118.6)^a = -1.26$	$d = 0.22$
Female gender (%)	67.6	64.2	$X^2(1) = 0.18$	$d = 0.07$
West-European (%)[b]	83.8	85.1	$X^2(1) = 0.04$	$d = 0.04$
Age in Memory, months (M, SD)	38.6 (12.7)	47.9 (17.6)	$t(119)^a = -3.55^{**}$	$d = 0.61$
Snapshots (%)	48.6	41.8	$X^2(1) = 0.67$	$d = 0.14$
Fragmentation (M, SD)	55.4 (28.2)	52.3 (31.9)	$t(139) = 0.60$	$d = 0.10$
Way of estimating years (%)[c]			$X^2(2) = 9.54^{**}$	$V = .26$
Used a strategy	54.1	62.7	$X^2(1) = 1.08$	$d = 0.18$
Just knew	13.5	25.4	$X^2(1) = 3.19$	$d = 0.30$
Wild guess	32.4	11.9	$X^2(1) = 8.42^{**}$	$d = 0.50$
Way of estimating months (%)[c]			$X^2(2) = 0.30$	$V = .046$
Used a strategy	21.6	19.4		
Just knew	6.8	9.0		
Wild guess	71.6	71.6		
Confidence				
Years (Median, Inter-quartile range)	64 (55)	74 (43)	$U = 2105$	$d = 0.26$
Months (Median, Inter-quartile range)	11.5 (37)	20 (53)	$U = 2304$	$d = 0.12$
Belief in memory $\leq$ age 2 (%)	36.5	35.8	$X^2(1) = 0.01$	$d = 0.01$

[a]Adjusted df.
[b]Percentage of participants with either a Dutch, German or English nationality.
[c]Only if the overall test was significant, follow-up comparisons are reported.
**$p < .01$.

agree") were used to indicate to which degree a memory was like a fragment and like an event memory with a narrative structure. The event memory rating was coded reversely and the average of both scales was used as an index of fragmentation. The reliability of this measure was good, Cronbach's $a = .82$.

Control questions. Three final questions asked the participants to indicate (1) what they thought the purpose of the study was (open question); (2) whether they filled in the questionnaire truthfully (yes/no) and (3) whether they believed that it is possible that people report memories from age 2 and below (yes/no).

Procedure

The participants were recruited for a study on first memories through an online research participant management system, which directed participants to the online Qualtrics questionnaire after signing up. Participants provided informed consent, as well as their gender, age, language and their month of birth. Because at the time we were unaware of the possibility of random assignment in Qualtrics, birth month was used for allocating participants to either the early or late condition (odd birth months – early condition; even birth months – late condition). This strategy rendered more participants in the early condition, and the final $n = 12$ were allocated to the late condition irrespective of birth month.

Coding

The memories were experimenter-coded based on the participants' verbal descriptions. We adapted Bruce et al.'s (2005) coding scheme, using four categories. A fragment referred to a disconnected piece of memory, lacking all background information (e.g., a sensory impression). A snapshot was defined as a mental picture without a temporal sequence, but possibly containing some context information (e.g., "My first memory goes back to when I was in my old parent's house, I remember myself in my room, looking at the shelf with my comics on it."). An event memory referred to a description containing a clear temporal sequence ("I am running down the hallway crying, I am sitting down to watch a movie. It is a movie about dinosaurs. My mom comes in the room and asks me why I'm crying. I point at the TV while crying"). A repetitive memory referred to multiple similar events (e.g., "I remember my great granddad buying me cola at the bar in his retirement home every time I went there"). One of the authors (TS) coded all memories. Two raters (TS and IW) coded 57 memories (38%) independently. Inter-rater reliability was good ($\kappa = .87$).

Analyses

Initially, 159 participants[2] initiated the online questionnaire. The data from 18 participants were discarded: $n = 6$ were non-completers; $n = 4$ indicated that they had not completed the questionnaire truthfully and inspection of the strategy questions revealed that $n = 8$ had asked their parents' help for dating their memory. Thus, the final sample consisted of 141 participants. Inspection of the control questions revealed that no-one guessed the purpose of the study (i.e., manipulating age through instructions).

For the analyses, a single age estimate in months was calculated by multiplying the number of years by 12 and adding the month estimate. Two extreme outliers were assigned a value of 1 unit above the second highest value (Tabachnick & Fidell, 2007). The same procedure was followed for outliers in the memory characteristic variables (sharing 1 outlier; preoccupation with emotion 1 outlier; continuity 2 outliers). Group differences were examined using analyses of variance (ANOVAs), *t*-tests and, if assumptions were not met, nonparametric Mann–Whitney *U* tests. We used a sequential Bonferroni–Holm procedure in the exploratory ANOVAs to control for family-wise error rates (Cramer et al., 2016).

Results and discussion

Age in the early and late conditions
As can be seen in Table 1, the early condition reported a lower average age in their in earliest memories than the late condition A *t*-test showed that this difference was statistically significant.

Exploratory analyses
Memory type in the early and late conditions. Regarding memory type, it was unexpected that none of the memories received a fragment coding. In total, 45.4% of the memories were coded as snapshots and three memories were coded as repetitive memories. We incorporated the repetitive memories in the event memory category. A X^2 test revealed that the percentages of experimenter-coded snapshots did not differ significantly between the conditions. Likewise, the conditions did not differ significantly with respect to self-reported fragmentation. Thus, the evidence for the predictions that the early condition would report more sketchy memories than the late condition was inconclusive at both the objective (experimenter-coded) and subjective (self-report) level.

Strategies and belief in very early memories. We first explored the participants' strategies for arriving at their estimate of the number of years in the age in their earliest memory. An overall X^2 test showed a statistically significant difference in strategy use between the early and late conditions. As can be seen in Table 1, more participants in the early condition said that they had guessed the number of years. Using a strategy or just knowing the number of years did not statistically differ between the groups. The majority of participants (71.6%) guessed the number of months. The conditions did not differ statistically.

As for confidence in estimates of the number of years and the number of months, nonparametric Mann–Whitney *U* tests showed no statistically significant differences between the early and late conditions.

Next, we explored the possibility that the reported ages were biased by the age information in the vignettes. That is, the participants may have inadvertently reported an age similar to the age in the instructions just because they read it prior to the estimation process and used it as input without actually probing their memory for information about their age. Indeed, Greenberg, Bishara, and Mugayar-Baldocchi (2017) found that asking whether someone's earliest memory was from before or after a certain age (e.g., 1 or 6 years) influenced reported ages dependent on the age provided in that question. Because such anchoring effects would especially play a role in judgements under uncertainty, we speculated that the effect of the instruction may be particularly pronounced in the participants who said to have guessed their age. In contrast, participants who relied on autobiographical knowledge (e.g., landmark events) in their age estimation might be less susceptible to context effects.

In order to explore this possibility, we concentrated on the strategies for arriving at the number of years in participants' age estimates. Inspection of these strategies suggested that the "I just knew" and "I used a strategy" options did not seem to yield descriptions of qualitatively different strategies. Therefore, we collapsed them into a category expressing the use of autobiographical knowledge for all participants (AK-users, $n = 108$), except for one participant in the late condition. He had chosen the "just knew" option, but answered that he did not know how he knew. This participant and the guessers were coded as non-AK-users ($n = 33$).

Next, we contrasted the age estimates of AK-users and non-AK-users. Testing this difference across the early and late conditions was complicated by the presence of only relatively few ($n = 9$) non-AK-users in the late condition. As widely varying cell sizes would render a 2 (condition: early vs. late) × 2 (strategy: using vs. not using autobiographical knowledge) ANOVA suboptimal, we limited the comparison of AK-users with non-AK-users to the early condition. In addition, we reasoned that scepticism about the possibility of very early memories (i.e., from age 2 or under) might interfere with a context-induced report bias. The percentages of participants saying that they believed it is possible that people have memories of age 2 and under (see Table 1) did not differ statistically between the early and late conditions, $p = .935$. However, a *t*-test revealed that overall, believers reported significantly younger ages ($M = 38.41$, $SD = 16.80$) than non-believers ($M = 45.63$, $SD = 14.77$), $t(139) = 2.65$, $p = .009$, $d = 0.45$. We therefore controlled for believing in memories from age 2 and under in a subsequent ANOVA comparing AK-users ($n = 50$) and non-AK-users ($n = 24$) users in the early condition.

The ANOVA showed that the non-AK-users ($M = 42.4$ months, $SD = 12.7$) reported to be significantly older in their memory than the AK-users ($M = 36.0$ months, $SD = 12.5$), $F(1, 71) = 4.37$, $p = .04$, $\eta_p^2 = .058$. The means adjusted for belief in memories of age 2 and under in the late condition were 50.8 months ($SD = 17.2$) for the non-AK-users ($n = 9$) and 45.8 months ($SD = 17.7$) for the AK-users ($n = 58$). Thus, the participants who estimated their age based on autobiographical knowledge reported earlier memories than the participants who guessed. This runs counter to the idea that the age information in the vignettes simply biased the reporting of age estimates: in that case we would have expected to see the age effects especially in guessers. Instead, we speculate that the age information in the vignettes primed participants to start their memory search in a particular life-time period. Of course, the results should be replicated in future studies. An alternative explanation is that the number of data-dependent decisions in our exploratory analyses resulted in inflated type I error, and thus reflects a spurious finding (see Gelman & Loken, 2014).

Age in snapshots and event memories across conditions. We also explored whether the age information affected the age in experimenter-coded snapshots and event memories differentially. Again, we controlled for belief in memories from age 2 or under in a 2 (Condition) × 2 (Memory Type) ANOVA. The main effect for condition, $F(1, 136) = 11.35$, $p = .001$, $\eta_p^2 = .077$, was statistically significant (adjusted $a = .0167$). This main effect is conceptually similar to the *t*-test reported earlier, but in this particular ANOVA it shows that age estimates in the early condition were significantly younger than in the late condition even when believing in the possibility of very early memories was controlled for. In addition, a significant (adjusted $a = .025$) main effect for memory type, $F(1, 136) = 11.63$, $p = .001$, $\eta_p^2 = .079$, indicated that age in snapshot memories ($m = 37.6$, SD = 14.6) was younger than in event memories ($m = 45.8$, SD = 14.5). The condition by memory type interaction effect was statistically significant (adjusted $a = .05$), $F(1, 136) = 5.50$, $p = .02$, $\eta_p^2 = .039$. To follow up on this interaction, we ran an ANOVA controlling for belief in memories age 2 and under with the condition by memory type interaction represented by four different levels (i.e., Early Snapshots; Late Snapshots; Early Event memories and Late Event memories). *Post hoc* Tukey tests suggested that especially event memories in the late condition differed from their counterparts in the early condition, mean difference = −13.82, SE = 3.23, $p < .001$, and from snapshot memories in both the late (mean difference = −13.85, SE = 3.51, $p = .001$) and early (mean difference = −16.33, SE = 3.28, $p < .001$) conditions. All other comparisons did not reveal significant differences, all p's > .872. Together, the finding that snapshots are from a younger age than event memories extend Bruce et al.'s (2005) findings on fragment memories. Moreover, the snapshot memories seemed relatively insensitive to the age manipulation.

Characteristics of snapshot and event memories. We also explored whether the phenomenological differences between fragment and event memories (Bruce et al., 2005) would extend to snapshot memories. Table 2 presents the characteristics for snapshots and event memories separately. It should be noted that the three repetitive memories were excluded from the analyses. Compared to earlier findings that fragments and event memories differed on many dimensions (Bruce et al., 2005), there were only a few statistically significant differences between the present memory types. Snapshot memories were rated as less often shared and more fragmented than event memories. The latter indicates that the experimenter-coded snapshot – event memory distinction matched the participants' subjective experience.

Table 2. Mean ratings of age in and characteristics of snapshots and event memories in Study 1.

	Memory type			
	Snapshot ($n = 64$)	Event ($n = 74$)	t (136)	Cohen's d
Vividness	3.81 (1.24)	4.05 (1.18)	−1.18	0.20
Belief in accuracy	4.26 (0.96)	4.60 (1.11)	−1.89	0.33
Accessibility	3.98 (1.74)	4.23 (1.73)	−0.83	0.14
Recollection	3.48 (1.16)	3.48 (1.27)	0.04	0
Sensory detail	3.59 (1.15)	3.55 (1.25)	0.19	−0.03
Sharing	3.01 (1.31)	3.73 (1.47)	−3.05[a]	0.52
Narrative coherence	4.15 (1.06)	4.51 (1.01)	−2.03	0.35
Observer perspective	4.03 (1.51)	3.73 (1.48)	1.18	−0.20
Field perspective	4.12 (1.54)	4.60 (1.47)	−1.85	0.32
Valence	5.37 (1.61)	4.79 (1.77)	1.99	−0.34
Emotional intensity	3.41 (1.06)	3.50 (1.31)	−0.46	0.08
Preoccupation with emotion	2.17 (0.95)	2.28 (1.10)	−0.65	0.11
Unique event	4.81 (1.74)	5.53 (1.75)	−2.45	0.41
Continuity	2.03 (1.08)	2.35 (1.25)	−1.61	0.27
Fragmentation	65.8 (27.6)	43.04 (28.3)	4.78[b]	−0.81

Note: Standard deviations are within parentheses.
[a]$p = .003$, adjusted $a = .0036$.
[b]$p < .001$, adjusted $a = .0033$.

Study 2

The results of Study 1 suggest that using a particular age in instructions for retrieving a first autobiographical memory may influence the subsequent estimate of the age in that memory. Study 2 further built upon the idea that the age information in the vignettes functions as a starting point for a deliberate search through an autobiographical knowledge base.

According to the self-memory system model of autobiographical memory (e.g., Conway, 2005; Conway & Pleydell-Pearce, 2000), autobiographical knowledge is hierarchically organised with layers running from general to specific information. An important organising principle for the more abstract layers is that of thematic life-time periods (e.g., "when I was in elementary school"). People may use a life-time period as a first entry for self-generating cues in an iterative search for a specific memory (cf. Conway, 2005). Age information referring to different life-time periods (e.g., "preschool" vs. "elementary school") may thus render different starting points. This first cue may be elaborated on by activating bits of self-knowledge from that particular life-time period ("Where did we live?").

In Study 2 we specifically examined whether activating self-related semantic knowledge from an early life-time period (i.e., the preschool years) affects the estimated age in earliest memories. There were three conditions. In the self-relevant knowledge condition participants answered questions about personal facts from their preschool period (e.g., the brand of the family car). To examine whether thinking back on a particular age-period is sufficient for affecting age estimates, a public-event knowledge condition asked about news events that occurred during the participants' preschool years (e.g., the fall of the Berlin wall). In the third condition, we just asked for participants' very first memory without age information. Study 1 lacked such a control and thus it is unknown whether the age-differences were due to the early instructions facilitating lower age estimates, or to the late instructions increasing them.

There were a number of additional methodological improvements compared to Study 1. To begin with, to prevent participants from using external information (e.g., asking parents) to generate age estimates, they were tested in the laboratory rather than online. In addition, not a single memory in Study 1 was coded as a fragment memory. Perhaps the instructions aiming at lowering the criterion for what counts as a memory had been too implicit. In Study 2 we explicitly defined fragment and event memories and clarified how they differed. Finally, we used a briefer measure of autobiographical memory characteristics in Study 2 (i.e., MCQ; Schaefer & Philippot, 2005) because anecdotal reports suggested that participants in Study 1 found the AMCQ (Boyacioglu & Akfirat, 2015) long and tedious.

In sum, Study 2 sought to replicate and extend the findings of Study 1 that the age in earliest memories is malleable. If the activation of self-relevant knowledge plays a critical role, we expected to find younger ages in earliest memories in the self-relevant knowledge condition than in the public-event knowledge and no-age conditions. Alternatively, if just thinking about a particular life-time period is sufficient for generating earlier memories, then the age estimates in the self-relevant and public-knowledge conditions should be younger than in the no-age controls. Additionally, we aimed at replicating the finding that especially snapshot (and fragment) memories are relatively insensitive to an age manipulation.

Method

Participants

Participants were 162 students (25.3% male) with a mean age of 21.65 years (range 18–25 years). The majority of the participants had a West-European nationality and were either German (42%), Dutch (27.2%) or British (1.9%). Twenty-nine per cent had various other cultural backgrounds. Participants were randomly assigned to a self-related knowledge ($n = 53$), a public-event knowledge ($n = 55$) or a control condition ($n = 54$). Participants in these conditions did not differ with respect to current age, gender and West-European nationality (see Table 3). The participants were reimbursed with either course credit ($n = 4$) or 5 Euros ($n = 158$). The study was approved by the departmental ethics committee.

Material and procedure

Participants were recruited through advertisements on a local Facebook group for paid research participants ($n = 115$) and the departmental online research participant management system ($n = 47$). For practical reasons related to the construction of the public-event questions, we only included participants between the ages of 18 and 25. Groups with a maximum of three participants were tested in the laboratory. Each participant was randomly allocated to one of three conditions. After signing informed consent, participants completed their digital questionnaires individually at separate desktop computers.

The questionnaire was constructed in Qualtrics (Version April, 2015). Following demographic information, it included the following sections.

Knowledge and age manipulation. There were 24 yes/no questions. The nature of these questions depended on condition. In two conditions the questions concerned knowledge related to the participants' first three years of life. Participants were informed that ages 0–3 would be referred to as their pre-kindergarten (or preschool for Dutch participants) years. In the *Self-related knowledge (SRK) condition*, the questions asked for facts from participants' lives during that time (e.g., whether they knew the brand of the family car; whether there was a pet in their household). In the *Public-event knowledge (PEK) condition*, the questions asked whether particular public events had occurred during the participants' first three years of life (e.g., the fall of the Berlin wall; the introduction of the Euro as European currency). To avoid response tendencies, 50% of the questions were tailored to the years matching each participant's preschool age (yielding a potential "yes" response), whereas 50% of questions referred to the three years before the participant was born (yielding a potential "no"). Thus, for a participant who was 18 years old at the time of the study (2015) half of the questions were about events that had happened in 1997–1999, whereas the other half reflected events from the years 1994–1996. In the *Control condition*, participants solved 24 arithmetical problems (e.g., "Is $(3 \times 2) + 1 = 6?$") taken from the Operation Span task (Conway et al., 2005). Participants indicated whether the suggested outcome was correct (Yes/No). Half of the solutions provided were correct, the other half was incorrect.

The remainder of the questionnaire was the same in all three conditions.

Earliest memory. Participants reported their earliest memory along the lines of the instructions in Study 1, but the vignettes in Study 2 contained one situation (the birthday party) that was described as both an event and a fragment memory. In addition, the differences between fragment and event memories were described, explicitly referring to the vignettes. Furthermore, participants were instructed to report an "experience that you can actually remember and not one that you merely know from narrations, photographs or videos for instance".

Age estimation, confidence and strategies. The questions about age estimates and confidence ratings were identical to Study 1. The strategy questions now contained two options (i.e., "It was a wild guess" and "I used a strategy"). In addition, participants were asked whether there were videos or photographs of the reported memory. Answers included one "no" option and three "yes" options (i.e., *the same specific scene; the same event but not the same scene; the same scene but not the same perspective*).

Table 3. Demographic variables, memory type and control variables in the self-relevant knowledge, public-event knowledge and control conditions in Study 2.

	Condition			Test statistic, DF	Effect size
	SRK ($n = 53$)	PEK ($n = 55$)	Control ($n = 54$)		
Current age in years (M, SD)	21.9 (1.80)	21.2 (1.66)	21.9 (1.60)	$F(2, 159) = 2.57$	$\eta_p^2 = .031$
Female gender (%)	77.4	74.5	72.2	$X^2(2) = 0.37$	$V = .048$
West-European (%)[a]	73.6	74.5	64.8	$X^2(2) = 1.51$	$V = .097$
Age in memory, months (M, SD)	38.2 (13.3)	37.2 (10.9)	45.7 (17.5)	$F(2, 159) = 5.83^{**}$	$\eta_p^2 = .068$
Snapshots (%)[b]	45.3	47.3	46.3	$X^2(2) = 0.04$	$d = .016$
Fragmentation (M, SD)	60.4 (34.5)	68.1 (29.7)	59.84 (32.6)	$F(2, 159) = 1.12$	$\eta_p^2 = .014$
Used AK (%)					
Year estimate	77.4	69.1	75.9	$X^2(2) = 1.11$	$d = .083$
Month estimate	28.3	38.2	38.9	$X^2(2) = 1.64$	$d = .101$
Confidence					
Years (Median, Inter-quartile range)	71 (41)	70 (45)	75 (30)	$X^2(2) = 0.18$	$\eta_{K-W}^2 = .001$
Months (Median, Inter-quartile range)	26 (88)	25 (63)	25 (71)	$X^2(2) = 0.29$	$\eta_{K-W}^2 = .002$
Photos of the event (%)	24.5	27.3	20.4	$X^2(2) = 0.72$	$V = .067$
Belief in memory $\leq$ age 2 (%)	49.1	38.2	44.4	$X^2(2) = 1.31$	$V = .090$

Notes: SRK = self-relevant knowledge; PEK = public-event knowledge and IQR = inter-quartile range.
[a]Percentage of participants with either a Dutch, German or English nationality.
[b]Includes four fragments.

Autobiographical memory characteristics

Memory Characteristics Questionnaire (MCQ). Different from Study 1, we used Schaefer and Philippot's (2005) version of the MCQ. It consists of 20 items asking for characteristics on different dimensions: (1) "Clarity" (6 items; Cronbach's $a = .81$)[3] representing general vividness of the memory depending on perceptual and sensory information; (2) "Sensory details" (4 items; Cronbach's $a = .57$) reflecting sound, smell, touch and taste; (3) "Time" (5 items; Cronbach's $a = .67$) addresses the memories' time context as year, season, day and hour; (4) "Spatial context" (3 items; Cronbach's $a = .67$) represents the location and spatial arrangements of their memory; and (5) "Thoughts and Feelings" (2 items; Cronbach's $a = .72$) the memory for what they thought and felt at the time. We added 10 items that were used by Bruce et al. (2005, 2007), asking for the extent to which participants recalled events before and after the event in their earliest memory (Continuity, 2 items, see Study 1; Cronbach's $a = .58$); valence ("The overall tone of the memory is negative/positive", "My feelings at the time were negative/positive"; Cronbach's $a = .95$); emotional intensity (1 item); vantage perspective (1 item); talking about the event (sharing, 1 item); thinking about it (rehearsal, 1 item); whether the setting was familiar (1 item) and whether the event seemed long (duration, 1 item). Each of the 30 items was rated using a 100-point slider scale.

Centrality. The short version of the Centrality of Event Scale (CES; Berntsen & Rubin, 2006) assessed how central the event in the earliest memory was to a person's identity and life story. The CES contains 7 items, rated on a 5-point Likert scale (1 = *totally disagree*–5 = *totally agree*). The total score ranges between 7 and 35 with higher scores indicating higher centrality. Internal consistency in the current sample was good (Cronbach's $a = .88$).

Fragmentation. We used the same measure of fragmentation as in Study 1. The internal consistency was excellent (Cronbach's $a = .93$).

Control questions. The same control questions as in Study 1 were used.[4]

Coding

The memories were coded following the criteria of Study 1 by two independent raters (TS and a research assistant) who were blind to condition. Their inter-rater reliability was high, $\kappa = .85$. Differences were resolved by discussion.

Analyses

Initially, 166 participants participated in the study. Inspection of the strategies revealed that four participants had learned the age in their memory from a family member on an earlier occasion. The data from these participants were discarded, leaving a final sample of $n = 162$. None of the participants guessed the purpose of the study (i.e., manipulating age estimates) and all said to have responded truthfully. The data-analytic strategies were similar to Study 1. The age estimate variable was adjusted as follows. Three extreme outliers were assigned a value of 1 unit above the second highest value and two outliers were given a value of 1 unit below the second lowest value of their condition (Tabachnick & Fidell, 2007). It should be noted that the latter two adjusted values concerned participants who said that they remembered their own birth and being 3 months old in their memory. Other variables that were adjusted for outliers in a similar way were the CES (three outliers); MCQ clarity (three outliers); Valence (four outliers); Event duration (five outliers) and Fragmentation (two outliers).

Results and discussion

Age and memory type across conditions

As can be seen in Table 3, a one-way ANOVA rendered a significant difference between the conditions regarding the age in earliest memories. *Post hoc* Tukey tests indicated that compared to the control condition, both the SRK (mean difference = 7.46, SE = 2.43) and the PEK (mean difference = 8.52, SE = 2.41) reported significantly younger ages. The SRK and PEK conditions did not differ significantly from each other. Thus, having participants think about an early life-time period (i.e., their preschool years) was sufficient to affect the age in their earliest memories. These results suggest that activating self-relevant knowledge is not crucial to elicit younger ages.

Overall six memories (3.7%) were coded as repetitive and four memories (2.5%) were fragments. Because of their low frequency, repetitive memories were incorporated in the event memory category and fragments were included in the snapshot memory category. The conditions did not differ significantly with respect to the number of experimenter-coded snapshot memories. Likewise, there were no significant differences with regard to self-reported fragmentation. Thus, in line with findings in the early condition in Study 1, participants reported younger ages in the conditions that referred to an early life-time period but the evidence that their memories were sketchier than those in controls was inconclusive.

Confidence, pictures, belief in memories from age 2 and under, and strategies

Table 3 also shows that there were no significant differences between the conditions regarding participants' confidence in their age estimates. In addition, 24.1% of the sample said that there were pictures or videos that were associated with their memories. Because of the relatively low number of participants that endorsed the various "yes" items (i.e., 6.8% same specific scene; 9.3% same event but other scene; 8% same event but other perspective), these percentages were collapsed into one "yes" category. The percentage of endorsers did not differ significantly between conditions. On average, the age in earliest memories did not significantly differ between participants who had photos or videos corresponding to the memory ($M = 42.0$, SD = 15.8) and those who did not ($M = 39.8$, SD = 14.2), $t(160) = -0.82$, $p = .412$, $d = 0.15$. Furthermore, the percentage of participants who believed that it is possible that people have memories of age 2 or under did not differ significantly across conditions. However, participants who said that they believed in the possibility of having memories from age 2 or under estimated their age as significantly younger ($M = 33.8$, SD = 13.1) in their memories than participants who did not ($M = 45.5$, SD = 13.6), $t(160) = 5.52$, $p < .001$, $d = -0.87$.

Similar to Study 1, we explored whether the use of autobiographical knowledge rendered different age estimates across condition. It can be seen in Table 3 that the percentages of AK-users did not differ significantly between conditions. A 2 (AK-use) × 3 (Condition) ANOVA controlling for belief in early memories showed no significant main effect of AK-use, $F(1, 155) = 0.06$, $p = .807$, $\eta_p^2 < .001$. Likewise, there was no significant AK-use by condition interaction, $F(1, 155) = 0.954$, $p = .387$, $\eta_p^2 = .012$. For AK-users, the ages were $M = 37.2$, (SD = 2.02); $M = 36.8$, (SD = 2.13) and $M = 45.7$ (SD = 2.02) for the SRK, PEK and Control conditions, respectively. For the non-AK-users, the ages were $M = 41.3$, (SD = 3.73) for SRK, $M = 33.6$ (SD = 3.13) for PRK and $M = 43.0$ (SD = 3.60) for controls.

Age in snapshots and event memories across conditions

Next, we checked whether the finding in Study 1 that the age in snapshots and event memories differed across conditions would also be evident in Study 2. As belief in memories from age 2 or under affected age estimates, we controlled for this variable in a 3 (Condition) × 2 (Memory Type) ANOVA. The main effect for Condition, $F(2, 155) = 7.49$, $p = .001$, $\eta_p^2 = 0.09$, was statistically significant (adjusted $a = .0167$). Thus, the difference between the conditions remained statistically significant after controlling for belief in very early memories. The main effect of memory type, $F(1, 155) = 9.17$, $p = .003$, $\eta_p^2 = .056$, was also significant (adjusted $a = .025$). Overall, participants reported to be younger in snapshot ($M = 36.4$, SD = 12.6) than in event memories ($M = 42.5$, SD = 12.7). The condition by memory type interaction $F(2, 155) = 0.85$, $p = .430$, $\eta_p^2 = .011$, was not statistically significant (adjusted $a = .05$). Thus, the finding in Study 1 that especially event memories were sensitive to the age manipulation was not replicated.

Characteristics of snapshot and event memories

Table 4 displays the subjective ratings of the phenomenological characteristics of snapshots and event memories. Repetitive memories were excluded from the analyses. Three out of 15 comparisons were significant after sequential Bonferroni correction. Snapshots were rated as containing poorer recall of what happened before and after, as more fragmented and as more positive than event memories.

General discussion

We report on two studies examining whether age information implied by the experimental context influences the reported age in participant's earliest memories. In Study 1 participants were presented with vignettes describing earliest memories that explicitly mentioned a specific age that was either early (1–2 years old) or late (5–6 years old). On average, participants in the early condition reported to be significantly younger in their first memories than participants in the late condition. Study 2 examined whether activating self-relevant knowledge from the preschool years is important for decreasing the age in earliest memories. Thinking about self-relevant information from this earliest life-time period indeed resulted in younger average ages than in a no-age control group. However, thinking about public events from this life-time period also rendered earlier ages. The age estimates in the public-event knowledge and self-relevant knowledge conditions did not differ in a statistically

Table 4. Mean or median ratings of age in and characteristics of snapshots and event memories in Study 2.

	Memory type		Test statistic	Cohen's d
	Snapshot (n = 75)	Event (n = 81)		
Event centrality (M, SD)	12.5 (4.78)	13.2 (5.52)	t(154) = −0.90	0.15
MCQ				
Clarity (M, SD)	59.1 (18.7)	63.23 (14.9)	t(154) = −1.53	0.24
Sensory Detail (Median, Interquartile range)	15 (32)	22.8 (21)	U = 2382	0.38
Time (M, SD)	33.7 (20.8)	36.0 (20.1)	t(154) = −0.69	0.11
Context (M, SD)	64.4 (22.0)	65.0 (21.8)	t(154) = −0.18	0.03
Thoughts & feelings (M, SD)	42.9 (29.3)	51.5 (24.9)	t(154) = −1.98	0.32
Field perspective (Median, Interquartile range)	84 (50)	74 (46)	U = 2767	0.15
Emotion				
Valence (M, SD)	77.4 (23.4)	53.3 (31.0)	t(154) = 5.51[a]	−0.87
Intensity (M, SD)	57.9 (25.6)	61.3 (24.6)	t(154) = −0.85	0.14
Thought about it (M, SD)	45.8 (24.2)	47.7 (28.0)	t(154) = −0.47	0.07
Talked about it (Median, Interquartile range)	19 (42)	20 (42)	U = 2984	0.03
Event duration (M, SD)	29.5 (24.6)	34.3 (23.8)	t(154) = −1.23	0.20
Setting unfamiliar (Median, Interquartile range)	20 (49)	18 (31)	U = 2789	0.14
Continuity (Med, IQR)	1.50 (14.5)	24.5 (38)	U = 1703[b]	0.82
Fragmentation (M, SD)	72.1 (30.1)	55.2 (32.7)	t(154) = 3.35[c]	−0.81

Notes: Standard deviations or inter-quartile ranges are within parentheses.
[a]$p < .001$, adjusted $\alpha = .0033$.
[b]$p < .001$, adjusted $\alpha = .0036$.
[c]$p = .001$, adjusted $\alpha = .0038$.

significant fashion. Thus, it seems that in itself, thinking about an early life-time period results in reporting earlier ages and that the type of information that is thought about is not particularly important.

In both studies the average ages in the conditions referring to an early life-time period were a little over 3 years old. At first sight this is younger than the grand average of 3.5 years in the literature (Tustin & Hayne, 2010). As Study 1 lacked a control condition that was silent about age, it is unknown whether the early instructions in Study 1 facilitated lower age estimates, or whether the late instructions increased them. The difference between the knowledge conditions and the no-age control condition in Study 2, however, suggests that the age in earliest memories can indeed be reliably decreased. This fits with earlier findings that participants reported earlier ages after manipulations introducing relatively young ages (Kingo et al., 2013; Peterson et al., 2009). The ages reported in these earlier studies were even slightly younger (i.e., about 32 months in the early condition in Kingo et al., 2013; 36 months in Peterson et al., 2009) than in our studies (i.e., between 37.2 and 38.6 months). This may have to do with the manner of asking the questions. In the previous studies participants just wrote down their age, whereas we asked for separate estimates of the number of years and months. Perhaps people are less inclined to write down the number of months spontaneously. Asking for the number of months on top of the number of years would then results in slightly older ages.

We also expected that the manipulations bringing down the age in earliest memories would yield more sketchy memories, in line with earlier work reporting that fragments are younger than event memories (Bruce et al., 2005). Contrary to expectations both studies yielded few fragment memories. In addition, the percentages of snapshot memories (i.e., isolated images) did not differ significantly between conditions. Yet, reminiscent of earlier findings in fragment memories (Bruce et al., 2005), both studies showed that irrespective of condition, snapshot memories were of a younger age than event memories. Moreover, the results of Study 1 suggested that the difference between the early and late condition was most prominent for the event memories. The age estimates of snapshots seemed to be less sensitive to the age manipulation. However, this pattern of results was not replicated in Study 2.

The present studies explored two types of explanations for observations that the average age in earliest memories is malleable. In Study 1, the possibility that age estimates reflect a context-induced report bias was explored. The idea was that once a childhood memory has been retrieved, people use the externally provided age information as an anchor for estimating their age in that memory (Greenberg et al., 2017). Usually people use highly salient experiences with a known age (i.e., landmark experiences, e.g., one's first day at school) as a reference point for estimating their age in autobiographical memories (Arbuthnott & Brown, 2009). This should inoculate age estimations against context effects. Thus, if indeed the age in the instructions were echoed in participants' age estimates, this should be especially apparent in people guessing their age. In the absence of autobiographical knowledge people might (inadvertently) use contextual information in their answers. However, Study 1 showed the opposite pattern: guessers in the early condition were *older* in their earliest memory than participants who had used autobiographical knowledge. This renders an explanation in terms of a context-induced report bias less likely. Yet, this interpretation is based on exploratory analyses that should be replicated independently. An explanation in terms of priming or anchoring cannot be excluded at this point and future studies may further shed light on this issue.

The second type of explanation for the malleability of age in earliest memories is that the search process is influenced by the age information in the experimental context. That is, participants may use the life-time period referred to as a starting point for a deliberate memory search. It is thought that in order to navigate the search, the process involves iterations of self-generating cues (e.g., Conway, 2005). Starting within a particular life-time period would increase the probability that these self-generated cues represent knowledge that is specific to that life-time period. This, in turn, would increase the probability of retrieving a memory from that particular life-time period. Study 2 examined whether self-related knowledge questions about an early life-time period would aid the search process and result in younger ages. The lack of difference between the self-related and public-event-related knowledge conditions suggests that focussing on personal knowledge is not crucial for generating earlier memories than when no life-time period at all is used. In itself, thinking about an early period in life seems to be sufficient to render memories of younger ages. Perhaps the public-event questions provided participants with an anchor point to start their search, after which they turned to self-generating cues relying on knowledge from that life-time period to an equal extent as the participants in the self-relevant knowledge condition. It seems that the notion that age information in the experimental context provides a starting point for a memory search suffices to explain age-differences in earliest memories in the present studies. Future studies may examine this explanation further. Future work may also compare the impact of using vignettes (Study 1) and activating life-time period knowledge (Study 2) directly.

It has been suggested that sketchy memories are indicative of a developmentally earlier stage (Bruce et al., 2005; Conway, 2005; Pillemer, 1998). However, we did not find that the early conditions in our studies rendered more fragment memories than late or control conditions. In fact, we obtained very few fragment memories according to the rather strict criterion that they should represent decontextualised snippets of previous experience (cf. Bruce et al., 2005). Instead, we found that just under half of the memories fitted a category that we termed snapshot memories, reflecting scenes that did have some context but lacked temporal order. The percentages of snapshot memories were fairly consistent across conditions and studies (i.e., ranging from 41.8% to 48.6%) and they were consistently of a younger age than event memories across conditions. A comparison of phenomenological characteristics yielded only a few meaningful differences between snapshots and events. In both studies snapshots were more fragmented than events. In Study 1, events were shared more often and in Study 2 they contained more continuity and were less positive than snapshots. However, Bruce et al. (2005) reported that fragments and event memories differed in many more aspects and this suggests that snapshots may qualitatively differ from fragments. It should be noted that a number of the characteristics (recalling what happened before and after; fragmentation) are implied by the definition of snapshots and event memories and differences would thus reflect our coding scheme. However, these definitions are silent about emotional valence. It is interesting that snapshots were rated as more positive than event memories as the findings regarding emotional valence in the broader literature on childhood amnesia have been mixed (West & Bauer, 1999). To inform theory, future studies may further explore the usefulness of a distinction between fragments and snapshots. In addition, future work may follow up on the finding in Study 1 that snapshots seemed to be less sensitive to the age manipulation.

There are some methodological considerations that deserve attention. For example, it may be that in general, participants do not consider fragment memories as memories because of their characteristics such as vagueness (Tustin & Hayne, 2010). In spite of our attempts to lower the criterion for accepting mental representations as memories we obtained only a few fragment memories. It should be noted that in Bruce et al.'s studies, participants were explicitly instructed to retrieve fragment memories, whereas we coded memory type in a *post hoc* fashion. Thus, the very low number of fragments obtained in the present studies may indicate that participants did not readily retrieve fragments spontaneously. Future studies may use explicit instructions to retrieve fragments. In addition, our criteria for coding fragments may have been more stringent than in Bruce et al.'s (2005, 2007) studies. More generally, a distinction between categories of fragment and snapshots may be rather arbitrary. Future work may rely on scoring on a continuum running from "fragment" to "event" as this might more closely reflect the richness of the participants' memory reports. Furthermore, we used different measures of autobiographical memory characteristics in Studies 1 and 2, rendering the results less comparable. Future studies may optimise the assessment of characteristics.

A further consideration is that our samples mainly consisted of Western participants. There is evidence that cultural background matters (see Mullen, 1994; Wang, 2014). On average, participants from Eastern cultures report later earliest memories than those from Western cultures. A minority of our samples (i.e., 16% in Study 1 and 29% in Study 2) indicated that their nationality as other than German, Dutch or English. It is unknown how many had an Eastern cultural background as we did not ask them to specify. Nationality is unlikely to be responsible for the present findings as it did not statistically differ between the conditions in either study. However, our findings cannot be generalised to other cultures. Future work may determine whether age estimates in early memories are malleable in Eastern cultures as well.

Finally, the finding that asking about public-event knowledge and self-relevant knowledge had a similar effect on age estimates seems to be at odds with findings that extensive cueing renders earlier memories (Jack & Hayne, 2010). However, our self-relevant questions may have been too generic to provide an advantage over a natural tendency to self-generate cues based on autobiographical knowledge. Cues are effective to the extent that they overlap with aspects of the representation in memory (Tulving & Thomson, 1973). It is thought that this specificity is especially prominent in infancy, and that with progressing development the power to reactivate memories generalises to more abstract cues (such as verbal reminders, Imuta, Scarf, & Hayne, 2013). Future studies may use more extensive idiosyncratic questions to see if activating self-knowledge yields earlier (sketchy) memories than questions about public events from an early life-time period.

Taken together, the results of the present studies show that on average, age information introduced by the experimental context affects subsequent estimates of the age in earliest memories. Perhaps this information is used as a starting point for initiating a memory search of a particular life-time period. In addition, the age in snapshot memories was younger than in event memories. The results of Study 1 suggest that snapshots might even be resistant to age manipulations, yet this was not confirmed in Study 2. Future studies may further explore the phenomenological properties of snapshot memories, including the estimates of the age in those memories. Overall, the results of the present studies add to the growing literature that the age in earliest memories is malleable.

Notes

1. These items were "I do not recall this event very often" for the subscale Accessibility and "As I think about the event, I actually remember it rather than just knowing that it happened" for the subscale Recollection.
2. There were 160 cases, but 1 participant started the questionnaire twice. Her incomplete record was discarded.
3. The Cronbach's alphas pertain to the current sample.
4. For exploratory purposes, the questionnaire concluded with the Beck's Depression Inventory-II (Beck, Steer, Ball, & Ranieri, 1996) and a question about the overall affective tone of participants' childhood ("All in all, I would describe my childhood as … ") using a slider scale ranging from 0 (Negative) to 100 (Positive). There were no differences between conditions, and there were no correlations between these measures and any of the other variables in Study 2. In the interest of space, we refrain from reporting these findings in detail. Information can be obtained from the first author.

Acknowledgements

We would like to thank Jonas Schöndorf for his help with data collection and coding. The materials and data reported are available from https://osf.io/fneuc/.

Disclosure statement

No potential conflict of interest was reported by the authors.

References

Arbuthnott, K. D., & Brown, A. A. (2009). The use of autobiographical knowledge in age estimation. Memory, 17(3), 279–287. doi:10.1080/09658210802665829

Bauer, P. J. (2014). The development of forgetting: Childhood amnesia. In P. J. Bauer, & R. Fivush (Eds.), The Wiley handbook on the development of children's memory, (1st ed., pp. 519–544). Chichester: Wiley-Blackwell.

Bauer, P. J., & Larkina, M. (2014). The onset of childhood amnesia in childhood: A prospective investigation of the course and determinants of forgetting of early-life events. Memory, 22(8), 907–924. doi:10.1080/09658211.2013.854806

Beck, A. T., Steer, R. A., Ball, R., & Ranieri, W. F. (1996). Comparison of Beck Depression Inventories – IA and –II in psychiatric outpatients. Journal of Personality Assessment, 67(3), 588–597. doi:10.1207/s15327752jpa6703_13

Berntsen, D., & Rubin, D. C. (2006). The Centrality of Event Scale: A measure of integrating a trauma into one's identity and its relation to post-traumatic stress disorder symptoms. Behaviour Research and Therapy, 44(2), 219–231. doi:10.1016/j.brat.2005.01.009

Boyacioglu, I., & Akfirat, S. (2015). Development and psychometric properties of a new measure for memory phenomenology: The autobiographical memory characteristics questionnaire. Memory, 23(7), 1070–1092. doi:10.1080/09658211.2014.953960

Bruce, D., Phillips-Grant, K., Wilcox-O'Hearn, L. A., Robinson, J. A., & Francis, L. (2007). Memory fragments as components of autobiographical knowledge. Applied Cognitive Psychology, 21(3), 307–324. doi:10.1002/acp.1275

Bruce, D., Wilcox-O'Hearn, L. A., Robinson, J. A., Phillips-Grant, K., Francis, L., & Smith, M. C. (2005). Fragment memories mark the end of childhood amnesia. Memory & Cognition, 33(4), 567–576. doi:10.3758/BF03195324

Conway, M. A. (2005). Memory and the self. Journal of Memory and Language, 53(4), 594–628. doi:10.1016/j.jml.2005.08.005

Conway, A. R. A., Kane, M. J., Bunting, M. F., Hambrick, D. Z., Wilhelm, O., & Engle, R. W. (2005). Working memory span tasks: A methodological review and user's guide. Psychonomic Bulletin & Review, 12(5), 769–786.

Conway, M. A., & Pleydell-Pearce, C. W. (2000). The construction of autobiographical memories in the self-memory system. Psychological Review, 107(2), 261–288. doi:10.1037/0033-295X.107.2.261

Cramer, A. O. J., van Ravenzwaaij, D., Matzke, D., Steingroever, H., Wetzels, R., Grasman, R. P. P. P., … Wagenmakers, E.-J. (2016). Hidden multiplicity in exploratory multiway ANOVA: Prevalence and remedies. Psychonomic Bulletin & Review, 23(2), 640–647. doi:10.3758/s13423-015-0913-5

Friedman, W. J. (1993). Memory for the time of past events. Psychological Bulletin, 113(1), 44–66. doi:10.1037/0033-2909.113.1.44

Gelman, A., & Loken, E. (2014). The statistical crisis in science. American Scientist, 102(6), 460–465. doi:10.1511/2014.111.460

Greenberg, D. L., Bishara, A. J., & Mugayar-Baldocchi, M. A. (2017). Anchoring effects on early autobiographical memories. Memory. doi:10.1080/09658211.2017.1297833

Howe, M. L. (2013). Memory development: Implications for adults recalling childhood experiences in the courtroom. Nature Reviews Neuroscience, 14(12), 869–876. doi:10.1038/nrn3627

Imuta, K., Scarf, D., & Hayne, H. (2013). The effect of verbal reminders on memory reactivation in 2-, 3-, and 4-year-old children. Developmental Psychology, 49(6), 1058–1065. doi:10.1037/a0029432

Jack, F., & Hayne, H. (2010). Childhood amnesia: Empirical evidence for a two-stage phenomenon. Memory, 18(8), 831–844. doi:10.1080/09658211.2010.510476

Janssen, S. M. J., Chessa, A. G., & Murre, J. M. J. (2006). Memory for time: How people date events. *Memory & Cognition, 34*(1), 138–147.

Kingo, O. S., Bohn, A., & Krøjgaard, P. (2013). Warm-up questions on early childhood memories affect the reported age of earliest memories in late adolescence. *Memory, 21*(2), 280–284. doi:10.1080/09658211.2012.729598

Malinoski, P. T., & Lynn, S. J. (1999). The plasticity of early memory reports: Social pressure, hypnotizability, compliance and interrogative suggestibility. *International Journal of Clinical and Experimental Hypnosis, 47*(4), 320–345. doi:10.1080/00207149908410040

Mullen, M. K. (1994). Earliest recollections of childhood: A demographic analysis. *Cognition, 52*, 55–79. doi:10.1016/0010-0277(94)90004-3

Peterson, T., Kaasa, S. O., & Loftus, E. F. (2009). Me too!: Social modelling influences on early autobiographical memories. *Applied Cognitive Psychology, 23*(2), 267–277. doi:10.1002/acp.1455

Pillemer, D. B. (1998). What is remembered about early childhood events? *Clinical Psychology Review, 18*(8), 895–913. doi:10.1016/S0272-7358(98)00042-7

Qualtrics. (Versions October 2014/April 2015) [Computer software]. Provo, UT: Qualtrics. Retrieved from http://www.qualtrics.com

Rubin, D. C. (2000). The distribution of early childhood memories. *Memory, 8*(4), 265–269. doi:10.1080/096582100406810

Schaefer, A., & Philippot, P. (2005). Selective effects of emotion on the phenomenal characteristics of autobiographical memories. *Memory, 13*(2), 148–160. doi:10.1080/09658210344000648

Tabachnick, B. G., & Fidell, L. S. (2007). *Using multivariate statistics* (5th ed.). Boston, MA: Allyn & Bacon/Pearson Education.

Tulving, E., & Thomson, D. M. (1973). Encoding specificity and retrieval processes in episodic memory. *Psychological Review, 80*(5), 352–373.

Tustin, K., & Hayne, H. (2010). Defining the boundary: Age-related changes in childhood amnesia. *Developmental Psychology, 46*(5), 1049–1061. doi:10.1037/a0020105

Wang, Q. (2014). The cultured self and remembering. In P. J. Bauer & R. Fivush (Eds.), *The Wiley handbook on the development of children's memory* (pp. 605–625). Chichester: John Wiley & Sons. Retrieved from https://doi.org/10.1002/9781118597705.ch26

Wang, Q., & Peterson, C. (2014). Your earliest memory may be earlier than you think: Prospective studies of children's dating of earliest childhood memories. *Developmental Psychology, 50*(6), 1680–1686.

Wang, Q., & Peterson, C. (2016). The fate of childhood memories: Children postdated their earliest memories as they grew older. *Frontiers in Psychology, 6*, 1–7. doi:10.3389/fpsyg.2015.02038

Wells, C., Morrison, C. M., & Conway, M. A. (2014). Adult recollections of childhood memories: What details can be recalled? *The Quarterly Journal of Experimental Psychology, 67*(7), 1249–1261. doi:10.1080/17470218.2013.856451

West, T. A., & Bauer, P. J. (1999). Assumptions of infantile amnesia: Are there differences between early and later memories? *Memory, 7*(3), 257–278. doi:10.1080/096582199387913

Looking at the past through a telescope: adults postdated their earliest childhood memories

Qi Wang, Carole Peterson, Angel Khuu, Carissa P. Reid, Kayleigh L. Maxwell and Julia M. Vincent

ABSTRACT
Our previous studies have consistently shown a telescoping error in children's dating of earliest childhood memories. Preschool children through adolescents systematically date their earliest memories at older ages, in comparison with the age estimates provided by their parents or by themselves previously. In the current study, we examined the dating of earliest childhood memories in two samples of college adults and collected independent age estimates from their parents. Consistent with our findings with children, adults significantly postdated their earlier memories by approximately 12 months (Study 1) and 6 months (Study 2). The actual age of earliest memories was 2.5 years after adjusted for telescoping errors, 1 year earlier than what is commonly believed at 3.5 years. These findings challenge commonly held theoretical assumptions about childhood amnesia and highlight critical methodological issues in the study of childhood memory.

Childhood amnesia has been a subject of lasting interest among psychologists for over a century. It refers to the common phenomenon where adults typically cannot remember any event from their childhood that took place before they were 3.5 years old on average (Bauer, 2007; Peterson, 2012; Pillemer & White, 1989). Developmental studies have further shown that childhood amnesia can be observed in children as young as age 8 or 9 years and becomes more pervasive as children get older (Cleveland & Reese, 2008; Jack, MacDonald, Reese, & Hayne, 2009; Peterson, Grant, & Boland, 2005; Peterson, Warren, & Short, 2011; Tustin & Hayne, 2010; Wang, 2004). Critically, the most commonly used method for studying childhood amnesia is to examine the age of earliest memory, dubbed as the offset of childhood amnesia. It is considered to be the turning point from which early memories become accessible to conscious recall. The age of earliest memory has served as the basis for major theoretical explanations for childhood amnesia and the development of memory in early childhood more generally (Bauer, 2007; Nelson & Fivush, 2004; Perner & Ruffman, 1995; Peterson, 2012; Pillemer & White, 1989; Wang, 2003). However, recent cross-sectional and longitudinal studies on children's recollection of early childhood have shown that the age of earliest memory is in fact systematically biased in estimate.

Children postdate their earliest childhood memories

In the first study that focused on the accuracy of children's age estimates of early childhood memories, Wang, Peterson, and Hou (2010) asked Chinese and European Canadian 8-, 11-, and 14-year-old children to recall and date memories for events that occurred before they went to school. Children's parents verified each of the memories children recalled and provided independent age estimates for these memories. For the memory events that parents verified as happening before children were 48 months, children dated the memories at significantly older ages than did their parents. In contrast, for the events that parents verified as happening after children were 48 months, children dated the memories at significantly younger ages than did their parents. This pattern was consistent across age and culture groups. Given that the single earliest memories mostly occurred before 48 months (Peterson, 2012; Pillemer & White, 1989; Rubin, 2000; Wang & Peterson, 2014), these memories tend to be postdated.

Notably, studies prior to Wang et al. (2010) had also attempted to verify the dating accuracy of early childhood memories by comparing dating information provided by participants and that provided by parents or other adults who were present at the time of the events (e.g., Bauer, Burch, Scholin, & Güler, 2007; Bruce, Dolan, & Phillips-Grant, 2000; Eacott & Crawley, 1998; Howes, Siegel, & Brown, 1993; Jack et al., 2009). The general conclusion was that there were no systematic dating errors in early childhood memories. The key methodological difference between these studies and Wang et al. (2010) is that in these studies, the *mean* age estimate provided by participants was compared against the *mean* age estimate provided by parents, whereas in Wang et al. (2010), children's dating of each memory was verified against the dating information provided by parents. Indeed, the mean age estimates provided by children and by parents were almost identical in Wang et al. (2010), just as in prior studies. Because children postdated earlier memories and predated later memories, these two trends largely cancelled each other out, so that calculations of mean ages of children's memories by children vs. parents ended up being almost identical.

Wang and Peterson (2014) subsequently conducted two prospective studies to examine children's recall and dating of their earliest memories for the same events longitudinally, at two different time points. They asked 4–13-year-old children to recall and date their three earliest memories at two time points, with a 1-year (Study 1) or 2-year interval (Study 2). It was found that across all age groups, children postdated their memories to significantly older ages at the follow-up interview, particularly for memories initially dated from earlier years of life. Thus, although children continued to remember many of the same events as their earliest memories, the location in time of the memories shifted to an older age as time went by.

Then, in a further 8-year longitudinal study with a group of 4–9-year-old children, Wang and Peterson (2016) examined children's recall and dating of their earliest memories at three time points: an initial interview, a 2-year follow-up, and an 8-year follow-up. They found that earliest memories continued to be postdated many years following the previous recalls and that the magnitude of postdating was especially sizable for earlier memories and among younger children. Importantly, many early memories were forgotten as children got older, consistent with the findings of other longitudinal studies (Jack et al., 2009; Peterson et al., 2005, 2009; Tustin & Hayne, 2010). Yet, for the memories that children continued to remember, the dating of the memories shifted upward in time. Based on these findings, Wang and Peterson (2014, 2016) suggest that the postdating of earliest childhood memories may eventually result in a period of childhood "amnesia" from which no memories are dated, instead of no memories available for recall. They further suggest that the postdating of earliest childhood memories may reflect the general cognitive bias of telescoping error.

The telescoping error

When people recall and date distant memories from a period of their lives (e.g., the first semester at college, or the past 6 months), older memories tend to be postdated, whereby the events are thought to have happened more recently than they actually have (Janssen, Chessa, & Murre, 2006; Loftus & Marburger, 1983; Rubin & Baddeley, 1989; Thompson, Skowronski, & Lee, 1988). This phenomenon is termed *telescoping*, as it resembles the situation where an object seems closer in distance when viewed through a telescope. On the other hand, a reverse telescoping effect is often observed with more recent memories from the same period, whereby events are thought to have happened earlier or in a more distant past than they actually have and, as a result, they tend to be predated. These dating errors eventually cause the estimated dates to move toward the middle of the target period (Janssen et al., 2006; Loftus & Marburger, 1983; Rubin & Baddeley, 1989; Thompson et al., 1988).

Importantly, information about "when" of an event is not always encoded with information about "where" and "what", but often reconstructed at the time of recall (Brewer, 1988; Brown, 1990; Thompson, Skowronski, Larsen, & Betz, 1996). Retention has been shown to be a critical determinant for the accuracy of event date estimation (Betz & Skowronski, 1997; Thompson et al., 1996). Thus, although the mechanism underlying telescoping and reverse telescoping is not entirely clear, there have been proposals that the incomplete retention of memories as a result of elapsed time may contribute to such imprecision in memory dating (Huttenlocher, Hedges, & Prohaska, 1988; Janssen et al., 2006; Rubin & Baddeley, 1989). Because all the events being dated have presumably happened during the target period (e.g., the first semester at college, or the past 6 months), whenever dating errors occur, older events are generally postdated (i.e., telescoping) and more recent events are generally predated (i.e., reverse telescoping) so that the recollected dates would fall in the requested period. Furthermore, because older events tend to be less well retained, the magnitude of dating errors for these events tend to be more pronounced, when compared with more recent events.

Our findings with children's age estimates of early childhood memories are consistent with this literature: When recalling events from the period of early childhood, preschool children through adolescents exhibited telescoping errors by postdating their earliest memories to older ages (Wang et al., 2010; Wang & Peterson, 2014, 2016), and exhibited reverse telescoping errors by predating their later memories to younger ages (Wang et al., 2010), in comparison with the age estimates provided by their parents or by themselves previously. The largest errors showing telescoping occurred for those memories that were children's earliest. Note that children may be particularly vulnerable to the dating errors due to their limited knowledge of time and memory dating strategies (Friedman, 2005; Scarf, Boden, Labuschagne, Gross, & Hayne, 2017). Nevertheless, given the relatively low accessibility and ease of interference of childhood memories (Bauer et al., 2007), it is possible that the same telescoping errors are present in adults' estimates of their age at the time of their earliest memories too. This would call into question the age of earliest memories commonly reported in the childhood amnesia literature. The present study set out to examine this question.

The present study

We examined the dating of earliest childhood memories in two samples of college adults and obtained independent age estimates from their parents. Participants reported their five earliest memories and estimated their ages at the time of the events. They further rated the characteristics of these memories (i.e., valence, vividness, personal significance, biographical importance). Parents were contacted via phone or email to verify these memories and to provide independent dating estimates.

Notably, although the memory dating information provided by parents is far from being an objective measure of veracity, there are a number of reasons why parents would provide more accurate age estimates of their children's childhood memories than children themselves. First, their children (now young adults) are recalling memories from their very earliest years, a period when children are typically first able to demonstrate long-term verbal recall of complex events (Bauer, 2007). In contrast, these memories date from the adulthood of parents whose memory has fully developed. Second, participants are recalling memories from a time when memories are scarce and typically fragmentary, whereas parents are recalling memories from a period of their lives that is likely to have high personal significance. Therefore, parents may retain and utilise more memory details as well as a multitude of memories to reconstruct event dates. Finally, parents have an additional advantage over their children for memory dating, whereby they can utilise the observable developmental differences in children's behaviour at various ages to inform their date reconstructions.

Following previous studies (Wang et al., 2010; Wang & Peterson, 2014), we used 48 months, the approximate median age estimate, as the cut-off point to examine participants' dating of earlier and later childhood memories. In line with our findings with children (Wang et al., 2010; Wang & Peterson, 2014, 2016), we expected the adult participants to exhibit telescoping errors in dating their earlier memories (before 48 months) and reverse telescoping errors in dating their later memories (after 48 months), when compared with the dating information provided by their parents. We further expected this pattern of results to persist, regardless of the characteristics of the memory events.

Study 1

Participants

A sample of 32 college students (22 females, 10 males; M age = 20.49, SD = 1.25) at Cornell University and their parents participated. They were part of a larger study on the strategy and accuracy of dating early childhood memories. All participants whose parents provided verifications of their memories were included in the current sample. The sample was ethnically diverse, including 18 (56.25%) Caucasian, 4 (12.5%) Asian, 4 (12.5%) Hispanic, 2 (6.25%) Black, and 4 (12.5%) other ethnic groups. All participants were proficient in English. They received course credits for their participation. Parents participated on a voluntary basis.

Procedure

Participants were individually interviewed in the lab by trained research assistants. The interviews were digitally recorded and later transcribed. After participants provided informed consent, the interviewer asked them to recall their five earliest memories in as much detail as possible, starting with what they would consider their very earliest memory. For each recollection, the interviewer followed up with standard prompts, "What else can you remember about this time?" and then, "Is there anything else?".

After completing the recall of all five memories, participants were asked to estimate the date of each event in month and year. They were instructed to verbalise their thoughts while dating the memories, thinking aloud as they tried to figure out when each event occurred. It was emphasised that participants should verbalise all their thoughts, regardless of how important or unimportant those thoughts might seem. The interviewer gave participants a prompt for each memory they recalled earlier (e.g., "Your earliest memory was X"), and then remained silent while participants engaged in the dating task. The recording ended after the last memory was dated.

Participants were then asked a number of questions regarding their memories and the interviewer took notes of their responses. They were first asked about their emotions at the time of each recalled event, which were categorised as positive, negative, neutral, or mixed. They then rated various characteristics of each memory on 7-point Likert scales, including vividness (1 = *very vague*, 7 = *very vivid*), personal significance (1 = *definitely not important*, 7 = *definitely important*), and biographical importance. For biographical importance, participants were instructed to imagine that they were famous and someone was writing a biography to tell their life story and then rate how likely they were to include each memory in that biography (1 = *definitely wouldn't include*, 7 = *definitely include*). Participants were further asked whether they had experienced a number of common landmark events before the age of 8. These data address separate research questions and were not included here. The entire interview took approximately 45 min.

Parents were contacted via phone or e-mail and provided informed consent either orally or in writing. They were given a brief summary of each of the memories recalled by their children (e.g., "Went to the mall with father the day younger sister was born"). These minimal descriptions provided no details of the memories beyond those necessary to pinpoint a particular event. For each memory, parents were asked whether it had occurred to their knowledge or, if they did not know for sure, whether it was a reasonable event. They were further asked to date each memory to the nearest year and month.

Results

A total of 160 memories were collected. Among the memories, 83% were confirmed by parents to have happened,

17% were deemed to be reasonable, and none was disputed. These results are consistent with previous studies that verified early childhood memories recalled by children or adults (e.g., Bauer et al., 2007; Bruce et al., 2000; Eacott & Crawley, 1998; Peterson, Wang, & Hou, 2009). The age estimate for each memory was calculated in months for both participants and their parents. If the age spanned a range of months, the midpoint for that range was used as the participant's age at the event. The memory that was the earliest according to the ages that the participants identified was selected as their first memory. This could be the memory that participants had explicitly identified as their first memory, or if one of their other memories occurred at a younger age, it was selected instead. Gender showed no effect on any variable in preliminary analysis and was not considered further.

The average ages of all five memories reported by participants ($M = 60.75$ months, $SD = 25.41$) and parents ($M = 56.05$, $SD = 27.28$) were not significantly different, $F(1, 131) = 1.98$, $p = .16$, $\eta_p^2 = 0.02$. Similarly, the average ages of the first memory reported by participants ($M = 41.41$ months, $SD = 15.37$) and parents ($M = 44.13$, $SD = 20.24$) did not differ significantly, $F(1, 29) = 1.79$, $p = .19$, $\eta_p^2 = 0.06$.

Following prior research (Wang et al., 2010; Wang & Peterson, 2014, 2016), memories were roughly medium split into those dated before 48 months (48.50%) and those dated after 48 months (51.51%) to index the age at encoding, based on parents' age estimates. The difference between participants' and parents' age estimates (i.e., participants' dating − parents' dating) was used to index the dating error. A mixed model analysis was conducted on the dating error of all five memories, with the age at encoding (i.e., before vs. after 48 months) being a within-subject factor and subject being a random factor. A significant main effect of age at encoding emerged, $F(1, 115) = 32.78$, $p < .0001$, $\Delta R^2 = 0.18$. Memories of younger age at encoding (i.e., before 48 months) were postdated for almost 12 months (for participants, $M = 48.38$, $SD = 17.54$; for parents, $M = 36.50$, $SD = 8.55$), $F(1, 63) = 36.96$, $p < .0001$, $\eta_p^2 = 0.37$, whereas memories of older age at encoding (i.e., after 48 months) were predated over 6 months (for participants, $M = 67.97$, $SD = 27.80$; for parents, $M = 74.44$, $SD = 26.04$), $F(1, 67) = 7.70$, $p = .007$, $\eta_p^2 = 0.10$. Thus, there was a telescoping effect for earlier memories and a reverse telescoping effect for later memories (see Figure 1).

Next, we tested the effect of age at encoding on the dating error of the first memory. Because of the small sample ($n = 32$; 67% dated before 48 months), memories were not split into two groups by age estimates. Instead, the age at encoding based on the age estimates of parents was entered as a continuous variable into a regression model to predict the dating error. A significant effect emerged, $B = -0.47$, $SE = 0.10$, $t = -4.60$, $p < .0001$. As the age at encoding increased, the dating error changed from primarily positive values (i.e., postdating)

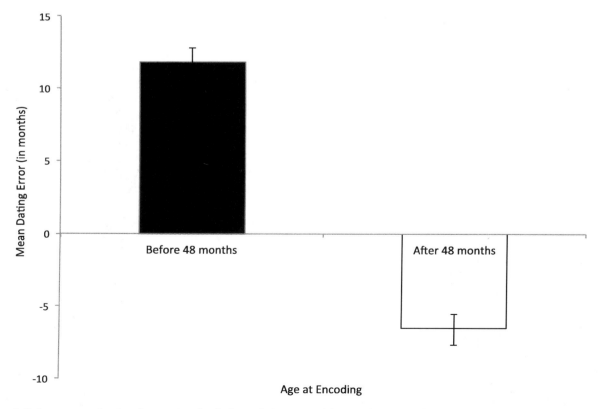

Figure 1. Dating error as a function of age at encoding (before and after 48 months) across all memories for Study 1.

to primarily negative values (i.e., predating), and among the memories that were postdated, the earliest memories showed largest telescoping errors (see Figure 2).

Additional analyses were conducted by including valence, vividness, personal significance, and biographical importance in the above models as covariates. The pattern of results remained identical: Across all five memories, those before 48 months were postdated and those after 48 months were predated, $F(1, 112) = 29.18$, $p < .0001$, $\Delta R^2 = 0.18$. For the first memory, the dating error changed from primarily telescoping to reverse telescoping as the age at encoding increased, $B = -0.41$, $SE = 0.12$, $t = -3.35$, $p = .003$.

Study 2

Findings from Study 1 thus showed telescoping dating errors for memories from earlier childhood and reverse telescoping dating errors for memories from later childhood. We replicated the findings in another sample in Study 2.

Participants

The sample consisted of 49 college students (39 females, 10 males; M age = 21.37, $SD = 2.06$) at Memorial University of Newfoundland. They were part of a larger study on the strategy and accuracy of dating early childhood memories. All participants whose parents provided verifications of their memories were included in the current sample. Almost all participants self-identified as Caucasian and all were proficient in English. They either received course credits for their participation or were entered in a draw for a $50 gift card. Parents participated on a voluntary basis.

Procedure

The procedure was identical to that in Study 1.

Results

A total of 245 memories were collected, of which 81% were confirmed by parents to have happened and 18% were deemed to be reasonable. Only 1% ($n = 3$) of the memories were disputed, which were excluded in analysis. These results are consistent with previous findings (e.g., Bauer et al., 2007; Bruce et al., 2000; Eacott & Crawley, 1998; Peterson et al., 2009). As in Study 1, the age estimate for each memory was calculated in months for both participants and their parents, and the memory that was the

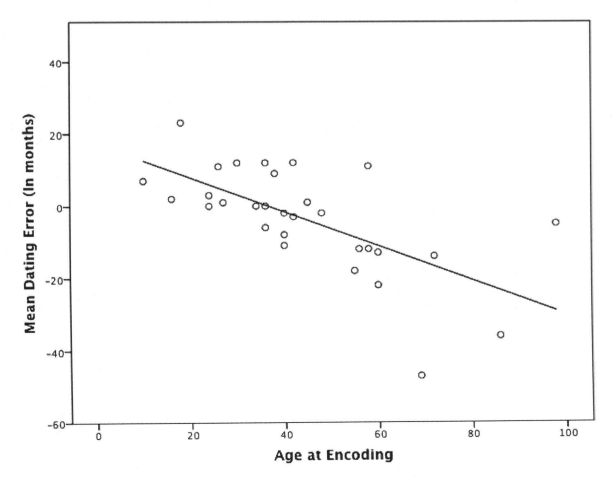

Figure 2. Dating error as a function of age at encoding for the first memory for Study 1.

earliest according to the ages that the participants identified was selected as their first memory. The average ages of all five memories reported by participants ($M = 61.69$ months, $SD = 31.67$) and parents ($M = 58.97$, $SD = 27.70$) were not significantly different, $F(1, 192) = 2.63$, $p = .11$, $\eta_p^2 = 0.01$. Similarly, the average ages of the first memory reported by participants ($M = 36.14$ months, $SD = 15.55$) and parents ($M = 40.27$, $SD = 20.74$) did not significantly differ, $F(1, 43) = 2.07$, $p = .16$, $\eta_p^2 = 0.05$.

Memories were divided into those dated before 48 months (41.45%) and those dated after 48 months (58.55%) to index the age at encoding, based on parents' age estimates. The difference between participants' and parents' age estimates for each memory was calculated to index the dating error. A mixed model analysis was conducted on the dating error of all five memories, with the age at encoding (i.e., before vs. after 48 months) being a within-subject factor and subject being a random factor. A significant main effect of age at encoding emerged, $F(1, 182) = 5.95$, $p = .016$, $\Delta R^2 = 0.04$. Memories of younger age at encoding (i.e., before 48 months) were postdated over 6 months (for participants, $M = 40.09$, $SD = 16.42$; for parents, $M = 34.10$, $SD = 10.09$), $F(1, 79) = 11.81$, $p = .001$, $\eta_p^2 = 0.13$, whereas there was no significant difference between participants' ($M = 76.30$, $SD = 28.38$) and parents' age estimates ($M = 76.58$, $SD = 22.12$) for memories of older age at encoding (i.e., after 48 months), $F(1, 112) = 0.02$, $p = .89$, $\eta_p^2 = 0.00$. Thus, there was a telescoping effect for earlier memories but a reverse telescoping was not significant for later memories (see Figure 3).

Next, we tested the effect of age at encoding on the dating error of the first memory ($n = 49$; 75% dated before 48 months). Again, the age at encoding based on the age estimates of parents was entered as a continuous variable into a regression model to predict the dating error. A significant effect emerged, $B = -0.56$, $SE = 0.09$, $t = -6.06$, $p < .0001$. Consistent with Study 1 results, the dating error changed from primarily positive values (i.e., postdating) to primarily negative values (i.e., predating) as the age at encoding increased, and among the memories that were postdated, the earliest memories showed largest telescoping errors (see Figure 4).

Additional analyses including valence, vividness, personal significance, and biographical importance in the above models as covariates yielded identical patterns of results. Across all five memories, those before 48 months were postdated and those after 48 months showed no significant dating errors, $F(1, 103) = 5.49$, $p = .02$, $\Delta R^2 = 0.06$. For the first memory, the dating error changed from primarily telescoping to reverse telescoping as the age at encoding increased, $B = -0.64$, $SE = 0.20$, $t = -3.23$, $p = .004$.

Discussion

Consistent with our previous findings of children's dating of early childhood memories (Wang et al., 2010; Wang &

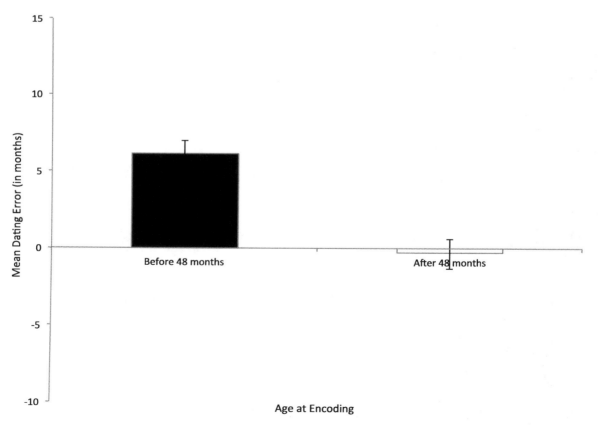

Figure 3. Dating error as a function of age at encoding (before and after 48 months) across all memories for Study 2.

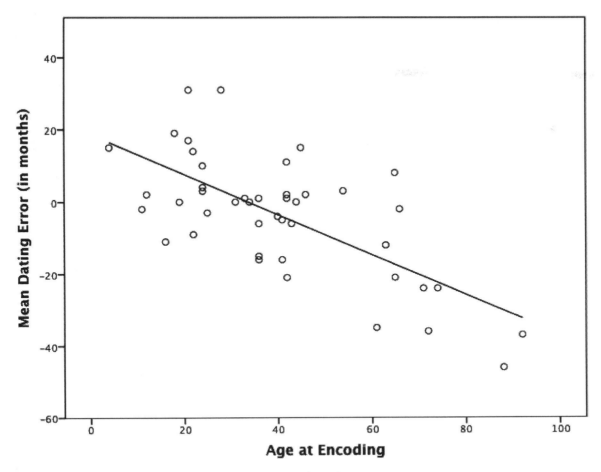

Figure 4. Dating error as a function of age at encoding for the first memory for Study 2.

Peterson, 2014, 2016), adult participants of two independent samples in the current study exhibited telescoping errors when dating memories from earlier childhood (before 48 months), when compared with the dating information provided by their parents. Adults also exhibited reverse telescoping errors when dating memories from later childhood (after 48 months), although the effect was only significant in Study 1. The pattern of results remained regardless of the characteristics of the memory events. The magnitude of dating errors was particularly pronounced for earlier memories, whereby participants postdated these memories for approximately 12 months in Study 1 and 6 months in Study 2. Interestingly, although adult participants of the two samples exhibited different degrees of telescoping errors, their parents dated the earlier memories at about the same age, at 36.5 months in Study 1 and 34.1 months in Study 2. If we assume that the parents' estimates approximate the actual time of occurrence of the events, then the age of earliest memories may indeed be 2.5 years. Alternatively, the average age of the first memory reported by participants was 41.4 months in Study 1 and 36.1 months in Study 2. After adjusting for their respective telescoping errors, the age of the first memory was again approximately 2.5 years for both samples. These findings have critical theoretical and methodological implications for research on childhood amnesia.

One major explanation for childhood amnesia is that over the course of development, early memories decrease in accessibility and eventually become inaccessible. This results in a period of childhood amnesia from which there are almost no memories available to conscious recall (Bauer, 2007; Peterson, 2012). This "forgetting" explanation has received empirical support, whereby many of the early memories indeed become inaccessible or forgotten as children grow older so that there is an increase in the age of earliest memory with increasing age of children (Jack et al., 2009; Peterson et al., 2005, 2009; Tustin & Hayne, 2010). However, our findings have shown that there is a second phenomenon at work too: children continued to remember many of their earliest memories years later and that, more importantly, they postdated the memories to considerably later ages as time passed, which results in an upward shift in the boundary of childhood amnesia over time (Wang et al., 2010; Wang & Peterson, 2014, 2016).

Findings from the current study further add to this body of research by showing that at young adulthood, earliest memories *continued* to be postdated to significantly later ages. They reaffirm our proposal of a "postdating" explanation of childhood amnesia: Some of the earliest memories remain accessible in the course of development, but they are telescoped when recalled at later time points as their retention weakened. This result in a period of "childhood amnesia" from which almost no memories are dated (Wang & Peterson, 2014, 2016). These findings further suggest that the widespread belief about childhood amnesia may be wrong and that adults' earliest memories may occur at approximately 2.5 years, 1 year earlier than the generally assumed average age of 3.5 years (e.g., Pillemer & White, 1989; Rubin, 2000). Theorists of childhood amnesia need to look beyond preschool ages and examine factors in toddlerhood and even infancy that influence memory formation and retention. Potential contributing factors include the development of a sense of agency, non-verbal representational skills, joint attention, and implicit and explicit emotional understanding. In addition, characteristics of an individual's experiences may also play a role in memory development, including multiple retrieval opportunities, the emotional valence of the experience, and the continuity of the early environment.

Methodologically, the current findings point to the importance of examining age estimates of individual memories as a function of age at encoding, rather than comparing group means across all memories. Prior studies that compared the *mean* age estimate provided by participants against the *mean* age estimate provided by parents have failed to identify systematic dating errors and come to the conclusion that the age estimates of earliest memories are generally accurate (e.g., Bauer et al., 2007; Bruce et al., 2000; Peterson et al., 2009). Indeed, the mean age estimates of memories provided by adult participants and their parents in the current study were almost identical as well. These findings are in line with the telescoping literature (Janssen et al., 2006; Loftus & Marburger, 1983; Rubin & Baddeley, 1989; Thompson et al., 1988), whereby memories from earlier childhood were postdated whereas memories from later childhood were predated, which cancelled each other out and caused the estimated dates to fall in the middle. Thus, it is critical in future research of childhood memory to take into consideration the age at encoding when evaluating dating accuracy.

Notably, parents might be subject to dating errors themselves. Just like their children, parents might postdate earlier memories and predate later memories from their children's childhood. If that was the case, the magnitude of actual memory dating errors by young adults might be even larger than what we observed. On the other hand, any dating errors parents made in our study might not be systematic. Parents were simply asked to date the memories that their children had recalled rather than generating and dating memories from a specific time period themselves, a usual condition for telescoping and reverse telescoping to occur (Janssen et al., 2006; Rubin & Baddeley, 1989). Thus, the overall pattern of results should not be affected by the parents' dating errors. Telescoping and reverse telescoping are observed when event date estimates are verified against objective measures such as dates recorded in diaries (Betz & Skowronski, 1997; Janssen et al., 2006). Nevertheless, future research should identify other means of verifying dating accuracy for early childhood memories.

In addition, it is interesting to note that although our two independent samples yielded similar patterns of results, participants in Study 1 exhibited larger telescoping and reverse telescoping errors than did participants in Study 2. We speculate that this might be due to the fact that the Study 1 sample was ethnically diverse whereas the Study 2 sample was composed of primarily Caucasians. The small number of participants in each ethnic group in Study 1 did not warrant reliable analysis of ethnicity. Yet inspection of the means showed that all groups showed telescoping for earlier memories and reverse telescoping for later memories, but the magnitude of errors varied across groups. The telescoping error was 8.00 months for Caucasians and 6.63 months for Asians, comparable with the Study 2 sample. This is also consistent with Wang et al.'s (2010) finding that European Canadian and Chinese children exhibited similar telescoping errors for their earliest memories. Of particular interest, the telescoping error was 26.58 months for Hispanics, 35.5 months for Blacks, and 5.29 months for others ethnic groups. Thus, Hispanic and Black participants appeared to have markedly larger telescoping errors than did Caucasians and Asians. These cultural differences, if confirmed, may reflect different retentions or memory dating strategies across groups. Given that culture plays an important role in childhood recollections and autobiographical memory development (for reviews, see Wang, 2003, 2013), it will be extremely important to study these ethnic groups in future research.

In sum, the present study yielded critical findings that even at adulthood people continue to postdate their earliest childhood memories to considerably later ages, and thus, postdating of earliest memories is not just found with children. It appears as if people are looking at their earliest childhood experiences through a telescope so that those experiences feel closer in time. The distortions in memory dating may have led to erroneous conclusions about when our earliest memories occurred, which has far-reaching theoretical and methodological implications.

Disclosure statement

No potential conflict of interest was reported by the authors.

References

Bauer, P. J. (2007). *Remembering the times of our lives: Memory in infancy and beyond*. Mahwah, NJ: Erlbaum.

Bauer, P. J., Burch, M. M., Scholin, S. E., & Güler, O. E. (2007). Using cue words to investigate the distribution of autobiographical memories in childhood. *Psychological Science, 18*, 910–916. doi:10.1111/j.1467-9280.2007.01999

Betz, A. L., & Skowronski, J. J. (1997). Self-events and other-events: Temporal dating and event memory. *Memory & Cognition, 25*(5), 701–714. doi:10.3758/BF03211313

Brewer, W. F. (1988). Memory for randomly sampled autobiographical events. In U. Neisser, E. Winograd, U. Neisser, & E. Winograd (Eds.), *Remembering reconsidered: Ecological and traditional approaches to the study of memory* (pp. 21–90). New York, NY: Cambridge University Press. doi:10.1017/CBO9780511664014.004

Brown, N. R. (1990). Organization of public events in long-term memory. *Journal of Experimental Psychology: General, 119*(3), 297–314. doi:10.1037/0096-3445.119.3.297

Bruce, D., Dolan, A., & Phillips-Grant, K. (2000). On the transition from childhood amnesia to the recall of personal memories. *Psychological Science, 11*, 360–364. doi:10.1111/1467-9280.00271

Cleveland, E. S., & Reese, E. (2008). Children remember early childhood: Long-term recall across the offset of childhood amnesia. *Applied Cognitive Psychology, 22*, 127–142. doi:10.1002/acp.1359

Eacott, M. J., & Crawley, R. A. (1998). The offset of childhood amnesia: Memory for events that occurred before age 3. *Journal of Experimental Psychology: General, 127*, 22–33.

Friedman, W. J. (2005). Developmental and cognitive perspectives on humans' sense of the times of past and future events. *Learning and Motivation, 36*, 145–158. doi:10.1016/j.lmot.2005.02.005

Howes, M., Siegel, M., & Brown, F. (1993). Early childhood memories: Accuracy and affect. *Cognition, 47*, 95–119.

Huttenlocher, J., Hedges, L. V., & Prohaska, V. (1988). Hierarchical organization in ordered domains: Estimating the dates of events. *Psychological Review, 95*, 471–484. doi:10.1037/0033-295X.95.4.471

Jack, F., MacDonald, S., Reese, E., & Hayne, H. (2009). Maternal reminiscing style during early childhood predicts the age of adolescents' earliest memories. *Child Development, 80*, 496–505. doi:10.1111/j.1467-8624.2009.01274.x

Janssen, S. J., Chessa, A. G., & Murre, J. M. J. (2006). Memory for time: How people date events. *Memory & Cognition, 34*, 138–147. doi:10.3758/BF03193393

Loftus, E. F., & Marburger, W. (1983). Since the eruption of Mt. St. Helens, has any one beaten you up? Improving the accuracy of retrospective reports with landmark events. *Memory & Cognition, 11*, 114–120. doi:10.3758/BF03213465

Nelson, K., & Fivush, R. (2004). The emergence of autobiographical memory: A social cultural developmental theory. *Psychological Review, 111*, 486–511. doi:10.1037/0033-295X.111.2.486

Perner, J., & Ruffman, T. (1995). Episodic memory and autonoetic consciousness: Developmental evidence and a theory of childhood amnesia. *Journal of Experimental Child Psychology, 59*, 516–548. doi:10.1006/jecp.1995.1024

Peterson, C. (2012). Children's autobiographical memories across the years: Forensic implications of childhood amnesia and eyewitness memory for stressful events. *Developmental Review, 32*, 287–306. doi:10.1016/j.dr.2012.06.002

Peterson, C., Grant, V. V., & Boland, L. D. (2005). Childhood amnesia in children and adolescents: Their earliest memories. *Memory (Hove, England), 13*, 622–637. doi:10.1080/09658210444000278

Peterson, C., Wang, Q., & Hou, Y. (2009). "When I was little": Childhood recollections in Chinese and European Canadian grade-school children. *Child Development, 80*, 506–518. doi:10.1111/j.1467-8624.2009.01275.x

Peterson, C., Warren, K. L., & Short, M. M. (2011). Infantile amnesia across the years: A 2-year follow-up of children's earliest memories. *Child Development, 82*, 1092–1105. doi:10.1111/j.1467-8624.2011.01597.x

Pillemer, D. B., & White, S. H. (1989). Childhood events recalled by children and adults. In H. W. Reese (Ed.), *Advances in child development and behavior* (Vol. 21, pp. 297–340). New York: Academic Press.

Rubin, D. C. (2000). The distribution of early childhood memories. *Memory (Hove, England), 8*, 265–269. doi:10.1080/096582100406810

Rubin, D. C., & Baddeley, A. D. (1989). Telescoping is not time compression: A model of the dating of autobiographical events. *Memory & Cognition, 17*, 653–661. doi:10.3758/BF03202626

Scarf, D., Boden, H., Labuschagne, L. G., Gross, J., & Hayne, H. (2017). "What" and "where" was when? Memory for the temporal order of episodic events in children. *Developmental Psychobiology, 59*, 1039–1045. doi:10.1002/dev.21553

Thompson, C. P., Skowronski, J. J., Larsen, S., & Betz, A. L. (1996). *Autobiographical memory: Remembering what and remembering when.* Mahwah, NJ: L. Erlbaum.

Thompson, C. P., Skowronski, J. J., & Lee, D. J. (1988). Telescoping in dating naturally occurring events. *Memory & Cognition, 16*, 461–468. doi:10.3758/BF03214227

Tustin, K., & Hayne, H. (2010). Defining the boundary: Age-related changes in childhood amnesia. *Developmental Psychology, 46*, 1049–1061. doi:10.1037/a0020105

Wang, Q. (2003). Infantile amnesia reconsidered: A cross-cultural analysis. *Memory (Hove, England), 11*(1), 65–80. doi:10.1080/741938173

Wang, Q. (2004). The emergence of cultural self-constructs: Autobiographical memory and self-description in European American and Chinese children. *Developmental Psychology, 40*(1), 3–15. doi:10.1037/0012-1649.40.1.3

Wang, Q. (2013). *The autobiographical self in time and culture.* New York, NY: Oxford University Press. doi:10.1093/acprof:oso/9780199737833.001.0001

Wang, Q., & Peterson, C. (2014). Your earliest memory may be earlier than you think: Prospective studies of children's dating of earliest childhood memories. *Developmental Psychology, 50*, 1680–1686. doi:10.1037/a0036001

Wang, Q., & Peterson, C. (2016). The fate of childhood memories: Children postdated their earliest memories as they grew older. *Frontiers in Psychology: Cognition, 6*, 597. doi:10.3389/fpsyg.2015.02038

Wang, Q., Peterson, C., & Hou, Y. (2010). Children dating childhood memories. *Memory (Hove, England), 18*, 754–762. doi:10.1080/09658211.2010.508749

Consistency of adults' earliest memories across two years

Berivan Ece, Burcu Demiray and Sami Gülgöz

ABSTRACT
The consistency of earliest memories in content, dating, and memory qualities was investigated. A total of 84 (27 males; $M_{age} = 24.93$, $SD = 1.36$) adults reported earliest memories, estimated ages, and rated their recollections on memory qualities with a two-year time lag. At Time 2, their original reports at Time 1 were presented and they were asked to report whether the earliest memories they recalled at Time 2 were the same. Fifty-six per cent of the participants reported the same earliest memories and those remembering the same events had earlier memories than those remembering different ones. Although no significant differences were observed in estimated ages on the basis of mean ages, a predating bias of later memories and a tendency to postdate earlier memories were observed on the basis of a 48-month cut-off point. Thus, how the data is analysed is critical in detecting dating biases or errors affecting conclusions and interpretations about the dating consistency of earliest memories. Finally, memory qualities of earliest memories displayed a high level of consistency with a two-year time lag regardless of remembering the same versus different event.

Childhood amnesia refers to the well-established observation that adults tend to have almost no autobiographical recollections from the first few years of life (Bauer, 2007; Freud, 1905/1953; Hayne, 2004; Nelson & Fivush, 2004; Peterson, 2002). This consistent observation dates back to the end of 1800s (Henri & Henri, 1898; Miles, 1895) and has evoked a large number of studies about the approximate age from which adults can remember their earliest memories throughout the 1900s. Although some studies have reported that adults can recall events from their childhood as early as two-and-a-half years of age (e.g., Eacott & Crawley, 1998, 1999; Usher & Neisser, 1993), the majority of childhood amnesia research has demonstrated that earliest memories tend to come from the period between the ages of three and four (e.g., Bruce, Dolan, & Phillips-Grant, 2000; Conway & Holmes, 2004; Dudycha & Dudycha, 1941; Jack & Hayne, 2007; Mullen, 1994; Pillemer & White, 1989; Rubin, 1982; Tustin & Hayne, 2010; Waldfogel, 1948; West & Bauer, 1999). There is considerable research interest in the age of earliest memories because it is considered a landmark in the offset of childhood amnesia and the onset of autobiographical memory. Moreover, once this landmark is roughly identified, it can promote our understanding of potential developmental changes in that particular period contributing to the emergence of autobiographical memory.

Multiple factors were proposed to play a role in the emergence of autobiographical memory and the disappearance of childhood amnesia. These factors include the development of the cognitive self (Howe, 2003; Howe & Courage, 1993, 1997), language development (Dahl, Kingo, & Krøjgaard, 2015; Nelson, 1993; Simcock & Hayne, 2002), forgetting (Bauer, 2015; Hayne & Jack, 2011), maternal reminiscing style (Fivush, Haden, & Reese, 2006; Nelson & Fivush, 2004), and brain maturation or neurological development (Bachevalier, 1992; Bauer, 2008; Newcombe, Lloyd, & Ratliff, 2007). Childhood amnesia has also been investigated as a function of numerous factors such as gender (e.g., Cowan & Davidson, 1984; Mullen, 1994; Peterson, Warren, Nguyen, & Noel, 2010; Waldfogel, 1948; West & Bauer, 1999), culture (e.g., MacDonald, Uesiliana, & Hayne, 2000; Wang, 2001; Wang, Conway, & Hou, 2004), event dating (Wang & Peterson, 2014, 2016), personality traits (e.g., Child, 1940; Crook & Harden, 1931; Waldfogel, 1948), and birth order (e.g., Mullen, 1994). In contrast to the wealth of research on many factors related to childhood amnesia, the consistency of earliest memories over time has received little attention. Thus, the major purpose of the present study is to fill this gap in the literature by exploring the consistency in the recalled event, the dating of these events, and the qualities of remembering when adults are asked for their earliest memories with a gap of two years.

Consistency of earliest memories

Consistency of earliest memories refers to whether participants recollect the same event across different time points.

In some studies, the recollections are considered consistent as long as the participants recall the same event but in others, the consistency in the event narratives and details are examined.

One of the earlier studies on the consistency of earliest memories was conducted by Kihlstrom and Harackiewicz (1982) who examined the memories of 105 high school students across 3 months and reported 58.1% consistency in recollections. They further reported that students who recalled the same earliest memories at both time points recalled earlier earliest memories ($M = 3.56$; $SD = 1.10$) than their counterparts who reported different earliest memories ($M = 4.02$; $SD = 1.06$). Finally, when the different earliest memories reported at Time 1 and Time 2 were compared, the ones reported at Time 2 were earlier and more pleasant than the earliest memories remembered at Time 1.

Jack and Hayne (2010) investigated the emergence of autobiographical memory by using a personalised timeline. In their research, six university students were interviewed in two sessions separated by one-week intervals and were asked to provide all of their memories of events before their sixth birthday. When the earliest memories were examined, five of the six participants reported the same events after a one-week interval. The use of such a short interval obviously raises the question of whether the consistency observed in the study is due to recalling one's response given only a week ago.

In contrast to studies examining the consistency of memories across 2 sessions, Bauer, Tasdemir-Ozdes, and Larkina (2014) examined the earliest memories of 34 women who were tested 2–4 times over a period of 4 years. Participants were mothers of children who were brought to the laboratory for experimental tasks. Consistency of the memories was analysed at three levels: event consistency, date consistency, and content consistency. In terms of event consistency, a high level of consistency was observed such that 82% of the 34 participants who were tested twice, 72% of the 29 participants tested thrice, and 82% of the 17 participants tested 4 times provided consistent events at each testing. If the participants were consistent about the event and they had an age estimate for the event, the consistency in these estimates was 100% when tested twice but dropped with repeated testing to 79% in the case of four testing sessions. They also displayed considerable content consistency. The unusually high levels of consistency in this study stand apart from other studies and it is not clear whether this is due to the all-female participant group, or due to the fact that they were mothers of young children who could have been primed about early experiences through their children's experiences. There is no evidence suggesting that people exposed to experiences of their children are primed for rehearsal of their own childhood experiences as yet but it certainly is a reasonable possibility.

Larkina, Merrill, and Bauer (2017) did not particularly focus on earliest memories but studied the consistency of memories coming from the ages 1–5 and 6–10 alongside those coming from the previous year and the memory of the most significant event of their lives with 2 groups of participants, adolescents (12–14-years-olds) and young adults (18–23-years-olds). They were tested twice with a gap of one month. In the second testing, the participants were reminded of the topic of the memory they reported in the first session and were asked for the event details and date. Evaluating three types of consistency, event, content, and date, they found that young adults were more consistent than adolescents in both event (82–79% for young adults and 91–87% for adolescents) and content consistencies (43–31% for young adults and 35–24% for adolescents) and both age groups were more consistent in their memories about ages 1–5. The only exception was that both groups showed the least amount of consistency in the dating of the events from ages 1–5. Larkina et al. (2017) found gender differences where females reported more consistent memories than males, the levels of consistency were considerably below those obtained in the study by Bauer et al. (2014) despite the fact that in the current study the participants were reminded of the topics from the previous session.

Other studies that examined the consistency of earliest memories included children as participants. For example, Peterson, Warren, and Short (2011) reported that older children had later earliest memories than younger children, supporting earlier findings (e.g., Peterson, Grant, & Boland, 2005; Peterson, Wang, & Hou, 2009) and they were also more consistent in their earliest memory reports. Among the youngest group, 7.4% reported the same event as their earliest memory, whereas this ratio was 38.5% in the oldest group. The researchers also examined the consistency in the content of memories that were reported in the two sessions and they observed that content consistency also increased with age.

Wang and Peterson (2014, 2016) conducted two longitudinal studies to explore the consistency and dating biases in children's earliest memory reports. In 2014, they ran two studies involving a one-year and a two-year time interval. With a one-year time lag, 33.3% of the children remembered the same earliest memory, but postdated their recollections compared to their original dating at Time 1. With a two-year interval, 83% of children reported the same earliest memory and postdated them at Time 2. In 2016, they investigated the recollection and dating over a longer period in 37 children (ages 4–9) who were tested 2 years and 8 years after the initial testing. Their results showed that 86.5% of children recalled at least one initial memory both at Time 2 and Time 3. Children displayed the same pattern of postdating their earliest memories as they got older and as the children got older the consistency in dating increased as well. In short, authors observed a clear postdating bias for earlier memories in independent samples.

Any systematic bias in dating early childhood memories may have several implications for earliest memory research as proposed by Wang et al. (In press). As dating consistency is one of the major focuses of the present study, any bias affecting how adults date their early childhood memories plays a critical role in our results and conclusions. For that reason, we examined the analyses applied by Wang and her colleagues in their earlier studies focusing on potential dating biases (Wang & Peterson, 2014, 2016; Wang, Peterson, & Hou, 2010). The major difference of their analyses is the 48-month cut-off point they used for the age at encoding. They argued that the postdating bias of earlier memories and the predating bias of later memories may not be revealed when analyses were based on overall mean ages as in the majority of previous studies on earliest memory. When they applied a cut-off point like 48-month, results supported their argument by displaying postdating of early childhood memories experienced before 48 months (Wang et al., 2010; Wang & Peterson, 2014, 2016) and predating of memories experienced after 48 months (Wang et al., 2010, in press, Study 1). Thus, considering the age at encoding is critical in detecting and understanding dating consistency or inconsistency in earliest memories.

These studies raise several issues regarding the recollection of earliest memories. One issue is whether a particular event that is remembered as the earliest retrievable memory is indeed the earliest memory and is consistently so or whether the earliest memory may change in time and according to context. A second issue is the consistency of event date. As dating processes act independently of the processes of recalling an event, the consistency in dating must be discussed in the context of these processes. Dating an event can be quite straightforward, if the event is the birth of a sibling as in the Eacott and Crawley (1999) study. Otherwise, dating is either informed by others (e.g., parents) or based on some form of estimation. Estimations may be anchored on some other information, such as the fact that the event took place in a particular city, where the respondent lived until she was four years old. Otherwise, they will be arbitrary. It is also important to distinguish between remembering the same earliest memory at two testing sessions (i.e., consistency) versus remembering the memory reported in the previous session. With a short interval between two testing sessions, participants could respond with the event reported in the previous session, drawing on the memory of that session rather than retrieving the earliest memory. Yet another issue the methodology used to analyse dating consistency. As studies by Wang and her colleagues showed dating biases may not be observed when analyses are based on mean ages as the postdating of earlier memories and predating of later memories will cancel out each other's effect (Wang et al., 2010, in press; Wang & Peterson, 2014, 2016).

The present study

The present study attempts to tackle some of these issues and has both similarities and differences with the studies reviewed above. The current study (a) has a large sample size, (b) examines adults rather than adolescents or children, (c) focuses on earliest memories rather than a targeted event, (d) has a time lag of two years which should allow for forgetting the previous response, (e) takes into account the respondents' own judgments of consistency rather than relying on assessment of reported events by the researchers, and (f) analyses data based on both mean ages and the 48-month cut-off point for the age at encoding.

In the present research, we aimed to develop an optimal design that will address the issues related to the consistency of adults' earliest memories. Young adults reported their earliest memory, dated them by indicating their age at the time of the event, and rated the qualities of their memories (i.e., importance, emotional valence, and intensity) twice with a two-year interval. Thus, we evaluated the event and date consistency of young adults' earliest memories as well as consistency in memory qualities. This is important because different qualities of earliest memories may display differential patterns regarding their consistency over time. Just as participants can remember the same event across two sessions but date them differently (Larkina et al., 2017; Wang & Peterson, 2014, 2016) memory qualities may vary even though the recalled memories are the same. More interestingly, memory qualities may be similar even the events are not the same. The current research will allow us to examine such potential differences in the consistency patterns of event, date, and qualities of earliest memories.

Another novel contribution of the current study is that we had participants' self-reports as a measure of event consistency alongside judgments by a trained research assistant who made the judgments on the basis of the brief event descriptions. Self-reports also had a novel aspect: at Time 2, participants were first asked whether the earliest memory they reported was the same as the one they reported at Time 1 and then, they were presented with the full text of their earliest memory from Time 1 and asked to indicate whether it was the same as the memory they reported at Time 2 (i.e., recognition). Therefore, we had a chance (a) to compare the event consistency of earliest memories on the basis of different sources (i.e., self-report versus judgments of research assistant) and (b) examine whether the participants were recalling memories reported earlier (i.e., recall versus recognition).

With respect to the event recalled as earliest memories, we predict that consistency rate among young adults would be similar to the one observed by (a) Kihlstrom and Harackiewicz (1982) in high school students with a 3-month interval (58%) and (b) Peterson et al. (2011) in 12–13 years old children with a 2-year time lag (56%). We further predict significant differences in the estimated ages reported by participants who will remember the same versus different earliest memories at two time points. More specifically, we predict that young adults remembering the same earliest memories after a two-year time lag will have earlier earliest memories than those remembering different earliest memories at Time 2. This prediction is based on previous research indicating that participants who consistently recall the same earliest memory over time tend to have earlier estimated ages than those who recall different earliest memories (Bauer et al., 2014; Kihlstrom & Harackiewicz, 1982). For dating consistency, our predictions were twofold as we had 2 different lines of analyses: based on mean ages versus 48-month cut-off point. When analysed on the basis of mean ages, we expect no significant differences in young adults' dating of their earliest memories over time. In other words, we predict that young adults will date their earliest memories consistently over time with a two-year time lag. When memories experienced before versus after 48 months old are analysed separately, however, we predict postdating of those before 48 months and predating of the ones after 48 months old based on recent studies on dating biases of early childhood memories (Wang et al., 2010, in press; Wang & Peterson, 2014, 2016). And finally for memory qualities, analyses will be exploratory in nature; hence, we have no specific predictions.

Method

Participants

A total of 181 participants completed the online survey (Qualtrics, Provo, UT). To ensure data quality, participants who (a) did not meet the inclusion criteria (e.g., younger than 18 years old), (b) did not follow instructions (e.g., did not date or rate their earliest memories), and (c) spent too little (less than 2 min) or too much time (more than 2 h) on the survey were excluded. The final sample at Time 1 consisted of 152 young adults (53 male) with an age range of 18–34 ($M = 22.22$, $SD = 3.05$). Two years later, 84 (27 male) of these 152 participants completed the survey again. This sample at Time 2 had an age range of 21–36 ($M = 24.93$, $SD = 1.36$). Participants who were undergraduate students at Koç University received credits from an introductory psychology course for their participation. All the remaining participants who were contacted by either e-mail or social media sites (i.e., Facebook) volunteered to take part in the study and received no compensation for their participation.

Materials

Earliest memory task
Participants were instructed to report briefly the earliest memory they could recall from their childhood. Once they wrote down their memory, they were asked to date the event and rate it in terms of importance (*How important was this event for you? From not important at all*, 1, *to very important*, 5), emotional valence (*from very negative*, 1, *to very positive*, 5) and intensity (*How emotionally intense was this event for you? From not intense at all*, 1, *to very intense*, 5), consequentiality (*How important were the consequences of this event for you? From not important at all*, 1, *to very important*, 5), effect on personality (*How important was this event for your personality development? From not important at all*, 1, *to very important*, 5), control over the event (*How much control over this event did you have? From none at all*, 1, *to very high*, 5), confidence (*How confident are you that this is the earliest event in your memory? From not confident at all*, 1, *to very confident*, 5), reality (*How confident are you that this event is a real event that you experienced? From not confident at all*, 1, *to very confident*, 5), vividness (emotions and images) (*How vivid are the emotions/images of this event right now? From not vivid at all*, 1, *to very vivid*, 5), and rehearsal (frequency of thinking and talking) (*How frequently did you think/talk about this event? From never*, 1, *to very frequently*, 5). Among these memory qualities, emotional valence had two separate ratings: for the time of experience (then) and the time of retrieval (now).

Procedure

The study was conducted online (Qualtrics, Provo, UT) and the survey link was shared by using social media tools and via standard e-mail sent by the researchers to the participant pool of Koç University. The survey consisted of three parts at Time 1. In the first part, participants were informed about the study and asked to provide their consent to participate. In the second part, they responded to demographic questions about their age and gender. In the third part, they completed the earliest memory task. Completion of the whole survey took approximately 15 min. The participants were not informed that they would be tested another time.

Time 2 data collection was carried out two years following Time 1. At Time 2, the first three parts were exactly the same with Time 1. The only difference was that there was an additional fourth part at the end of the same survey in which participants were asked whether the earliest memory they reported was the same as the one they reported at Time 1 (i.e., recall question). Following that question, they were presented with their original earliest memory at Time 1 and asked to indicate if it was the same as the memory they reported at Time 2 (i.e., recognition question). For both recall and recognition questions, participants responded by selecting one of the three options: "yes", "no", or "I don't remember what I reported at Time 1". Completion of the whole survey took approximately 20 min at Time 2. After data collection, a trained research assistant compared the earliest memory reports at Time 1 and Time 2 and rated them as "same" or "different".

The time interval between the first session and the second one varied between 603 and 742 days with a mean of 684.7 days (SD = 26.1).

Results

Consistency of earliest memories across Time 1 and Time 2 was examined by three separate lines of analyses measuring consistency in the reported event, memory qualities, and dating.

Event consistency

We had two types of event consistency measures: participants' self-reports and ratings by a trained research assistant. Because the participants were asked to report the earliest events briefly, they were judged only in terms of event consistency; the accounts did not allow for a detailed content analysis. The level of agreement between the participants and the rater was 95%. One memory that participants reported as the same event was rated as different by the rater and three pairs of memories that participants indicated as being different was rated as the same by the rater. Due to the high level of agreement between the participants and the rater, further analyses were based on the participants' judgments.

When the participants were asked in the second session without any prompts whether the events they recalled in that session were the same as the ones in the first session 31.0% reported they were the same, 11.9% reported they were different, and 57.1% reported that they could not remember what they reported at Time 1. When, subsequently, they were presented with the brief event description they had written in the first session, 56% reported they were the same, 42.9% reported they were different, and 1.1% could not decide. When male (59.3%) and female (55.4%) participants were compared in their consistency, the ratios were not significantly different from each other.

Dating of events

The second line of analyses included the consistency of estimated ages at the time of earliest memory across Time 1 and Time 2. Two different methods were used in the analysis of dating consistency. First, estimated ages at two different time points were compared based on mean ages for all memories. Second, memories were categorised as earlier versus later based on the age at encoding with the cut-off point of 48 months.

The estimated ages at Time 1 and Time 2 were compared for the whole sample. A paired samples t-test displayed no significant difference in estimated ages of earliest memories across the two time points, $t(80) = -0.90$, $p = .372$, $d = .10$. As expected, adults dated their earliest memories similarly at Time 1 ($M = 4.21$, SD = 1.56) and Time 2 ($M = 4.09$, SD = 1.38). The same comparison was conducted separately for the participants who reported the same versus different earliest memories at Time 2 based on their recognition responses. The pattern in the overall data remained unchanged with no significant difference in dating across Time 1 versus Time 2 between the participants reporting the same, $t(45) = -1.14$, $p = .261$, $d = .17$, or different, $t(33) = -0.40$, $p = .689$, $d = .07$, earliest memories. Moreover, consistency of dating was also explored on the basis of the correlation between Time 1 and Time 2 regarding the reported ages at the time of event age at event. Results showed that age at event reported at Time 1 and Time 2 were significantly correlated not only for the overall sample ($r(83) = 0.652$, $p < .001$) but also for those who remembered the same ($r(46) = 0.829$, $p < .001$) or different ($r(33) = 0.427$, $p = .012$) earliest memory.

Between-group comparison of the same versus different earliest memory groups showed significant differences in estimated ages at event at both Time 1, $F(1,79) = 6.20$, MSE = 14.39, $p = .015$, $\eta_p^2 = 0.074$, and Time 2, $F(1,82) = 7.61$, MSE = 13.19, $p = .007$, $\eta_p^2 = 0.086$. As predicted, participants reporting the same earliest memory had earlier earliest memories both at Time 1 ($M = 3.85$, SD = 1.38) and Time 2 ($M = 3.72$, SD = 1.21) compared to those reporting different earliest memories (Time 1: $M = 4.71$, SD = 1.70 and Time 2: $M = 4.53$, SD = 1.44).

A surprising finding was that both participants who reported the same memory and those who reported different ones had similar consistency levels for the age at earliest memory. To further investigate this, we compared the difference between the ages at the first reported memory and the later memory across two groups. However, variations in the estimations would result in negative and positive values for differences and these would not be indicative of how far the estimations deviated in the second session in comparison to the first. Therefore, we took absolute values of the differences and compared these values for the groups reporting the same or different memories. The group that reported the same memory had lower variation in estimation ($M = 0.48$, SD = 0.62) than the group reporting different memories ($M = 1.06$, SD = 1.32; $t(78) = 2.61$, $p = .01$, $d = .59$). We further examined this finding to see whether participant age was a factor in this difference. An ANOVA was conducted using the groups reporting the same and different memories as an independent variable and participant age as a covariate which we also included in an interaction with group variable. The results indicated that the difference between the two groups was further qualified by participant age. The group variable was not significant, $F(1,76) = 3.16$, MSE = 0.89, $p = .080$, $\eta_p^2 = 0.040$, the covariate of participant age was, $F(1,76) = 5.63$, MSE = 0.89, $p = .020$, $\eta_p^2 = 0.069$, but more importantly, the interaction between participant age and whether they reported the same memory was significant, $F(1,76) = 4.62$, MSE = 0.89, $p = .035$, $\eta_p^2 = 0.057$. To understand the interaction we looked at the correlations between the absolute value of differences in age estimations at two times and the age of participants for those who reported the same event and for those who reported different events. The correlation was not significant for those reporting the same event, $r(46) = 0.04$, $p = .795$, whereas, for those reporting different events, the difference in age estimations was higher for older participants, $r(34) = 0.37$, $p = .034$.

Dating consistency was also examined on the basis of the reported age at the time of encoding. For that aim, earliest memories experienced before and after 48 months old were analysed separately. Although earliest memories during which participants were younger than 48 months were not significantly different in their dating across Time 1 and Time 2 ($t(48) = 1.82$, $p = .075$, $d = .26$). More specifically, participants who were younger than 48 months at the time of the reported earliest event tended to date their memories later at Time 2 ($M = 3.55$, $SD = 1.36$)) compared to Time 1 ($M = 3.24$, $SD = 0.86$) but this tendency did not reach significance level. For memories during which participants were older than 48 months, however, earliest memories were significantly predated at Time 2 ($M = 4.91$, $SD = 0.96$) compared to Time 1 ($M = 5.69$, $SD = 1.20$) ($t(31) = -4.25$, $p < .001$, $d = .75$). In short, adults predated their later memories (after 48 months old and displayed a tendency to postdate earlier ones (before 48 months old).

Finally, we explored whether the differences between memories experienced before and after 48 months will change the group differences we observed between participants who remembered the same versus different earliest memories at Time 2. To be more specific, we checked if participants who remembered the same earliest memories at two different time points still had earlier earliest memories than those who remembered different memories at Time 2 when earlier and later memories are examined separately. Results remained unchanged only for the earlier memories reported at Time 2 ($F(1,46) = 5.07$, $MSE = 8.73$, $p = .029$, $\eta_p^2 = 0.010$). Participants who were younger than 48 months old at the time of the experience and remembered the same earliest memories at Time 2 had significantly earlier memories than those who reported different ones at Time 2. The difference was not observed for Time 1 ($F(1,46) = 2.14$, $MSE = 1.53$, $p = .150$, $\eta_p^2 = 0.045$). For memories experienced after 48 months old, no differences in dating were observed between participants who remembered the same versus different memories at 2 time points both at Time 1 ($F(1,30) = 1.65$, $MSE = 2.33$, $p = .209$, $\eta_p^2 = 0.052$) and Time 2 ($F(1,30) = 0.91$, $MSE = 0.84$, $p = .348$, $\eta_p^2 = 0.029$). In short, analysing dating separately on the basis of 48-month cut-off point affected the majority of group differences we observed on the basis of average estimated ages.

Consistency of memory qualities

A set of 2 × 2 mixed ANOVAs were conducted to compare the consistency of memory qualities across Time 1 and Time 2 and the potential differences between same versus different earliest memory groups in terms of their memory qualities at both Time 1 and Time 2. More specifically, the within-subjects factor was the time of testing (Time 1 versus Time 2) and the between-subjects factor was the consistency of earliest memories (same versus different). The alpha level was set as 0.01 for all analyses and the means and standard deviations are displayed in Table 1 with sample size, MSE, F and p values.

Results displayed a significant difference between same versus different earliest memory groups only in terms of the effect on personality quality. As seen in Table 1, participants who reported different earliest memories rated the effect of the reported earliest events on their personality higher both at Time 1 ($M = 3.41$, $SD = 1.08$) and Time 2 ($M = 3.24$, $SD = 1.10$) compared to their counterparts who consistently reported the same memory at Time 1 ($M = 2.72$, $SD = 1.15$) and Time 2 ($M = 2.76$, $SD = 0.97$) ($F(1,78) = 8.56$, $MSE = 13.35$, $p = .004$, $\eta_p^2 = 0.099$). Same versus different earliest memory groups were not significantly different from each other in any of the remaining memory qualities. No significant differences were observed across Time 1 and Time 2 for remaining memory qualities (see Table 1).

Discussion

Consistency of the content, dating, and qualities of earliest memories was investigated in young adults across two years. We asked participants to recall their earliest memory, to date it and to rate its qualities, such as its importance, emotional valence and intensity. Two years later, we applied the same procedure, but also asked participants whether their earliest memory was the same as the one they reported at Time 1. Next, we presented them with their original earliest memory from Time 1 and asked them to indicate if it was the same as the memory they just reported at Time 2. Our aim was to examine what percentage of people recalled the same earliest memory at both time points, and whether people dated and rated their memories similarly at both time points.

In terms of content of the earliest memory, 56% of the participants reported the same earliest memory when tested two years later. This consistency rate is similar to that of 58% observed in high school students over a period of three months (Kihlstrom & Harackiewicz, 1982) and exactly similar to the consistency obtained in 12–13-year-old children across two years (Peterson et al., 2011). When compared with previous studies reporting consistency rates of 83% (Jack & Hayne, 2010) and 79–100% (Bauer et al., 2014), the current rate is low. However, the consistency rate of 83% was based on a sample of only six adults with a one-week interval between the two time points and the rates of 79–100% were based on only women. Wang and Peterson (2014) also reported a consistency rate of 83% among children with a two-year time lag.

Table 1. Within-subjects comparison of memory qualities across Time 1 and Time 2 and their between-subjects comparison across the same versus different earliest memory groups at both Time 1 and Time 2.

Memory quality	Time 1 M	Time 1 SD	Time 2 M	Time 2 SD	N	Time 1 versus Time 2 MSE	F	p	Same versus different MSE	F	p
Importance						0.57	0.95	.333	1.83	1.15	.288
Same	3.73	1.09	3.66	1.26	46						
Different	4.00	0.82	3.82	0.9	34						
Valence then						0.06	0.08	.782	0.24	0.07	.790
Same	2.78	1.41	2.91	1.50	46						
Different	3.03	1.34	2.82	1.47	34						
Valence now						0.72	1.80	.184	0.01	0.01	.943
Same	3.33	1.10	3.26	1.02	46						
Different	3.41	1.05	3.21	0.98	34						
Emotional intensity						0.38	0.60	.442	1.20	0.76	.387
Same	3.61	1.13	3.72	1.17	46						
Different	3.79	1.04	3.88	0.77	34						
Consequentiality						0.52	0.53	.468	11.63	5.02	.028
Same	3.22	1.37	2.96	1.51	46						
Different	3.62	0.95	3.65	1.13	34						
Effect on personality						0.17	0.23	.632	13.35	8.56	.004
Same	2.72	1.15	2.76	0.97	46						
Different	3.41	1.08	3.24	1.10	34						
Control over the event						0.90	3.67	.059	5.32	2.71	.104
Same	2.28	1.15	2.39	1.13	46						
Different	2.91	1.19	2.50	1.19	34						
Confidence						0.17	0.38	.539	5.49	4.14	.045
Same	3.54	0.94	3.50	0.94	46						
Different	3.06	0.92	3.24	0.99	34						
Reality						0.75	1.97	.164	0.03	0.04	.836
Same	4.43	0.58	4.30	0.89	46						
Different	4.47	0.62	4.32	0.77	34						
Vividness of emotions						0.06	0.12	.731	0.43	0.27	.604
Same	3.33	1.12	3.35	0.88	46						
Different	3.41	1.10	3.47	0.99	34						
Vividness of images						0.25	0.60	.440	0.07	0.09	.768
Same	3.83	0.71	3.61	0.68	46						
Different	3.65	0.95	3.71	0.72	34						
Frequency of thinking						1.28	2.70	.104	0.01	0.01	.921
Same	2.52	0.89	2.13	0.89	46						
Different	2.29	0.94	2.32	0.95	34						
Frequency of talking						0.46	0.88	.351	1.78	1.16	.285
Same	2.13	1.07	1.91	0.87	46						
Different	2.24	1.16	2.24	0.99	34						

Thus, there is no agreement on the average consistency rate of earliest memories due to a limited number of studies, which vary in sample size and characteristics, methodology, and interval length. In addition to the diversity in sample size, sample characteristics, the interval between memory reports that may have led to different levels in consistency, studies also vary in their assessment of consistency. For example, Kihlstrom and Harackiewicz (1982) and Jack and Hayne (2007, 2010) examined whether the participants were reporting the same event, Bauer et al. (2014) and Peterson et al. (2011) analysed both whether they were reporting the same event and whether the event narratives were similar in content. Therefore, these studies do not avail themselves for a direct comparison.

Based on our results, earliest memories do not seem to be highly consistent over time, at least among young adults across two years. It is notable that the current study has a unique contribution by assessing the consistency of earliest memories by self-reports based on both recall and recognition. All previous studies were based on the content comparisons by researchers rather than participants' self-reports. In the present research, we compared participants' own evaluations of the consistency of the content (56%) with that of an independent judge (59.5%), which were highly similar.

Estimated ages at the time of the reported earliest memories were investigated to evaluate the consistency of dating over time. For that aim, we applied two different methods. The first one is the typical analyses conducted in earliest memory research on the basis of mean ages. The second one is the method used by Wang and her colleagues on the basis of the 48-month cut-off point for the age at encoding (Wang et al., 2010; Wang & Peterson, 2014, 2016). The first method yielded no significant differences in the dating of earliest memories across two years. Young adults reported approximately the same age for their earliest memories at two different time points independent of remembering the same versus different earliest memories at second testing on the average. The second method, however, displayed a predating bias for later memories (after 48 months old) and a tendency to postdate earlier memories (before 48 months old). These results are in line with previous findings (Wang et al., 2010, in press, Study 1). Wang and Peterson (2014, 2016) examined children's dating of their earliest memories longitudinally found out that children postdated their earlier memories as they got older resulting in a shift in the age at the time of the event. As they further pointed, this has implications for earliest memory research since the typical age observed for earliest memory, which is around 3.5 (e.g., Bruce et al., 2000; Conway & Holmes, 2004; Jack & Hayne, 2007; West & Bauer, 1999) may be an already shifted one as a result of this postdating bias. Therefore, future studies focusing on dating consistency of earliest memories should consider the age at encoding in their analyses.

Another prediction about the estimated age was regarding the differences between participants remembering the same versus different earliest memories over time. Young adults reporting the same memories at both time points were expected to have earlier earliest memories than those remembering different earliest memories at repeated testing. Results confirmed this prediction indicating differences in estimated ages of the same versus different earliest memory groups at both Time 1 and Time 2. When analysed separately for earliest memories experienced before and after 48 months old, the pattern remained the same only for earlier memories at Time 2. This finding is in line with earlier studies reporting that participants remembering the same earliest memories over time have memories from younger ages compared to those who remember different ones (Bauer et al., 2014; Kihlstrom & Harackiewicz, 1982). Bauer et al. (2014) explained this observation on the basis of the *density of event pool* suggesting that the event pool for earlier events is narrower; hence, when individuals remember events from a smaller pool, they are more likely to remember the same event later on. Similarly, the event pool gets richer by age making it more likely to remember a different event over time from a period with a larger pool.

Young adults who remembered the same versus different earliest memories were compared in terms of the qualities of the events they reported. The aim was to investigate if the earliest memories recalled consistently over time were different in their qualities compared to those that were not recalled consistently. Earliest memories reported by participants who remembered the same versus different events were different in only one memory quality: effect on personality. Young adults who remembered different earliest memories rated their memories higher in terms of its effect on their personality compared to those who remembered the same earliest memory. It is possible that when these participants actively searched for an earliest memory at second testing, they came up with an event that is important for whom they have become. In sum, however, young adults remembering the same versus different earliest memories were similar in majority of the qualities at both time points.

Qualities of earliest memories were also examined in terms of their consistency across two years. This part of the study was exploratory, with no specific expectations. Overall, results displayed consistency in all qualities over time regardless of remembering the same versus different earliest memories at two time points. More specifically, young adults who remembered the same earliest memories rated the qualities of importance, emotional valence and intensity, consequentiality, effect on personality, control over the event, confidence, reality, vividness (emotions and images), and rehearsal (frequency of thinking and talking) similarly across Time 1 and Time 2.

Conclusions

Current study contributed to the autobiographical memory literature in general and earliest memory research in particular by investigating the consistency of earliest memories in terms of content, dating, and memory qualities over a period of two years. It further contributed to the literature by measuring consistency via self-reports on the basis of both recall and recognition, in addition to the typically used same versus different memory judgments by coders. Results demonstrated moderate consistency in content as 56% of the participants reported the same earliest memories following a two-year time lag. Although dating seemed to be highly consistent on the basis of mean ages, the results were different when analysed separately for earlier and later childhood memories with the cut-off point of 48 months old. There was a predating bias for later memories and a tendency to postdate earlier ones. Moreover, young adults remembering the same earliest memories consistently had earlier earliest memories than those who remembered different earliest memories at two time points. However, the group differences between participants who remembered the same versus different earliest memories at two separate time points in terms of estimated ages did not remain the same when analysed on the basis of 48-month cut-off point. Thus, the final contribution of the present work was to support previous findings by Wang and her colleagues (Wang et al., 2010, in press; Wang & Peterson, 2014, 2016) regarding the dating biases in remembering early childhood memories in a sample of young adults with a within-subjects design. In general, postdating of earlier memories was stronger in earlier studies (Wang et al., 2010) but this may result from the fact that they had children samples. Future studies may explore further dating bias differences between children and adults. More specifically, children may be more likely to postdate earlier memories and adults may be more likely to predate later ones due to their ages at retrieval. Thus, age at retrieval may gain more importance in case of adult samples in addition to the age at encoding.

In conclusion, the way we analyse the data is critical in exploring and detecting potential dating biases and errors. For that reason, future studies on early childhood memories should to take into account the role of the age at encoding on dating.

Disclosure statement

No potential conflict of interest was reported by the authors.

References

Bachevalier, J. (1992). Cortical versus limbic immaturity: Relationship to infantile amnesia. In M. R. Gunnar & C. A. Nelson (Eds.), *Developmental behavioral neuroscience* (pp. 129–153). Hillsdale, NJ: Lawrence Erlbaum.

Bauer, P. J. (2007). *Remembering the times of our lives: Memory in infancy and beyond*. Mahwah, NJ: Erlbaum.

Bauer, P. J. (2008). Toward a neuro-developmental account of the development of declarative memory. *Developmental Psychobiology, 50*, 19–31. doi:10.1002/dev.20265

Bauer, P. J. (2015). A complementary processes account of the development of childhood amnesia and a personal past. *Psychological Review, 122*, 204–231. doi:10.1037/a0038939

Bauer, P. J., Tasdemir-Ozdes, A., & Larkina, M. (2014). Adults' reports of their earliest memories: Consistency in events, ages, and narrative characteristics over time. *Consciousness and Cognition, 27*, 76–88. doi:10.1016/j.concog.2014.04.008

Bruce, D., Dolan, A., & Phillips-Grant, K. (2000). On the transition from childhood amnesia to the recall of personal memories. *Psychological Science, 11*, 360–364. doi:10.1111/1467-9280.00271

Child, I. L. (1940). The relation between measures of infantile amnesia and of neuroticism. *The Journal of Abnormal and Social Psychology, 35*, 453–456.

Conway, M. A., & Holmes, A. (2004). Psychosocial stages and the accessibility of autobiographical memories across the life cycle. *Journal of Personality, 72*, 461–480. doi:10.1111/j.0022-3506.2004.00269.x

Cowan, N., & Davidson, G. (1984). Salient childhood memories. *The Journal of Genetic Psychology, 145*, 101–107. doi:10.1080/00221325.1984.10532254

Crook, M. N., & Harden, L. (1931). A quantitative investigation of early memories. *The Journal of Social Psychology, 2*, 252–255. doi:10.1080/00224545.1931.9918973

Dahl, J. J., Kingo, O. S., & Krøjgaard, P. (2015). The magic shrinking machine revisited: The presence of props at recall facilitates memory in 3-year-olds. *Developmental Psychology, 51*(12), 1704–1716. doi:10.1037/dev0000050

Dudycha, G. J., & Dudycha, M. M. (1941). Childhood memories: A review of the literature. *Psychological Bulletin, 38*(8), 668–682. doi:10.1037/h0055678

Eacott, M. J., & Crawley, R. A. (1998). The offset of childhood amnesia: Memory for events that occurred before age 3. *Journal of Experimental Psychology: General, 127*, 22–33. doi:10.1037/0096-3445.127.1.22

Eacott, M. J., & Crawley, R. A. (1999). Childhood amnesia: On answering questions about very early life events. *Memory (Hove, England), 7*, 279–292. doi:10.1080/096582199387922

Fivush, R., Haden, C. A., & Reese, E. (2006). Elaborating on elaborations: Role of maternal reminiscing style in cognitive and socioemotional development. *Child Development, 77*, 1568–1588. doi:10.1111/j.1467-8624.2006.00960.x

Freud, S. (1905/1953). Three essays on the theory of sexuality. In J. Strachey (Trans., Ed.), *The standard edition of the complete psychological works of Sigmund Freud* (Vol. 7, pp. 135–243). London: Hogarth Press.

Hayne, H. (2004). Infant memory development: Implications for childhood amnesia. *Developmental Review, 24*, 33–73. doi:10.1016/j.dr.2003.09.007

Hayne, H., & Jack, F. (2011). Childhood amnesia. *Wiley Interdisciplinary Reviews: Cognitive Science*. doi:10.1002/wcs.107

Henri, V., & Henri, C. (1898). Earliest recollections. *Popular Science Monthly, 21*, 108–115.

Howe, M. L. (2003). Memories from the cradle. *Current Directions in Psychological Science, 12*, 62–65. doi:10.1111/1467-8721.01227

Howe, M. L., & Courage, M. L. (1993). On resolving the enigma of infantile amnesia. *Psychological Bulletin, 113*, 305–326. doi:10.1037/0033-2909.113.2.305

Howe, M. L., & Courage, M. L. (1997). The emergence and early development of autobiographical memory. *Psychological Review, 104*, 499–523. doi:10.1037/0033-295X.104.3.499

Jack, F., & Hayne, H. (2007). Eliciting adults' earliest memories: Does it matter how we ask the question? *Memory (Hove, England), 15*, 647–663. doi:10.1080/09658210701467087

Jack, F., & Hayne, H. (2010). Childhood amnesia: Empirical evidence for a two-stage phenomenon. *Memory (Hove, England), 18*(8), 831–844. doi:10.1080/09658211.2010.510476

Kihlstrom, J. F., & Harackiewicz, J. M. (1982). The earliest recollection: A new survey. *Journal of Personality, 50*, 134–148. doi:10.1111/j.14676494.1982.tb01019.x

Larkina, M., Merrill, N. A., & Bauer, P. J. (2017). Developmental changes in consistency of autobiographical memories: Adolescents' and young adults' repeated recall of recent and distance events. *Memory (Hove, England), 25*, 1036–1051. doi:10.1080/09658211.2016.1253750

MacDonald, S., Uesiliana, K., & Hayne, H. (2000). Cross-cultural and gender differences in childhood amnesia. *Memory (Hove, England), 8*, 365–376. doi:10.1080/09658210050156822

Miles, C. (1895). A study of individual psychology. *The American Journal of Psychology, 6*, 534–558. doi:10.2307/1411191

Mullen, M. K. (1994). Earliest recollections of childhood: A demographic analysis. *Cognition, 52*, 55–79. doi:10.1016/0010-0277(94)90004-3

Nelson, K. (1993). The psychological and social origins of autobiographical memory. *Psychological Science, 4*, 7–14. doi:10.1111/j.1467-9280.1993.tb00548.x

Nelson, K., & Fivush, R. (2004). The emergence of autobiographical memory: A social cultural developmental theory. *Psychological Review, 111*, 486–511. doi:10.1037/0033-295X.111.2.486

Newcombe, N., Lloyd, M. E., & Ratliff, K. R. (2007). Development of episodic and autobiographical memory: A cognitive neuroscience perspective. *Advances in Child Development and Behavior, 35*, 37–85.

Peterson, C. (2002). Children's long-term memory for autobiographical events. *Developmental Review, 22*, 370–402. doi:10.1016/S0273-2297(02)00007-2

Peterson, C., Grant, V. V., & Boland, L. D. (2005). Childhood amnesia in children and adolescents: Their earliest memories. *Memory (Hove, England), 13*, 622–637. doi:10.1080/09658210444000278

Peterson, C., Wang, Q., & Hou, Y. (2009). "When I was little": Childhood recollections in Chinese and European Canadian grade-school children. *Child Development, 80*, 506–518. doi:10.1111/j.1467-8624.2009.01275.x

Peterson, C., Warren, K., Nguyen, D. T., & Noel, M. (2010). Infantile amnesia and gender: Does the way we measure it matter? *Procedia – Social and Behavioral Sciences, 9*, 1767–1771. doi:10.1016/j.sbspro.2010.12.397

Peterson, C., Warren, K. L., & Short, M. M. (2011). Infantile amnesia across the years: A 2-year follow-up of children's earliest memories. *Child Development, 82*, 1092–1105. doi:10.1111/j.1467-8624.2011.01597.x

Pillemer, D. B., & White, S. H. (1989). Childhood events recalled by children and adults. *Advances in Child Development and Behavior, 21*, 297–340.

Rubin, D. C. (1982). On the retention function for autobiographical memory. *Journal of Verbal Learning and Verbal Behavior, 21,* 21–38. doi:10.1016/S00225371(82)90423-6

Simcock, G., & Hayne, H. (2002). Breaking the barrier? Children fail to translate their preverbal memories into language. *Psychological Science, 13,* 225–231. doi:10.1111/1467-9280.00442

Tustin, K., & Hayne, H. (2010). Defining the boundary: Age-related changes in childhood amnesia. *Developmental Psychology, 46,* 1049–1061. doi:10.1037/a0020105

Usher, J. A., & Neisser, U. (1993). Childhood amnesia and the beginnings of memory for four early life events. *Journal of Experimental Psychology: General, 122,* 155–165. doi:10.1037/0096-3445.122.2.155

Waldfogel, S. (1948). The frequency and affective character of childhood memories. *Psychological Monographs: General and Applied, 62*(4), 1–39. doi:10.1037/h0093581

Wang, Q. (2001). Culture effects on adults' earliest childhood recollection and self-description: Implications for the relation between memory and the self. *Journal of Personality and Social Psychology, 81,* 220–233. doi:10.1037/00223514.81.2.220

Wang, Q., Conway, M., & Hou, Y. (2004). Infantile amnesia: A cross-cultural investigation. *Cognitive Sciences, 1,* 123–135.

Wang, Q., & Peterson, C. (2014). Your earliest memory may be earlier than you think: Prospective studies of children's dating of earliest childhood memories. *Developmental Psychology, 50,* 1680–1686. doi:10.1037/a0036001

Wang, Q., & Peterson, C. (2016). The fate of childhood memories: Children postdated their earliest memories as they grew older. *Frontiers in Psychology: Cognition, 6,* 2038. doi:10.3389/fpsyg.2015.02038

Wang, Q., Peterson, C., & Hou, Y. (2010). Children dating childhood memories. *Memory (Hove, England), 18,* 754–762. doi:10.1080/09658211.2010.508749

Wang, Q., Peterson, C., Khuu, A., Reid, C. P., Maxwell, K. L., & Vincent, J. M. (In press). Looking at the past through a telescope: Adults postdated their earliest childhood memories. *Memory (Hove, England).*

West, T. A., & Bauer, P. J. (1999). Assumptions of infantile amnesia: Are there differences between early and later memories? *Memory (Hove, England), 7,* 257–278. doi:10.1080/096582199387913

Thirty-five-month-old children have spontaneous memories despite change of context for retrieval

Trine Sonne, Osman S. Kingo, Dorthe Berntsen and Peter Krøjgaard

ABSTRACT
Many parents have experienced incidents in which their preschool child spontaneously (i.e., without prompting of any kind) recall a previously experienced event. Until recently, such spontaneous memories had only been examined in non-controlled settings (e.g., diary studies). Using a novel experimental paradigm, a previous study has shown that when young children are brought back to a highly distinct setting (same room, same experimenter, same furnishing), in which they previously experienced an interesting event (a Teddy *or* a Game event), spontaneous memories can be triggered. However, exactly *which* cues (or combination of cues) are effective for the children's memory, remains unknown. Here, we used this novel paradigm to examine the possible impact of contextual cues at the time of retrieval. We manipulated whether the 35-month-old children returned to the same room ($n = 40$) or to a different, but similarly furnished, room ($n = 40$) after one week. The results revealed that although the children returning to a new room produced fewer spontaneous memories than the children returning to the same room, the difference was not significant. Interestingly, despite changing rooms, the children still produced spontaneous memories. Taken together the results may shed new light on the mechanisms underlying childhood amnesia.

Introduction

For decades, researchers interested in memory and the development hereof have sought to map out the developmental course of the ability to remember previously experienced events. Today, we know that children and even infants are capable of remembering events over longer delays (see e.g., Bauer, 2007). This knowledge has been an important step in order to understand the phenomenon of childhood amnesia. The term *childhood amnesia* refers to the inability in adults to recall memories of specific events from the first years of their lives (e.g., Bauer, 2015; Pillemer & White, 1989). Due to the many studies providing evidence of memory in early childhood, we now know that this phenomenon is not due to an inability to form memories in the first place. Rather, childhood amnesia should probably be attributed to a multitude of contributing factors including *neurological development* (Bauer, 2008), *socio-emotional development* including *maternal reminiscence style* (Fivush, Haden, & Reese, 2006; Nelson & Fivush, 2004), the development of a *cognitive self* (Howe, 2003), differences in basic attentional and cognitive orientation, that is, the *different lenses explanation* (Bauer, 2007) including *language development* (Dahl, Kingo & Krøjgaard, 2015; Simcock & Hayne, 2002), as well as *forgetting* (Bauer, 2015; Hayne & Jack, 2011). What remains unknown seems to be the relative contribution of these factors and how they may interact.

So far, the predominant method for investigating childhood amnesia has been to *ask* children or adults to recall and talk about their past experiences (Hayne, Scarf, & Imuta, 2015). However, in order to comply with this standard methodology, the subject – regardless of age – would have to engage in a deliberate and strategic retrieval process requiring executive control involving activity in the frontal lobes. Meanwhile, the frontal lobes are known to mature late in the ontogenesis (e.g., Johnson, 2005) making the default task of deliberate and strategic recall harder for young children than for adults.

Deliberate and strategic retrieval is, however, not the only route to memories of past events. At times, such memories come to our mind suddenly and uninvited, almost "out of the blue". Such memories are referred to as *involuntary* or *spontaneous* memories and healthy adults frequently experience such memories in daily life, often triggered by distinct environmental cues (Berntsen, 1996, 2009). When dealing with young children, who are unable to report whether a memory is retrieved strategically or spontaneously, we define spontaneous memories from a third person perspective as (i) verbally produced, (ii) socially unprompted, and (iii) environmentally cued (Krøjgaard, Kingo, Dahl, & Berntsen, 2014). Involuntary or spontaneous retrieval differs from deliberate and strategic retrieval by being based primarily on simple associative mechanisms and is therefore less dependent on mature frontal lobes (Hall et al., 2014). Consequently, involuntary or spontaneous retrieval is likely to be less cognitively demanding and has recently been proposed to be a basic mode of remembering present early in the ontogenesis (Berntsen, 2009, 2012). Thus, for young children, spontaneous retrieval may constitute an easier path to past experiences. As a consequence, in young children, memories that may be inaccessible through voluntary retrieval may be reachable through the less demanding spontaneous retrieval route, in response to relevant distinctive cues. Following this, the number of childhood memories forgotten, as the children grow older, may have been underestimated. If so, this would have implications for our understanding of childhood amnesia. In the discussion we will return to this possibility.

Spontaneous retrieval in children

Until very recently spontaneous recall in children had almost exclusively been documented using semi-structured methodologies, as for instance diary studies (e.g., Nelson & Ross, 1980; Reese, 1999; Todd & Perlmutter, 1980). One exception is an unpublished study cited in Leichtman (2006) in which children between 4 months and 3 years of age on 5 consecutive days were exposed to a puppet with an edible treat hidden in a mitten. When returning to the lab 3 or 6 months later, 12% of the 17–18 month olds and 45% of the 3–4 year olds spontaneously talked about the previously experienced event (Leichtman, 2006).[1]

Recently, a novel experimental procedure provided evidence that spontaneous memories can be induced in young children under controlled conditions (Krøjgaard, Kingo, Dahl, & Berntsen, 2014) – even for unique events (Krøjgaard, Kingo, Jensen, & Berntsen, in press). The development of this novel experimental paradigm provides a unique opportunity for investigating spontaneous memories in children more closely. As the present study makes use of the same design as the one used in the most recent version of this paradigm (Krøjgaard et al., in press), it is outlined here in some detail: A group of 35- and 46-month olds visited the lab twice separated by one week. At the first visit, the children were presented with one of two highly unique and entertaining events: either a *Teddy event*, involving two mechanical teddies capable of singing and wiggling with their ears, or the *Game event*, in which the children were invited to try two different types of throwing games for which they always won medals. When not used for demonstration, the props for each of the two events were locked away in their own distinct box. At the second visit, the children returned to the exact same setting and were left alone with their parent for two minutes right in front of the two opaque boxes of which they knew the contents of only *one* of the boxes. The parents had been carefully instructed not to prompt the children in any way during this waiting period, allowing us to record possible spontaneous utterances from the children for later analyses.

Compared to an equivalent baseline measure obtained at the first visit prior to being presented with the given event, the children spontaneously talked about the event they had seen at the first visit, while they never talked about the event they had not seen when returning to the lab at the second visit (Krøjgaard et al., in press). The 35-month-olds performed poorly relative to their 46-month-old peers, when asked control questions requiring strategic recall at the very end of the second visit, whereas age had little effect on the children's *spontaneous* recall.

While the recent study by Krøjgaard et al. (in press) showed that spontaneous recall can indeed be induced in young children, we do not know exactly what type of cues made the children spontaneously remember the target event. The experimental set-up used in Krøjgaard et al. (2017) allows us to investigate this more thoroughly. In the present study, we therefore focus on the possible impact of *contextual cues* (i.e., manipulating whether or not the children return to the same room). Focusing on cues is important not only when attempting to understand the mechanisms of spontaneous recall, but also, from a broader perspective, in relation to childhood amnesia to which we will turn in the discussion. In the following, we review the existing evidence on the possible impact of contextual cues for recall.

Are contextual cues important?

In a seminal paper, Tulving and Thomson (1973) proposed the *encoding specificity principle* stating that retrieval depends on the overlap between the information available during encoding and the information present at retrieval. Inspired by this principle, Pipe and collaborators (among others) have examined the possible impact of returning to the exact location where the to-be-remembered event took place, when young children were asked to recall a previously experienced event (e.g., La Rooy, Pipe, & Murray, 2007; Pipe & Wilson, 1994; Wilkinson, 1988). La Rooy et al. (2007) for instance examined 5- and 6- year-olds' verbal recall of a "visiting the pirate" event experienced six months earlier. The test interviews were conducted either in (a) a perfect-context reinstatement (same room, same objects), (b) an imperfect-context reinstatement (same room, but with some objects replaced), or (c) an imperfect-context (different room, no objects). The results revealed that being interviewed in the same room in which the to-be-remembered event had taken place reduced forgetting, and that children in the perfect-context reinstatement condition outperformed their peers in the two other conditions with regard to accuracy (La Rooy et al., 2007). Additional converging evidence has been obtained in the forensic literature in which returning to the original crime scene of alleged abuse led 3–14-year-old children to provide additional details (Hershkowitz et al., 1998, although see Orbach, Hershkowitz, Lamb, Sternberg, & Horowitz, 2000; for a general review of context-facilitation in memory, see Smith, 2014).

Very little however, is known regarding the possible impact of contextual cues for *spontaneous*, verbal retrieval. In a diary study with 25-month-old children, Reese (1999) showed that spontaneous recall was predominantly evoked by cues from the environment (as opposed to verbal and internal cues). Reese (1999) did not distinguish between different environmental cues (e.g., objects vs. contexts), but two of the examples she provided involved specific contexts as cues (e.g., when passing a stadium, a child said *Go go go Otago*, a chant from a rugby game) suggesting that contextual cues may be salient.

However, to our knowledge it has however never been investigated systematically whether contextual cues are also important when dealing with spontaneous retrieval in children. We set out to examine exactly this possibility.

The present study

In the present study we followed and extended the procedure developed by Krøjgaard et al. (in press) in which spontaneous memories of a previous lab visit were induced in young children by reinstating the context. Here we extend this paradigm to specifically examine the potential impact of contextual cues by manipulating which room the children returned to at their second visit (see Figure 1).

Accordingly, at the second visit half of the children returned to the exact same room (Room A) with the exact same boxes (Same-Room Condition), whereas the other half returned to a new room (Room B) with the exact same boxes (Different-Room Condition). The reasoning behind the furnishing of the rooms was the following: We wanted to have the basic setup with the two adjacently arranged boxes present in both rooms. This was primarily to avoid possible ambiguities with regard to remembering the hidden props, which then could be based on either landmarks (e.g., "inside the red box") or spatial placement (e.g., 'to the left"). Besides the arrangement of the two adjacent boxes, the two rooms were different and distinct (see Figure 1): Whereas the far end in Room A was dominated by light-grey room dividers in soft cloth, the far-end in Room B was substantially dominated by the large floor-to-ceiling mat-black eye tracker booth in particle board. In addition, whereas the room dividers in Room A were positioned straight across the room, the eye tracker booth in Room B was positioned in a "V-configuration". Thus, because the far ends of the two rooms differed with respect to shape, size, colour, and texture we assumed that the two rooms would be easily distinguishable.

Because the original experiment already provided evidence that both 35-month-olds and 46-month-olds spontaneously remembered the target event, we decided to only focus on the youngest age group in the present study.

Since no evidence exists from controlled studies on spontaneous recall regarding the possible effect of contextual cues, our tentative hypothesis was based on the studies conducted using strategic verbal recall (e.g., La Rooy et al., 2007). We thus hypothesised that returning to a different room would reduce spontaneous recall. Our expectation was therefore that the children in the Different-Room Condition would produce fewer spontaneous memories of the target event compared with their peers in the Same-Room Condition.

The experiment

Participants

Eighty 35-month-olds (45 female, $M_{age} = 35.15$ months, $SD = .42$; range: 34.13–36.60 months) participated. The children were recruited from birth registries from the National Board of Health and were predominantly Scandinavian Caucasian living in families with middle to higher SES.

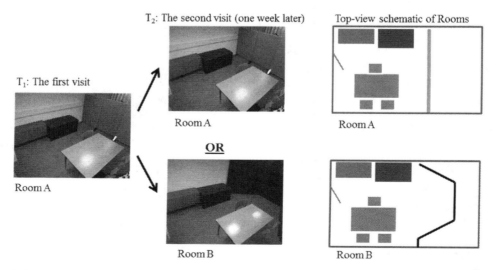

Figure 1. Displays the basic design in which the children in the Same-Room Condition ($n = 40$) returned to Room A for testing, whereas the children in the Different-Room Condition ($n = 40$) returned to the Room B for testing. The rooms were of the same size, and were similar with respect to the arrangement of the boxes containing the two events, whereas the rooms differed with respect to location in the building as well additional furnishing.

All children were healthy, full-term, and had an Apgar score ≥ 7. The children were randomly assigned to one of two conditions: the Same-Room Condition ($n = 40$) or the Different-Room Condition ($n = 40$). In each condition half of the children ($n = 20$) were exposed to the Teddy event, whereas the other half ($n = 20$) were exposed to the Game event (see below). Seven additional children were tested but later excluded due to: fussiness (4); experimental error (2); speaking a foreign language at test (1). Each child received a small gift for participating when returning for the second visit.

Materials

Two sparsely furnished 16 m² rooms were used: Room A and Room B. Both rooms were located in the same corridor (see Figure 1 as well as the previous description of the differences between the two rooms).

In both rooms, along one side, two boxes were placed right next to each other: To the left a red metal box with doors and to the right a grey plastic box with a top lid. Both boxes had locks. Each box contained specific props to provide a unique and distinct experience dependent on whether the child had been allocated to the Teddy event (the red metal box) or the Game event (the grey plastic box). A table with chairs was placed along the opposite wall of the room to make sure that the child had a clear view to both boxes. All sessions were recorded for later coding.

The *red metal box* contained two distinct mechanical toy teddies: A blue elephant named Elly capable of singing a song while wiggling its ears when pressing a button; a light-brown coloured dog called Alfred, who could sing a song while wiggling its ears and clapping its paws when activated. The *grey plastic box* contained props for two different games: A throwing game (involving three coloured buckets and three soft balls), and a bowling game (involving plastic balls and 10 pins).

Procedure

All children visited the lab twice separated by one week (±1 day). For all children the first visit (T_1) took place in Room A. When returning for the test (T_2) the room was condition specific: The children in the Same-Room Condition were tested in Room A, whereas the children in the Different-Room Condition were tested in Room B. During recruitment, the parents were carefully informed that the study concerned spontaneous recall and they were instructed not to talk about the study and not in any way let the children know that the study was about memory. In case the child should ask about the visits, the parents were instructed to simply reply "I don't know". In addition we had ensured that none of the children had participated previously in any studies in our lab. The purpose was to avoid that the children would guess or be left with the impression that the study was about memory.

T_1 – Encoding

At the first visit (T_1) the procedure involved two steps: (1) A two-minute baseline measure, and (2) an encoding session involving the specific event to which the child had been allocated. When picked up in the waiting room, the parent was handed a written note reminding him or her not to initiate any conversation with the child and only to respond briefly without following up on any statements from the child during the baseline assessment. The child and the parent were taken to Room A and seated next to each other facing the two locked boxes. The experimenter then stated: "I have to do something, but I'll be right back". The child and the parent were left alone in front of the two boxes for exactly two minutes (timed by use of a stop watch). The sequence was recorded for subsequent coding and any verbal utterances produced by the child served as a baseline measure (see below).

When the two minutes had passed, the experimenter returned. A BLINDED version of the MacArthur Communicative Development Inventory: Words and Sentences (CDI) was handed out in order to assess the productive vocabulary of the children, and the parents were asked to return it at the second visit.[2] At the second step (the event specific encoding), each child was presented with *one* of the events: either the Teddy or the Game event. Both events lasted approximately six minutes. The basic idea was to engage the child in a funny and memorable event. Importantly, at no time during the encoding session, were the children left with the impression that they had to remember anything; the word "remember" (or equivalent) did not appear in the two distinct event demonstrations. These precautions were made in order to avoid that the children would feel socially prompted to remember anything when returning for the test a week later.

The Teddy event. The experimenter opened the red metal box with a key and demonstrated the two very special teddies that could sing, clap, and wiggle their ears to the child. The child was encouraged to say which animals the teddies were, to say their names (Elly the elephant, and Alfred the dog), and to activate the teddies.

The Game event. The experimenter brought out the two games (a throwing and a bowling game) from the grey plastic box, one at a time. The child was asked whether he or she knew the name of the items and was encouraged to say it out loud and praised when doing so. No matter how the games went the child was praised and received a "gold medal" for participating in each game.

T_2 – test

The second visit (T_2) involved two steps: (1) a two minute test of spontaneous recall and (2) control questions involving strategic retrieval. The two minute test was an exact replication of the baseline procedure administered at T_1.

The only difference (besides the change of location for half of the participants) was that this time, the children had actually been in the lab once before and had therefore experienced the contents of *one*, of the boxes, depending on which event the children had seen at T_1.

When the two minutes had passed, the experimenter returned to ask control questions to examine what the children could remember when asked directly about the event. The control questions were deliberately asked *after* the two-minute spontaneous memory test in order to conceal that the study was about memory until after the test for possible spontaneous utterances. The control questions used here were of a focused "yes/no" format. For each of the two boxes (of which each child had only seen the contents of one), the child was asked two questions that required the child to search his or her memory to provide an answer. The order of the questions addressing the two events was balanced across subjects and conditions. The experimenter began by asking: "Remember last time you were here ... :

> Q1: 'Did you see what was in the red cabinet/grey plastic box?' [If the response was 'no', or if a 'yes' was accompanied by a description of the contents, question #2 was left out. If only a 'yes' or no response was given, then question #2 was asked]
>
> Q2: 'What was in the red cabinet/grey plastic box?'"

Coding and data reduction

Two kinds of data were collected: (i) spontaneous verbal responses produced while waiting at both T_1-baseline and T_2-test, (ii) responses to the control questions at T_2. We first consider possible spontaneous verbal responses.

Coding of spontaneous verbal responses
Central for the coding of spontaneous verbal responses was the two videos of two-minute duration from each child: One video from T_1-baseline and one from T_2-test. Prior to the coding, all video recordings had been edited so they only contained the two-minute excerpts from when the child and parent were left alone in the room. As a result, the coders were blind to which event a given child had seen, as well as whether a given video originated from T_1-baseline or from T_2-test. Finally, the coders were unaware of the two conditions and the related hypotheses.

Based on the coding strategy employed in Krøjgaard et al. (in press), all spontaneous verbal utterances produced by the children during the two-minute waiting time at both baseline and test were coded by two measures: a Word List and a Coding Scheme.

Coding by Word List. From the edited recordings the coders coded verbally communicated spontaneous memories related to the to-be-remembered events from the children based on a Word List (see Appendix). The Word List consisted of words related specifically to each of the two events (Teddy and Game) and an additional Unspecific list referring to utterances indicating that the child had been in the lab before, but without specifically referring to one of the two events (e.g., when returning, one child said: "we did that last time too"). The Word List was fixed and developed prior to the coding. Any mentioning of a word from the Word List (see Appendix) resulted in the score of either a "T" (Teddy), "G" (Game), or "U" (Unspecific) dependent of which of the three lists the word belonged to. Note that these distinctions were necessary as both the event specific scores, as well as the event-unspecific scores, were indicative of having been in the lab before. Sum scores were calculated for each child.

Coding by Coding Scheme. Following Krøjgaard et al. (in press), we also coded possible utterances by a Coding Scheme. The rationale was to obtain an additional measure in case there might be spontaneous verbal utterances indicative of memory for the events that would not be captured by the words from the fixed Word List. Each two-minute video sequence from both the T_1-baseline and the T_2-test "waiting" phase was divided into 12 time-slots of 10 seconds' duration each. For each 10 second time-slot the coder had to reply to seven specific questions regarding possible mnemonic content in the video segments. These questions concerned the following seven dimensions: (1) *language*, (2) *gestures*, (3) *reliving*, (4) *action details*, (5) *object details*, (6) *spatial details*, and (7) *social details*. The Coding Scheme was inspired by the coding of internal (episodic) details developed by Levine, Svoboda, Hay, Winocur, and Moscovitch (2002) in order to distinguish between episodic and semantic components of memories of events. The exact wording of the seven questions was as follows:

(1) Does the child by means of *language* refer to knowledge that originates from a previous visit?
(2) Does the child by means of *gestures* refer to knowledge that originates from a previous visit?
(3) Does the child's verbal and/or non-verbal behavior indicate that the child mentally *relives* parts of a previous visit?
(4) Does the child refer to specific *action details* from a previous visit?
(5) Does the child by means of specific *object details* refer to knowledge that originates from a previous visit?
(6) Does the child by means of specific *spatial details* refer to knowledge that originates from a previous visit?
(7) Does the child by means of specific *social details* refer to knowledge that originates from a previous visit?

For each question, each 10 second time-slot could lead to either a single score or no score. For each of the seven questions, a sum score based on the results from the 12 ten second time-slots was calculated (range: 0–12). Thus, seven sum scores were derived for each child. Note that the possible responses to the seven questions were not mutually exclusive. To illustrate, when returning at T_2, one boy who had been presented with the Game event, pointed to the grey box and said "There is a bucket inside", which led to hits in dimension 1, 2, 3, and 6, but not in 4, 5, and 7.

The coding by Word List and the coding by Coding Scheme were conducted by one primary and one secondary coder for each condition. After being trained together on a coding manual, the primary coder coded all participating children, whereas the secondary coder re-coded 20% of the children. Interrater agreement was very high: Same-Room Condition: 99.5%; Different-Room Condition: 97.9%.

Coding of control questions. Here it was simply noted whether the child's answer was correct ("yes" or "no"), and this part was therefore coded online by the experimenter. Re-coding was not considered necessary.

Results

Preliminary analyses

An ANOVA with Condition (Same-Room vs. Different-Room) and Event (Teddy vs. Game) as between-subjects factors and the children's productive vocabulary as the dependent variable revealed neither main effects nor interactions (all $ps > .18$) indicating that the children in the groups did not differ with respect to productive vocabulary ($M_{\text{Same-room\_Teddy}} = 552.28$, SD = 133.35; $M_{\text{Diff-room\_Teddy}} = 551.50$, SD = 139.39; $M_{\text{Same-room\_Game}} = 534.95$, SD = 137.17, $M_{\text{Diff-room\_Game}} = 487.74$, SD = 112.53). This analysis was conducted to ensure that any possible difference in results obtained by means of the experimental manipulation between the two conditions could not be attributed to differences in the children's productive vocabulary.

Results from the Word List and Coding Scheme

The central part of the data was from the two-minute waiting periods at T_1-baseline and T_2-test. Based on our hypotheses, three questions were crucial: First, did the number of possible spontaneous verbal utterances obtained at the T_2-test differ reliably from the equivalent data obtained at the T_1-baseline? Second, were the possible spontaneous verbal utterances *congruent* (see below) or incongruent with the specific event (Teddy *or* Game), the child was presented with at T_1-baseline? And third, did the room that the children were tested in at T_2 affect the results?

We define a *congruent* spontaneous utterance as referring specifically to the event (Teddy *or* Game) that the child was presented with at T_1-baseline (or by a condition *un*specific utterance just indicating that the child had been there before), and not to the other event, whereas an *incongruent* utterance refers specifically to the event to which the child was *not* exposed at T_1-baseline. Because the analyses focused on whether the children at T_2 spontaneously talked about the event (Teddy or Game) they had been presented with at T_1, and since the two events were counterbalanced across children and conditions, the two events were collapsed in the subsequent analyses (cf. Krøjgaard et al., in press).

Table 1 displays the descriptive statistics and *t*-tests, from both events combined, based on the congruent spontaneous utterances (both from the Word List and the Coding Scheme) obtained while waiting for the experimenter to return at the T_2-test. Data from the measures obtained at T_1-baseline as well as incongruent measures from the T_2-test are not displayed, simply because there were *no* hits – except for a single incident. This single exception came from a boy from the Same-Room Condition who, during the T_1-baseline (i.e., *before* being presented with the Game event), talked about animals in cabinets. During the subsequent demonstration of the Game event, it turned out that this boy earlier the very same day, by sheer coincidence, had seen stuffed animals in cabinets! Hence, this boy talked about animals in cabinets while waiting and was credited (coding-wise correctly) by the naïve coder for doing so. Except for this single exception, no false positives were obtained. In addition, during the T_2-test there was not a single incident in which a child spontaneously talked about the event that the child had *not* seen at T_1. Consequently, the analyses from the congruent hits obtained at the T_2-test were generally analysed by simple One-Sample *t*-tests tested against the test value of "0" (i.e., "no hits"), except in the Word List measure and in three dimensions in the Coding Scheme measure in the Same-Room Condition in which the test value were slightly above zero (equivalent to the exact means obtained in these scales as a consequence of the one boy mentioned previously and straight zeroes for all the remaining measures).

Overall, the results revealed that the children at the T_2-test in both conditions spontaneously and reliably talked about the event they had seen at T_1, whereas they never talked about the event they had not seen at T_1. The results were clear, systematic, and significant in both conditions and for both the Word List and the Coding Scheme (only the social dimension in the Same-Room Condition was not significant).

Did the room that the children were tested in at T_2 affect the results? When looking at the means obtained in the two conditions, there was a systematic tendency that the children in the Different-Room Condition obtained numerically lower sum scores for the spontaneous utterances (the social dimension was the single exception) relative to the peers in the Same-Room Condition (see Table 1). However, probably due to the large variance in the scores, this tendency was not statistically significant. Thus, contrary to our expectations, returning to a different context (the Different-Room Condition) did not have a reliable detrimental effect on the number of produced spontaneous utterances at the T_2-test.

As can be seen from Table 1, the obtained congruent scores for the seven Coding Scheme dimensions were highly systematic and clear. Because they addressed

Table 1. Descriptive statistics and t-tests based on the Congruent Word List measures and the Congruent Coding Scheme measures for Teddy and the Game event combined at the T_2 test.

	Same-Room Condition (n = 40)						Different-Room Condition (n = 40)						Same-Room vs. Different Room			
	Descriptives		One-sample t-tests (tested against the value x)				Descriptives		One-sample t-tests (tested against the value x)				Independent samples t-test			
Measure	M	SD	x	t	df	p	r	M	SD	x	t	df	p	r	t	df	p	r
Word List	1.15	1.72	.05	3.79	39	=.001	0.51	0.73	1.20	0	3.83	39	<.001	0.52	1.28	78	=.203	0.14
Coding Scheme																		
Language	0.70	0.94	.05	4.38	39	<.001	0.57	0.58	0.81	0	4.47	39	<.001	0.58	0.64	78	=.526	0.07
Gesture	0.45	0.60	0	4.77	39	<.001	0.61	0.38	0.57	0	4.05	39	<.001	0.54	0.57	78	=.572	0.06
Reliving	0.70	0.94	.05	4.38	39	<.001	0.57	0.55	0.78	0	4.44	39	<.001	0.58	0.78	78	=.440	0.09
Action	0.23	0.53	0	2.68	39	=.011	0.39	0.18	0.39	0	2.88	39	=.006	0.42	0.48	78	=.631	0.05
Object	0.28	0.55	0	3.14	39	=.003	0.45	0.15	0.43	0	2.22	39	=.032	0.34	1.13	78	=.262	0.12
Spatial	0.48	0.60	.03	4.70	39	<.001	0.60	0.40	0.63	0	4.00	30	<.001	0.54	0.55	78	=.588	0.06
Social	0.03	0.16	0	1.00	30	=.323	0.16	0.23	0.58	0	2.47	39	<.018	0.38	-2.12	78	=.038	0.23

Notes: The Congruent hits are based on the condition specific hits (e.g., "teddy," "elephant") as well as condition unspecific hits (e.g., "last time", "again"). Note further that some of the variables obtained in the Same-Room Condition are not tested against "0" in the One-sample t-tests. The reason is that for these variables, the single false positive scores during baseline originating from the one boy who coincidentally talked about the Teddy event.

memory for the same underlying event, we expected them to be correlated with one another to some extent and, consequently, that they might be treated as a scale as was the case in the Krøjgaard et al., (in press) study. In the present dataset, an item analysis led to a Cronbach's a = .915, replicating Krøjgaard et al., (in press) and justifying treating the dimensions as a scale. We then computed a total sum score of hits based on sums of each of these seven dimensions (sum of condition specific *and* condition unspecific hits). First, we analysed whether the results obtained by each of the dimensions would replicate when running the analysis on the computed sum scores. As expected they did. For the children in the Same-Room Condition (n = 40), the mean sum score of congruent hits (condition specific hits and unspecific hits combined) at the T_2-test (M = 2.85, SD = 3.75) clearly differed from the means obtained at T_1-baseline (One-Sample t-test tested against "0.13": $t(39)$ = 4.59, p < .001, r = 0.59). Similarly, for the children in the Different-Room Condition (n = 40) the mean sum score of congruent hits (condition specific hits and unspecific hits combined) at the T_2-test (M = 2.45, SD = 3.59) also reliably differed from the means obtained at T_1-baseline (One-Sample t-test tested against "0": $t(39)$ = 4.32, p < .001, r = 0.57). However, the sum scores obtained did not differ across conditions (independent samples t-test: $t[78]$ = 0.49, p = .627, r = 0.06). Thus, the results based on the sum scores replicate the pattern of results obtained when looking at the individual dimensions: In both conditions, the children at the T_2-test reliably and systematically produced spontaneous utterances about the events they had been presented with at T_1-baseline, while never talking about the event they had *not* seen. Similarly, although the children returning to the same room for the test on average had higher sum scores than the peers returning to a different room, the difference was not statically significant.

Results from the control questions

The control questions addressed whether the children would respond correctly when asked directly about the contents of the two boxes. By means of non-parametric binomial tests (against p = .50, two-tailed) we analysed whether the distribution of correct replies regarding the contents of the two boxes across conditions was significant. The "known" box refers to the box to which the child was exposed to during T_1, whereas the "unknown" box refers to the box to which the child was *not* exposed to at T_1. The results are displayed in Table 2.

Overall, the children in both conditions tended to respond correctly when asked about whether they knew the contents of the "known" box (i.e., the box they had seen the contents of), whereas they only responded at chance level when asked about whether they knew the contents of the "unknown" box (i.e., the box, they had never seen the contents of).

Table 2. Descriptives and binominal statistics from the results from for the control questions asked (did the child know the contents of the boxes?) at T_2.

Condition	Box asked about first?	N Known/unknown	Correct replies regarding known box			Correct replies regarding unknown box		
			Count	%	p*	Count	%	p*
Same-room	Known	20	14	70	$p = .115$	12	60	$p = .503$
	Unknown	20	16	80	$p = .012$	8	40	$p = .503$
	(Both boxes)	40	30	75	$p = .002$	20	50	$p = 1.00$
Different-room	Known	16	15	94	$p = .001$	4	25	$p = .077$
	Unknown	24	18	75	$p = .023$	10	42	$p = .541$
	(Both boxes)	40	33	83	$p < .001$	14	35	$p = .081$
Both conditions	Known	36	29	81	$p < .001$	16	44	$p = .618$
	Unknown	44	34	73	$p < .001$	18	41	$p = .291$
	(Both boxes)	80	63	79	$p < .001$	34	43	$p = .219$

*Binomial test, test-value: $p = .50$ (two-tailed).

In order to examine whether the results differed across conditions, we computed a sum score for the number of correct responses regarding whether the children knew the contents of each of the two boxes (the known and the unknown box; range 0–2). An independent samples t-test revealed that although the children in the Same-Room Condition tended to have slightly higher sum scores, the difference was not significant, $t(78) = 0.71$, $p = .478$, $r = .07$, $M_{Sum\_score\_Same-Room} = 1.25$, $SD = 0.49$; $M_{Sum\_score\_Diff-Room} = 1.18$, $SD = 0.47$. Thus, changing the room at recall did not affect how the children responded to the control questions.

Discussion

In accordance with previous studies using the same overall design (Krøjgaard et al., 2014, in press), the results showed that spontaneous memories can indeed be induced in an experimental setting, and that 35-month-old children at the T_2-test spontaneously talked about the event they were presented with at T_1, whereas they never talked about the event, they had not seen. Further, the dimensions used for the Coding Scheme again turned out to constitute a reliable scale. By systematically replicating previous results regarding spontaneous memories, the present findings lend further support to the credibility of the new paradigm.

In the present study we expanded on the previous findings by specifically examining the possible impact of contextual cues operationalised here as having half of the children return to a different room at the test. Although the number of spontaneous memories was numerically smaller, returning to a different room did – in contrast to our prediction – not reliably reduce the number of spontaneous memories. Potentially, this null finding could be due to lack of statistical power. Although possible, we consider this unlikely. Even the largest effects size ($r = 0.14$) obtained from the comparison of the Word List measure outcome from the two conditions (see Table 1, last column), was "small" from a conventional point (Cohen, 1988). Given the obtained M's and SD's for the two conditions, a power analysis showed that 190 subjects in each condition would have been needed in order to obtain a power of 0.8 for a two-tailed test with an $\alpha = .05$.

Thus, although the children in the Different-Room Condition numerically obtained fewer hits than their peers in the Same-Room Condition, the difference was of small magnitude, and therefore we find it unlikely that the results were due to lack of statistical power. Even if a study with about 190 subjects in each condition might reach a statistically reliable difference with $p < .05$ (as suggested by our power analyses), the effects of the manipulation is under all circumstances very small. It should also be noted that our sample sizes were in the range of the sample sizes normally used in this field.

Although no previous studies specifically have examined the possible impact of changing the context for spontaneous retrieval, other studies have found effects of contextual reinstatement, as reviewed in the introduction. For instance La Rooy et al. (2007), showed clear effects of changing the context at retrieval on children's memories. How should this discrepancy in results be explained? The design in La Rooy et al., (2007) and the present study differed in at least three respects, that is, age of the participants (5–6 year olds vs. almost 3-year olds), the retention interval (6 months vs. 1 week), and retrieval mode (strategic vs. spontaneous). In addition, the manipulation of context may have been stronger in the La Rooy et al. (2007) study. In the present study, the two rooms used in the Different-Room Condition differed with regard to their location in the corridor and the furnishing of the far end of each room. Theory predicts that in order to serve as a strong cue, the cue needs to be *distinct* (cf. Watkins & Watkins, 1975; Smith, 2014). In retrospect, the children's perception of the distinctiveness of the setting may have been mainly tied to the setup of the two boxes – which was preserved across the two rooms – rather than to the rooms as such. This agrees with the fact that very few of the children in the Different-Room Condition commented on returning to a different room. Although this is only anecdotal evidence, it may suggest that the change of room at test in the present study was not particularly prominent to the children. In hindsight, we regret that we did not – after the test was over – ask the children in the Different-Room Condition whether they had noticed the change of rooms. When considering the environmental cues in a broader perspective, many cues were actually the same across the two conditions (same campus, same parking lot, same waiting room, same corridor, and same two boxes in the test rooms). Thus, greater effects of the retrieval context manipulation might have been obtained with a more prominent difference between the encoding and retrieval contexts in the Different Room Condition.

Control questions

In general, the children reliably confirmed that they knew the contents of the box they had been exposed to during the first visit. In contrast, the children's responses to whether they knew the contents of the box, they had never seen the contents of, did not exceed chance level. These results are in accordance with the results obtained previously employing the same overall design and with children in the same age group (Krøjgaard et al., in press).

Importantly, however, condition (i.e., Same-Room vs. Different-Room) had no effect on this pattern of results. Although the children in the Different-Room Condition numerically fared slightly worse than their peers in the Same-Room Condition, the difference was not significant. Thus, replicating the pattern in results from the spontaneous measures, changing the room at retrieval did not reliably diminish the children's ability to respond to the control questions.

Broader implications

The present findings add to a growing literature showing that spontaneous memories are common in young children's lives and may be their most dominant way of rehearsing and remembering their personal past. Viewed from a broader perspective, these findings appear consistent with explanations of childhood amnesia centring on *forgetting* (Bauer, 2015; Hayne & Jack, 2011). Given the fact that the great majority of studies on children's memory of events have been based on children's strategic retrieval (i.e., asking the children, see Hayne, Scarf, & Imuta, 2015), in which the process of retrieval *by itself* is particularly demanding for young children, researchers may have underestimated the magnitude of young children's memories. Provided that this argument is valid, then a larger amount of memories than hitherto assumed may have been lost as children grow older and eventually become adults.

However, this suggestion calls for an explanation regarding the possible fate of these additional memories and underlying forgetting mechanisms. In other words: Why should such memories in particular be disproportionally prone to forgetting in early childhood? There is evidence that the forgetting rate of younger children is faster than older children, even with the initial level of learning kept constant (Bauer, 2012, 2015). According to Bauer (2012, 2015) this is likely to reflect fragile memory traces early in childhood due to poorer consolidation, and reconsolidation. As suggested by Berntsen and Rubin (2012), more rapid forgetting due to less efficient reconsolidation processes in early childhood may reflect a dominance of involuntary rehearsal of past events in young children. According to Berntsen (2012), involuntary remembering is an important form of rehearsal that is likely to support consolidation and reconsolidation of past events. However, it is also an uncontrollable and context-sensitive type of recall, driven by associative mechanisms. This type of rehearsal therefore is likely to lead to a different, and probably more fragile, type of consolidation of past events, as compared to voluntary, strategic recall. Accelerated forgetting of events during early childhood may be the result (Berntsen & Rubin, 2012).

Consequently, although young children may have more (spontaneous) memories than hitherto assumed, these memories may be especially vulnerable to forgetting as their rehearsal seems more coincidental and cue dependent, and the effects on subsequent consolidation and reconsolidation therefore more fragile. Thus, based on this reasoning, we propose that *forgetting* (the "forgotten explanation", Hayne & Jack, 2011) may indeed be a central explanation in order to understand childhood amnesia.

In addition, the present results suggest that some environmental cues, that most adults would definitely notice (i.e., returning to a different room for a test), at times may pass more or less unnoticed by young children. In this respect the results also may lend support to the "different lenses" explanation of childhood amnesia (e.g., Bauer, 2007), or at least be consistent with this idea. Viewed in this perspective the results provide a specific example of how a given aspect of the environment is likely to be processed differently in adults and young children respectively. This is interesting because noticing the change of rooms is not dependent on advanced knowledge of a kind that one would only attribute to adults, while at the same time acknowledging that children in this age range *are* capable of registering differences between rooms (e.g., Hayne & Imuta, 2011; Newcombe, Balcomb, Ferrara, Hansen, & Koski, 2014). In short: Whereas the children most likely were capable of noticing the difference between Room A and Room B, changing rooms at test had no impact on their inclination to retrieve and talk about memories spontaneously.

Finally, the results from the present experiment may be interpreted to suggest how the "different lenses" explanation of childhood amnesia (Bauer, 2007) could *interact* with the "forgetting" explanation (Bauer, 2012, 2015; Hayne & Jack, 2011): If the processing of the distinctive cues undergo changes from childhood to adulthood as suggested above, then this aspect by *it-self* may lead to accelerated forgetting, because some of the cues may have their "cuing potential" reduced as the child grows older. However, we acknowledge that this suggestion is indeed speculative. Further research on which cues remain effective as the child matures and which will not, will be needed to pursue this hypothesis.

To conclude, we have provided further evidence that spontaneous memories can indeed be induced in young children in an experimental setting. In addition, we have provided evidence that changing the spatial context for retrieval – at least as operationalised in the present study – does not diminish the children's ability to retrieve memories spontaneously in young children. However, additional experiments using a more radical change of the retrieval context are warranted before a firm conclusion regarding to what extent the context for retrieval affects spontaneous recall can be drawn. Taken together, the results obtained here and in previous work using the same paradigm may shed new light on childhood amnesia and potential underlying mechanisms. One possible explanation that would be consistent with the present results is forgetting due to a dominance of incidental and associative rehearsal of past events in young children.

Notes

1. Numerous infant studies have provided evidence, that infants by means of behavioral responses are capable of remembering aspects of previously experienced events without being socially prompted to do so (e.g., Perris, Myers, & Clifton, 1990; Rovee-Collier, Griesler, & Earley, 1985). However, these demonstrations of memory among infants should not be considered spontaneous memories as defined here, because the memory manifestations in these infant studies were not verbal but exclusively motor-based.
2. We failed to collect CDI reports from four of the children.

Acknowledgements

We would like to thank Maiken Venø and Anne Rytter Christiansen for recruiting and testing participants as well as Julie Ardahl, Caroline Beyer, Mette Sørensen, and Louise Jensen for coding the video material. We would also like to thank the children who participated in this study and their parents for letting them participate.

Funding

This research was supported by Velux Fonden [Grant 10386] and the Danish National Research Foundation [Grant DNRF89].

References

Bauer, P. J. (2007). *Remembering the times of our lives*. Mahwah, NJ: Laurence Erlbaum Associates.
Bauer, P. J. (2008). Toward a neuro-developmental account of the development of declarative memory. *Developmental Psychobiology, 50*, 19–31.
Bauer, P. J. (2012). The life I once remembered: The waxing and waning of early memories. In D. Berntsen, & D. C. Rubin (Eds.), *Understanding autobiographical memory: Theories and approaches* (pp. 205–225). Cambridge: Cambridge University Press.
Bauer, P. J. (2015). A complementary processes account of the development of childhood amnesia and a personal past. *Psychological Review, 122*, 204–231.
Berntsen, D. (1996). Involuntary autobiographical memories. *Applied Cognitive Psychology, 10*, 435–454.
Berntsen, D. (2009). *Involuntary autobiographical memories: An introduction to the unbidden past*. Cambridge: Cambridge University Press.
Berntsen, D. (2012). Spontaneous recollections: Involuntary autobiographical memories are a basic mode of remembering. In D. Berntsen & D. C. Rubin (Eds.), *Understanding autobiographical memory: Theories and approaches* (pp. 290–310). Cambridge: Cambridge University Press.
Berntsen, D., & Rubin, D. C. (2012). Understanding autobiographical memory: An ecological theory. In D. Berntsen & D. C. Rubin (Eds.), *Understanding autobiographical memory: Theories and approaches* (pp. 333–355). Cambridge: Cambridge University Press.
Cohen, J. (1988). *Statistical power analysis for the behavioral sciences* (2nd ed.). Hillsdale, NJ: Lawrence Erlbaum Associates.
Dahl, J. J., Kingo, O. S., & Krøjgaard, P. (2015). The magic shrinking machine revisited: The presence of props at recall facilitates memory in 3-year-olds. *Developmental Psychology, 51*, 1704–1716.
Fivush, R., Haden, C. A., & Reese, E. (2006). Elaborating on elaborations: Role of maternal reminiscing style in cognitive and socioemotional development. *Child Development, 77*, 1568–1588.
Hall, S. A., Rubin, D. C., Miles, A., Davis, S. W., Wing, E. A., Cabeza, R., & Berntsen, D. (2014). The neural basis of involuntary episodic memories. *Journal of Cognitive Neuroscience, 26*, 2385–2399.
Hayne, H., & Imuta, K. (2011). Episodic memory in 3- and 4-year-old children. *Developmental Psychobiology, 53*, 317–322.
Hayne, H., & Jack, F. (2011). Childhood amnesia. *Wiley Interdisciplinary Reviews: Cognitive Science, 2*, 136–145.
Hayne, H., Rovee-Collier, C., & Borza, M. (1991). Infant memory for place information. *Memory and Cognition, 19*, 378–386.
Hayne, H., Scarf, D., & Imuta, K. (2015). Childhood memories. In J. D. Wright (Ed.), *International encyclopedia of the social & behavioral sciences* (pp. 465–470). Oxford: Elsevier.
Hershkowitz, I., Orbach, Y., Lamb, M. E., Sternberg, K. J., Horowitz, D., & Hovav, M. (1998). Visiting the scene of the crime: Effects on children's recall of alleged abuse. *Legal and Criminological Psychology, 3*, 195–207.
Howe, M. L. (2003). Memories from the cradle. *Current Directions in Psychological Science, 12*, 62–65.
Johnson, M. H. (2005). *Developmental cognitive neuroscience* (2nd ed.). Oxford: Blackwell.
Krøjgaard, P., Kingo, O. S., Dahl, J. J., & Berntsen, D. (2014). "That one makes things small": Experimentally induced spontaneous memories in 3.5-year-olds. *Consciousness and Cognition, 30*, 24–35.
Krøjgaard, P., Kingo, O. S., Jensen, T. S., & Berntsen, D. (in press). Bypassing strategic retrieval: Experimentally induced spontaneous episodic memories in 35- and 46-month-old children. *Consciousness and Cognition*.
La Rooy, D., Pipe, M.-E., & Murray, J. E. (2007). Enhancing children's event recall after long delays. *Applied Cognitive Psychology, 21*, 1–17.
Leichtman, M. D. (2006). Cultural and maturational influences on long-term event memory. In C. Tamis-LeMonda & L. Balter (Eds.), *Child psychology: A handbook of contemporary issues* (2nd ed., pp. 565–589). Philadelphia, PA: Psychology Press.
Levine, B., Svoboda, E., Hay, J. F., Winocur, G., & Moscovitch, M. (2002). Aging and autobiographical memory: Dissociating episodic from semantic retrieval. *Psychology and Aging, 17*(4), 677–689. http://dx.doi.org/10.1037//0882-7974.17.4.677
Nelson, K., & Fivush, R. (2004). The emergence of autobiographical memory: A social cultural developmental theory. *Psychological Review, 111*, 486–511.
Nelson, K., & Ross, G. (1980). The generalities and specifics of long-term memory in infants and young children. *New Directions for Child and Adolescent Development, 10*, 87–101.
Newcombe, N. S., Balcomb, F., Ferrara, K., Hansen, M., & Koski, J. (2014). Two rooms, two representations? Episodic-like memory in toddlers and preschoolers. *Developmental Science, 17*, 743–756.
Orbach, Y., Hershkowitz, I., Lamb, M. E., Sternberg, K. J., & Horowitz, D. (2000). Interviewing at the scene of the crime: Effects on children's

recall of alleged abuse. *Legal and Criminological Psychology, 5*, 135–147.

Perris, E. E., Myers, N. A., & Clifton, R. K. (1990). Long-term memory for a single infancy experience. *Child Development, 61*, 1796–1807.

Pillemer, D. B., & White, S. H. (1989). Childhood events recalled by children and adults. *Advanced in Child Development and Behavior, 21*, 297–340.

Pipe, M.-E., & Wilson, J. C. (1994). Cues and secrets: Influences on children's event reports. *Developmental Psychology, 30*, 515–525.

Reese, E. (1999). What children say when they talk about the past. *Narrative Inquiry, 9*, 215–241.

Rovee-Collier, C., Griesler, P. C., & Earley, L. A. (1985). Contextual determinants of retrieval in three-month-old infants. *Learning and Motivation, 16*, 139–157.

Simcock, G., & Hayne, H. (2002). Breaking the barrier? Children fail to translate their preverbal memories into language. *Psychological Science, 13*, 225–231.

Smith, S. M. (2014). Effects of environmental context on human memory. In T. Perfect & S. Lindsay (Eds.), *Handbook of Applied Memory* (pp. 162–182). London: SAGE.

Todd, C. M., & Perlmutter, M. (1980). Reality recalled by preschool children. *New Directions for Child and Adolescent Development, 10*, 69–85.

Tulving, E., & Thomson, D. (1973). Encoding specificity and retrieval processes in episodic memory. *Psychological Review, 80*, 352–373.

Watkins, O. C., & Watkins, M. J. (1975). Build up of proactive inhibition as a cue-overload effect. *Journal of Experimental Psychology: Human Learning and Memory, 1*, 442–452.

Wilkinson, J. (1988). Context effects in children's event memory. In M. M. Gruneberg, P. E. Morris, & R. N. Sykes (Eds.), *Practical aspects of memory: Current research issues* (Vol. 1, pp. 107–111). New York, NY: Wiley.

Appendix

Word List in alphabetical order for each of the two conditions as well as an "Unspecific" list of words each indicating that the child had been there before without being specific about any of the two conditions. Note that synonyms and conjugations of the words presented in the lists counted as well.

Teddy event	Game event	Unspecific
Alfred	Ball	"Always"
Animal	Blue	"Have been"
Button	Bowling	"Again"
Clap	Bucket	"Last time"
Dog	Game	"New/other room/place"
Elephant	Green	"Same/other boxes"
Elly	Hit	"Moved/changed"
Flip	Medal	
Hug	Pin	
Lives	Play	
Music	Prize	
Push	Red	
Sing	Roll	
Take/bring out or get	Throw	
Teddy	Turn over	
Turn on	Win	
Wiggle	Yellow	

What happened in kindergarten? Mother-child conversations about life story chapters

Michelle D. Leichtman, Kristina L. Steiner, Kaitlin A. Camilleri, David B. Pillemer and Dorthe Kirkegaard Thomsen

ABSTRACT
Research indicates that adults form life story chapters, representations of extended time periods that include people, places and activities. Life chapter memories are distinct from episodic memories and have implications for behaviour, self and mental health, yet little is known about their development during childhood. Two exploratory studies examined parent–child conversations about life chapters. In Study 1, mothers recorded naturalistic conversations with their 5–6 year old children about two chapters in the child's life. In Study 2, mothers recorded conversations with their 6–7 year old children about a particular life chapter—the child's kindergarten year—and also about a specific episode of their choice. The results indicated that young children are able to recall and discuss information about life chapters and that parents actively scaffold children's discussion of general information in chapters as well as specific events. Mothers' conversational style when discussing chapters (e.g., elaborativeness) predicted children's memory contributions, and was also positively correlated with their style when discussing specific events. The results suggest new avenues for research on the ontogeny of life chapters, the factors that shape them, and their role in development.

In the decades following the publication of Neisser's (1982) paradigm-changing book, *Memory Observed: Remembering in Natural Contexts*, systematic studies of autobiographical memory for events occurring outside the laboratory have become an increasingly prominent part of academic psychology in general and developmental psychology in particular. One important line of research examines how parent–child conversations about specific past events shape both what young children remember about those events and their more general memory styles. Across studies, parents' natural ways of talking about the past, and in particular the degree to which they adopt an "elaborative" conversational style when probing their children's memories, are associated with the quality of children's recall (Fivush, Haden, & Reese, 2006). The results of these studies support a "social construction model" of autobiographical memory development (Fivush & Nelson, 2004; Nelson & Fivush, 2004; Pillemer & White, 1989; Wang, 2013) that is consistent with Neisser's (1982) vision of an ecologically valid psychology of memory.

Although research on parent–child memory conversations has produced a compelling theoretical account of how social interaction shapes autobiographical memory, its potential value and impact are limited by an almost exclusive focus on children's memories of specific, one-moment-in-time special events. The present studies broaden the scope of this research to include, for the first time, parent–child conversations about extended lifetime periods. In the introduction that follows, we first identify possible reasons for the current focus on memories of specific events. Second, we describe the concept of "life story chapters" and briefly describe recent research with adult participants illustrating its potential scientific value. Third, we summarise research and theory on the development of the life story, including life story chapters, in middle childhood and adolescence. Fourth, we offer a rationale for including life story chapters in research on parent–child conversations about the past. Then, we present two initial studies that explore how parents and children co-construct memories of chapters in the child's emerging life story.

Why the research focus on parent–child conversations about specific events?

An extensive research literature documenting how parents scaffold their children's recall of the personal past has focused almost exclusively on memories of specific events. Participating parents are encouraged to engage their child in talk about unique episodes, as in Reese, Haden, and Fivush's (1993) seminal empirical study:

> the researcher then requested that the mother choose three past events to talk about that spanned no more than 1 day and were one-time occurrences the child had experienced neither before or since. Thus, the mothers were asked to avoid talking about events that were extended in time. (p. 408)

The privileging of specific memory is also a prominent component of social cultural developmental theory, where autobiographical memory is defined as "an explicit memory of an event that occurred in a specific time and place in one's personal past" (Nelson & Fivush, 2004, p. 486).

The origins of the pervasive research emphasis on young children's recall of specific episodes may be traced to earlier attempts by developmental psychologists to account for the phenomenon of infantile or childhood amnesia—Freud's (1905/1953) observation that adults frequently have difficulty remembering their earliest life experiences. Freud's preferred explanation was that early memories are inaccessible in adulthood because they are repressed, but developmental science offered seemingly more plausible and powerful scientific accounts focused on age-related changes in cognition, language and social circumstances (for more complete descriptions of alternative theories, see Bauer, 2007; Pillemer, 1998; Pillemer & White, 1989; Wang, 2013; White & Pillemer, 1979). Attempting to solve the childhood amnesia puzzle provided a rationale and impetus for new research and theory on autobiographical memory development (Pillemer, 1998). Accordingly, earlier (e.g., Pillemer, Picariello, & Pruitt, 1994) and recent (e.g., Bauer & Larkina, 2016) studies focusing on children's autobiographical memory are frequently framed as efforts to explain childhood amnesia. Importantly, because childhood amnesia refers to adults' inability to recall specific episodes rather than extended events or common routines, the focus on particular events was a natural outgrowth of efforts by developmental psychologists to understand it.

Although the primary focus on parent–child conversations of specific past events has produced a wealth of valuable findings, several important questions remain unanswered. When parents and children talk about temporally extended lifetime periods in the child's life—such as the kindergarten year or last summer's vacation at the lake—do parents scaffold the conversation in ways that are similar to or different from talk about specific events, such as the first day of kindergarten or the time a violent storm interrupted a family picnic? Do parents' styles of probing about the temporally extended past also shape how the child remembers these experiences? Recent research involving adults and older children, to be described in the following section, suggests that new research on parent–child conversations about lifetime periods could have important theoretical and practical implications.

Life story chapters

Recent research and theory has introduced the concept of "life story chapters," defined as "abstract, conceptual memory representations that refer to subjectively defined temporally extended life periods with beginnings and endings ... They include information about the people, places, activities, and objects associated with the period" (Thomsen & Pillemer, 2017, p. 468); in addition, chapters are often associated with a characteristic overall emotional tone (Thomsen, Steiner, & Pillemer, 2016). For example, a chapter describing "the first year of my marriage" could include general information about living circumstances ("our apartment was cozy, not crowded"), relationships with one's spouse ("we agreed on everything except money"), activities ("we loved cooking together"), as well as specific recollections that fit within the chapter structure ("I remember the night when she said she wanted to get pregnant in the next year"). Life story chapters are similar conceptually to "lifetime periods," a prominent component of Conway and Pleydell-Pearce's (2000) influential theoretical model of autobiographical memory. Adults naturally use chapters when orally describing their life stories (Thomsen, 2009), they readily provide life story chapters in response to direct probes (Thomsen & Berntsen, 2008), and they can segment transcripts of their spoken life narratives into distinct chapters (Pillemer, Krensky, Kleinman, Goldsmith, & White, 1991; Steiner, Pillemer, Thomsen, & Minigan, 2014).

Chapters contain general knowledge of people, activities, locations, and emotions typical of an extended period, whereas vivid memories of specific events often represent episodes that are novel or unique (Thomsen & Pillemer, 2017). Accordingly, adults rate chapters as more central to personal identity than specific memories (Steiner, Pillemer, & Thomsen, 2017; Thomsen & Pillemer, 2017). In several studies, the emotional tone of chapters was more strongly and consistently associated with trait measures of personality and self-esteem than the emotional tone of specific memories (Steiner et al., 2017; Thomsen & Pillemer, 2017). Taken together, these recent findings suggest that life story chapters are both familiar to adults and tied to their enduring conceptions of self.

Development of life story chapters

Although many studies have documented how parent–child conversations may enhance development of autobiographical memory for specific personal episodes, researchers have yet to explore parent–child talk about life story chapters. Research on the development of the life story suggests that the concept of a "life chapter" should be challenging for very young children. Habermas and Bluck (2000) proposed that a coherent life story does not emerge until early adolescence, when single events are incorporated into a meaningful and integrated narrative. Follow-up empirical studies demonstrated that narrative coherence increases in middle childhood through late adolescence (Habermas & de Silveira, 2008; Habermas & Paha, 2001; Habermas, Ehlert-Lerche, & de Silveira, 2009). When 9-year-olds were asked to write their life narratives, a majority simply described lists of personal episodes, with some participants providing a single event memory; narrative coherence increased substantially by the age of 12 (Bohn & Berntsen, 2008). Chen, McAnally, and Reese (2013) asked children ages 8–12 to describe personal chapters in their life beginning in the present and working backwards; 12-year-olds were less likely than younger children to have chapters composed entirely of single event descriptions. Steiner and Pillemer (2018) elicited spoken life stories from early adolescents ages 10–14; in a second session participants divided their transcribed narratives into self-defined chapters. Ten-year-olds were more likely than older children to include at least one chapter consisting of a single event. These studies indicate that young children may be unlikely to think about the past as a sequence of abstract, thematically organised chapters. Nevertheless, it is possible that children may show higher levels of proficiency when constructing a life story chapter with parental guidance.

Parent–child conversations about specific memories and chapters

Nelson and Fivush (2004; Fivush & Nelson, 2004) proposed a socio-cultural model of autobiographical memory development. Beginning in the preschool years, children develop the ability to construct and retain memories of specific events through verbal interactions with adults. When engaging in joint reminiscing with their children, adults provide an organising structure, or scaffolding, as they co-construct the child's memories. These dialogues help the child learn that memories are mental representations of events that occurred at a particular time and place and can be experienced from multiple perspectives; the conversations also carry the implicit or explicit meta-message that remembering and sharing personal details is a highly valued and potentially useful activity.

Parents differ systematically in the way that they reminisce about specific events with their young children. Specifically, research studies have identified two basic styles of maternal reminiscing (see Fivush et al., 2006, for a review). High elaborative mothers listen carefully to their children's input and expand on what has been said, using rich descriptive language. These mothers ask open-ended questions, encouraging the child to take an active role in creating a full and detailed account of past events. In contrast, low elaborative mothers tend to repeat their own questions, oftentimes in a yes-no format. The exchanges produce less information, there is less collaboration, and the co-constructed memory may not have a story-like quality. Children of high elaborative mothers have richer and more detailed autobiographical memories (Farrant & Reese, 2000; Newcombe & Reese, 2004; Reese et al., 1993; Reese, Levya, Sparks, & Grolnick, 2010), and they also recount earlier memories of childhood once they reach adolescence (Jack, MacDonald, Reese, & Hayne, 2009).

The socio-cultural model provides a theoretically plausible and empirically supported account of how parent–child conversations foster the development of autobiographical memory for specific events beginning in the preschool years. Parent–child conversations also may contribute to young children's ability to construct and remember temporally extended time periods, here labelled life story chapters (Thomsen, 2015). By engaging children in conversations about temporally extended time periods and asking elaborative questions about the people, locations, and activities associated with these periods, parents may support the development of life story chapters. Based on these ideas, we examined whether elaborative questioning would enhance the informational richness of children's chapter descriptions. Studies on the development of the life story, described earlier, suggest that very young children may be more adept at describing specific past events than describing temporally extended life chapters. Will parent–child conversations hold a focus on general chapter themes and recurrent activities or will they move to the potentially more familiar and developmentally appropriate terrain of specific episodes? More generally, are the patterns of associations between styles of parent–child memory talk and children's recall that have been consistently found for specific memories also evident when the research focus is on parent–child talk about life story chapters? To begin to address these questions, we conducted two studies of parent–child conversations about life story chapters.

The current studies

In two studies, parents engaged their children in talk about chapters from the child's life that the parent had identified prior to the conversations. Parents were not instructed how to structure the conversations; rather, they were encouraged to talk with their child as they might in a naturally occurring setting. Study 1 was an initial exploratory effort to examine how mothers and children discuss extended autobiographical periods. We investigated the content of the chapters, qualities of maternal elaboration, and whether the discussions focused on specific episodes or general chapter-relevant topics. In addition, we examined correlations between indices of maternal conversational styles and children's memory production. In Study 2, parents talked with their children about both a life story chapter and a specific memory; this design enabled direct comparisons between parents' conversational styles and children's memory when the target event is either temporally extended or pinpointed in time.

Study 1

Study 1 was an exploratory examination of how mothers and children talk about life story chapters. The first purpose was descriptive. We were interested in the primary topics of parent-defined children's chapters (e.g., sports activities; vacations; preschool); whether the children's chapters focused on types of information that are evident in adults' chapters: people, activities and locations (e.g., Brown, Hansen, Lee, Vanderveen, & Conrad, 2012; Conway & Pleydell-Pearce, 2000; Thomsen & Pillemer, 2017); whether the memory conversations tended to focus on temporally extended events rather than specific episodes; and whether mothers' and children's talk about chapters could be reliably coded using categories employed in studies of conversations about specific memories (e.g., memory/elaborative questions, evaluations). The second purpose was to assess whether associations between parental conversational styles and children's memory production that are evident when targeting specific memories in prior studies would also be apparent in conversations about temporally extended chapters. Although we expected to find a positive correlation between mothers' elaborativeness and children's recall of life chapters, this was not an a priori necessity. Since conversational style is often inconsistent across contexts (Fivush et al., 2006), it was possible that parents would not adopt elaborative conversational strategies when engaging their children in talk about temporally extended events, or that children's memory production would be less responsive to parental elaboration in this context than in typical studies of specific episodes.

Participants

Twenty-three mothers participated with their 5- to 6-year-old kindergarten children (12 boys, 11 girls; age *range* 60–81 months; $M = 73$, $SD = 5.97$). Kindergartners were chosen for participation because prior research on parent–child conversations about specific past events has included children in this age range (e.g., Reese et al., 1993), and because they were presumably old enough to have experienced identifiable life chapters (e.g., a preschool year). The majority of mothers (96%) and children (92%) were white, with the remainder reported as "other ethnicity." Mothers were highly educated, with 96% having completed a college degree or higher.

Procedure

Participants were recruited via information distributed through local school systems or via word of mouth and were paid for their participation. Mothers provided written consent at the outset of the study. Data collection took place either at children's homes or at a university research laboratory, depending on mothers' preferences. The same researcher collected all of the data and the procedure was the same for all participants. First, mothers completed a short demographic questionnaire. Next, out of earshot of the child, they were told that they were going to be asked to talk with their child about life chapters, and before doing so should identify life chapters to discuss. Mothers were instructed:

> Think back over the course of the child's life and identify four chapters in his or her life story. A chapter should describe an extended period of time in the child's life, lasting weeks, months or years, and may include information about people, locations and activities that were involved. For example, when doing this task for himself or herself, an adult might describe a life chapter focusing on his or her first year of college, a summer trip to Maine, or his or her marriage.

Mothers were told that they were allowed to choose chapters focusing on any topic or theme so long as they covered an extended time period lasting weeks, months, or years. The researcher reviewed mothers' chapter selections to ensure that they met these criteria. Mothers then wrote several sentences describing the chapters on a piece of paper to use as a cue during the conversation with their child in order to make sure the conversation went smoothly. Mothers also gave their child's age at the beginning and ending of the chapter or indicated that the chapter was still ongoing.

Next, mothers were instructed to select the two most recent chapters of the four to discuss with their child. They were provided with a digital audio recorder and instructed to discuss the two chapters in any way that they would naturally or normally talk with their child, with no time limit. The researcher left for the duration of the mother–child conversation, so that the conversation could take place as naturally as possible. The session lasted approximately 30 min.

Coding

Mother–child conversations were transcribed verbatim, and trained coders coded all variables by hand from the transcriptions. To characterise the general topic of the chapters, a coder first identified six mutually exclusive topical categories by reading through the transcriptions. Each chapter was then scored as focusing on a time period associated with one of these categories: the child's preschool or kindergarten year, an activity (e.g., a sport season or other seasonal activity), moving to a new residence, a family vacation, the birth of a sibling, or other (e.g., an injury, care of a pet). To further assess content, each chapter was coded for the presence or absence of the following features: references to people (other than the child), locations, activities and emotion.

Prior to coding the conversations, off-topic talk (12% of conversational turns in the original transcriptions) and talk about the future (<4% of conversational turns) was eliminated from the transcriptions, so that all analysed speech pertained to the life story chapters. To evaluate the extent to which conversations referred to extended time periods versus specific episodes, mothers' and children's conversational turns were coded separately as referring to either "general" or "specific" memory, in a coding scheme adapted from Pillemer, Goldsmith, Panter, and White (1988). Conversational turns were coded as general if they focused on information or events that were part of the extended life story chapter but were not tied to a one-point-in-time event that took place at a particular date and time. For example, a turn might refer to repeated events that happened more than once or over the course of many days (e.g., learning to ice skate, going to the library), or to other information that was part of the chapter as a whole (e.g., living in Maryland, liking butterflies). Conversational turns were coded as specific when they referred to events that were tied to a specific date and time that happened once during the course of a single day, usually characterising a unique experience (e.g., making a gingerbread man in class, finding a monarch butterfly). If a conversational turn referred to a specific event but contained information associated with a general memory (e.g., the day we captured a monarch butterfly in our net when we lived in Maryland), it was coded as specific.

Mothers' and children's speech was also coded separately in a coding scheme adapted from past research on mother–child conversations about specific episodes (Fivush & Fromhoff, 1988; Leichtman et al., 2017; Leichtman, Pillemer, Wang, Koreishi, & Han, 2000; Reese et al., 1993; Reese & Fivush, 1993). Descriptions of mother and child conversational variables and examples of how they were coded are shown in Table 1. Each sentence mothers spoke (which included statements and questions) was coded as referring to one of the following mutually exclusive categories: memory/elaborative questions, yes/no questions, context statements or evaluations. A composite variable entitled *elaborativeness* was calculated by summing across these four categories.

In line with our central goal of assessing how well children could contribute to discussions of life chapters, and how this was related to mothers' elaborativeness, coding of children's speech focused on memory responses (Reese et al., 1993). Each sentence children spoke was coded as either a memory response—in which the child contributed new information to the conversation—or as a non-memory response, in which they did not. Non-memory responses included sentences in which the child provided an evaluation (e.g., confirming or disconfirming information the mother provided without adding new information, for example by just saying yes or no) or in which they repeated previous content or made an observation without contributing new information.

One coder first coded all of the variables for the entire dataset. To assess reliability, an additional hypothesis-blind coder recoded the entire dataset. The interrater reliability estimate for specific vs. general memory was kappa = .75, with 97% agreement for specific and 99% agreement for general. Interrater reliability for the *elaborativeness* variable was calculated by computing kappa across mutually exclusive categories including: memory/elaborative questions, yes/no questions, context statements, evaluations and other; kappa = .94. Percent agreements were 96% for memory/elaborative questions, 99% for yes/no questions, 99% for context statements, and 98% for evaluations. Interrater reliability for children's memory responses was kappa = .90, with 98% agreement for memory responses and 96% agreement for non-memory responses.

Results

All analyses reported below are based on transcriptions with off-topic talk and future talk removed, as described in the coding section. Chapter conversations for the two selected chapters combined ranged from 47 to 167 ($M = 83.22$, $SD = 33.87$) conversational turns for mothers and 41–163 ($M = 81.09$, $SD = 34.07$) conversational turns for children.

Chapter content

Analysis of chapter content indicated that the most common topic of focus was the preschool or kindergarten year (43%), followed by discussion of an activity (13%), moving to a new residence (13%), a family vacation (9%), the birth of a sibling (9%), or other (13%). Consistent with

Table 1. Mothers' and children's main conversational variables, coded for conversations about life story chapter (Study 1) and conversations about chapter and specific event (Study 2).

Variable	Description	Example
Mothers' variables (Mutually exclusive):		
Memory/elaborative questions	Questions focusing on "what", "where", or "who"; open-ended; repetitions of the same question not counted	"What were some of the best parts of being in kindergarten?"
Yes/no questions	Questions requiring children to confirm or deny information; repetitions not counted	"Do you remember the beach house?"
Context statements	Statements requiring no response from the child; repetitions not counted	"I remember you telling me about that."
Evaluations	Statements confirming or disconfirming information provided by the child; repetitions not counted	"That's right."
(Composite):		
Elaborativeness	Composite measure equal to the sum of memory/elaborative questions, yes/no questions, context statements and evaluations	
Children's variable		
Memory responses	Conversational turns in which the child provided new information or moved the conversation to a new aspect of the event	"We saw whales."

literature on adults' life story chapters (e.g., Thomsen et al., 2016), the majority of conversations contained references to people other than the child (95%), specific locations (83%), and activities (87%). Many of the conversations (65%) also contained references to emotions.

In line with instructions to mothers to discuss chapters, on average 21.61 ($SD = 19.68$) or 25% of mothers' conversational turns and 16.43 ($SD = 15.14$) or 30% of children's memory responses referred to one-point-in-time events within chapters, while the remaining 75% of mothers' conversational turns and 70% of children's memory responses referred to general chapter information. All chapter conversations contained at least one conversational turn referring to a specific event. The first mention of a specific event occurred on average in the 15th conversational turn ($M = 14.95$, $SD = 13.26$; range 2–48). The mention of a specific event was first made by the mother in 57% (13/23) of transcriptions, and by the child in the remaining 43%.

Mothers provided estimates of the timing of chapters in the child's life, and identified whether or not chapters were ongoing. Based on this information, children were between 1 month and 78 months at the start of the chapters, $M = 53.37$, $SD = 15.97$ months. The majority (54%) of chapters began when children were between 48 and 60 months of age, i.e., when children were 4–5 years old, within 1–2 years of the time of the parent–child conversations. The duration of chapters was between 3 weeks and 6 years, with a mean of 12.61 months ($SD = 14.16$); the duration of the majority of the chapters (54%) was between 9 and 24 months. Mothers reported that 65% of chapters were ongoing, while 35% were completed. Ongoing chapters were on average longer in duration ($M = 15.54$ months) than completed chapters ($M = 7.13$ months), $t(44) = 1.98$, $p = .05$. There was no difference in children's ages at the start of ongoing and completed chapters, $t(44) = .73$, $p = .47$.

Mother–child conversational variables

In the following analyses of mother–child conversational variables, we collapsed across the two chapters that each dyad discussed. Mothers' speech ranged substantially in overall elaborativeness, and its subcomponents. Children also varied substantially in the degree to which they provided memory responses. (See Table 2 for means, standard deviations and ranges of mother and child variables.) Memory responses constituted 63% of children's conversational turns.

Subcomponents of mothers' elaborativeness were intercorrelated (in particular, mothers' memory/elaborative questions and yes/no questions), consistent with the concept of an "elaborative style" that researchers have documented in conversations about specific one-point-in-time past events. With the exception of context statements, each component of mothers' elaborativeness, as well as the composite elaborativeness variable, was also significantly positively correlated with children's memory responses (Table 3). This pattern of associations was similar when partial correlations were conducted controlling for the percentage of mothers' conversational turns that referred to a specific event memory, as opposed to general chapter information, suggesting that relationships between maternal conversational style and children's chapter memory performance were not dependent on the degree to which mothers questioned their children about particular episodes.

We then examined whether this pattern of results would hold when controlling for number of words in the conversation. The number of words in the entire parent–child conversation, including the speech of both mother and child, was calculated using Microsoft Word. In Study 1, number of words was highly correlated with number of mothers' conversational turns ($r = .51$, $p = .01$), and with mothers' elaborativeness ($r = .87$, $p < .001$). Regarding sub-components of elaborativeness, number of words was not significantly correlated with memory/elaborative questions ($r = .09$, $p = .66$) or yes/no questions ($r = .34$, $p = .08$), but was significantly correlated with context statements ($r = .84$, $p < .001$) and evaluations ($r = .46$, $p = .03$).

We conducted a series of analyses examining relationships between mothers' conversational variables and children's memory responses controlling for the total number of words in the conversation. With number of words partialled out, correlations between mothers' elaborativeness and children's memory responses ($r = .24$, $p = .29$), yes/no questions and memory responses ($r = .32$, $p = .45$) and context statements and memory responses ($r = -.37$, $p = .09$) were not significant. In contrast, the correlation between mothers' memory/elaborative questions and children's memory responses remained significant ($r = .64$, $p < .001$), as did the correlation between mothers' evaluations and children's memory responses ($r = .64$, $p < .001$).

Discussion

The results of this exploratory study provided several important insights. First, mothers were able to engage their young children in discussions of life story chapters, and children participated by providing additional memory information. The selected chapters were about extended periods in the child's life defined by a number

Table 2. Means, standard deviations and ranges of mothers' and children's main conversational variables, collapsed across the two chapter conversations (Study 1), $N = 23$.

Variable	Mean	SD	Range
Mothers' variables			
Memory/elaborative questions	23.30	12.79	0–51
Yes/no questions	44.26	21.11	14–103
Context statements	61.13	50.97	15–260
Evaluations	9.70	5.60	3–24
Elaborativeness[a]	138.39	62.19	60–303
Children's variable			
Memory responses	51.26	21.07	23–112

[a]Elaborativeness is a composite variable equal to the sum of memory/elaborative questions, yes/no questions, context statements and evaluations.

Table 3. Correlations between mothers' conversational variables and children's memory responses, collapsed across the two chapter conversations (Study 1), $N = 23$.

		1	2	3	4	5
1	Memory/elaborative questions					
2	Yes/no questions	.67**				
3	Context statements	−.21	.10			
4	Evaluations	.22	.23	.44*		
5	Elaborativeness	.28	.58**	.85**	.57**	
6	Memory responses	.63**	.41*	.10	.70**	.42*

*$p < .05$, **$p < .01$.

of different themes, with the preschool or kindergarten school year being particularly prominent. They included components such as discussion of people, locations, and activities that are similar to how the contents of life story chapters are described in the literature on adults.

In line with instructions to mothers to discuss children's life story chapters, the majority of the conversational turns within the mother–child conversations focused on general information, including repeated events. This general discussion of chapter content was punctuated by references to one-point-in-time events, which constituted a quarter of the conversational turns for mothers and less than a third of children's memory responses.

Analyses of mothers' elaborativeness and children's memory responses showed a pattern of results reminiscent of well-documented findings regarding parent–child conversations about specific memories. Mothers who engaged in more elaborative memory talk, including asking more memory/elaborative and yes/no questions, had children who provided more responses that contributed new chapter information. These results persisted in analyses controlling for the percentage of mothers' conversational turns that were focused on specific events within the chapters, suggesting that correlations between maternal conversational style and children's memory production were not a function of mothers shifting the focus to specific episodes rather than temporally extended chapters.

Study 2 explored whether these findings would replicate in a new sample of mothers and children, and included a comparison of conversations about life story chapters and specific past episodes.

Study 2

Study 2 investigated mother–child conversations about both a particular life chapter—the kindergarten year—and also a specific, one-point-in-time past event of the mother's choosing that occurred during the same general time period as the kindergarten chapter. Our first purpose was to examine the same variables in the chapter conversation as in Study 1 with a fresh sample of mothers and children and with an added degree of control. Since all mothers in Study 2 talked with their child about the same chapter of the child's life and the elapsed time since the chapter occurred was roughly equivalent for all children, the potential impact of content differences was minimised. Further, because we selected children for the sample who were in the spring semester of first grade, we were assured that all children had completed the life story chapter their mothers discussed with them.

A second purpose of Study 2 was to compare the variables in the chapter conversation with the same variables in the specific event conversation. We were interested in the similarities and differences between the two conversations, including the extent to which the conversations would refer differentially to specific versus general memory information, and whether the relationship between mothers' conversational variables and children's memory responses would be similar in the two conversational contexts. We also examined whether mothers' conversational variables and children's memory responses would be correlated across the two conversations. Theorists have noted that while stable individual differences in parental elaboration when reminiscing about specific past events have been documented, these differences do not necessarily extend to conversations during other parent–child interactions, for example, while parents are engaged in playing or caregiving (Fivush et al., 2006; Haden & Fivush, 1996). Therefore, we were interested in whether individual differences would be consistent across conversations about chapters and specific memories.

Participants

Twenty-eight parents (26 mothers, 2 fathers) participated with their 6- to 7-year-old first grade children (8 boys, 20 girls; age *range* 78–92 months; $M = 86$, $SD = 3.50$). First graders were chosen for participation because they had all experienced and completed the same life chapter (kindergarten) with a similar delay interval. Two additional mother–child dyads initially took part, but were eliminated before the data were coded due to the fact that the children were still in kindergarten. We included data from two fathers who returned recordings, despite the fact that we recruited only mothers (and for simplicity continue to refer to the participating parents as "mothers"). The majority of mothers and children (90% each) were white, with the remainder reported as Hispanic (7%) or "other ethnicity" (3%). Mothers were highly educated, with 90% having completed a college degree or higher.

Procedure

Participants were recruited via information distributed through local school systems or word of mouth and were paid for their participation. Mothers provided written consent at the outset of the study. Mothers who agreed to participate received a packet that included written step-by-step instructions on how to participate in the study, along with a digital recorder and instructions on how to use it.

All data collection took place in children's homes. Mothers were instructed to choose a moment that was convenient for them when they had a quiet time alone with their child to record two conversations. The packets for mothers contained three sealed envelopes, labelled "open first", "open second" and "open third." The envelope labelled "open first" contained instructions for the first conversation, which mothers were told to complete before opening the second envelope. The second envelope contained instructions for the second conversation, which mothers were told to complete before opening the third envelope. The two conversations mothers were asked to complete included the kindergarten chapter and a specific memory ("a particular event that was special or fun for your child"), following the protocol of previous research (e.g., Leichtman et al., 2017; Sahin-Acar & Leichtman, 2015; Wang, Leichtman, & Davies, 2000). Instructions to mothers for both conversations are presented in Appendix A.

The order of the conversations was counterbalanced across participants using random assignment so that half of participants received instructions to talk about the chapter first, and half received instructions to talk about the specific event first. The third envelope contained a brief demographic questionnaire.

Coding

Mother–child conversations were transcribed verbatim, and trained individuals coded all variables by hand from the transcriptions. Chapter conversations and specific event conversations were coded separately.

Chapter conversations

Coding of the chapter conversations was similar to coding in Study 1. All chapters focused on the kindergarten year of the child's life, as per instructions, so it was not necessary to further code the topic of the chapter. Each chapter was coded for descriptions of people, locations, activities and emotions, as in Study 1.

As in Study 1, off-topic speech (representing 2% of conversational turns in the original transcriptions) was eliminated from the transcriptions, so that all analysed speech pertained to the kindergarten chapter. The conversations contained no talk about the future that required removal. Mothers' and children's conversational turns were coded separately as referring to either "general" or "specific" memory, using the same criteria as in Study 1.

Mothers' and children's speech was also coded separately using the same coding scheme as in Study 1 for the variables shown in Table 1 (e.g., mothers' elaborativeness and children's memory responses).

Specific event conversations

As in the protocol for coding the chapter conversations, before the specific event conversations were coded, off-topic talk (<4% of conversational turns) and future event talk (<2% of conversational turns) was eliminated. Coding of specific event conversations focused on similar variables as coding of the chapter conversations. Conversational turns were coded as either specific or general, and mothers' and children's conversational variables (e.g., elaborativeness, memory responses) shown in Table 1 were coded.

Interrater reliability

One coder first coded all of the variables for the entire dataset. To assess reliability, an additional hypothesis-blind coder coded 9 randomly-selected transcriptions (32%) each of the chapter and specific event conversations. Interrater reliability for specific vs. general memory was as follows: in the chapter conversation, kappa = .89, with 94% agreement on specific and 96% agreement on general; in the specific event conversation kappa = .87, with 99% agreement on specific and 96% agreement on general. Interrater reliability for the *elaborativeness* variable was again calculated by computing kappa across memory/elaborative questions, yes/no questions, context statements, evaluations and other. In the chapter conversation, reliability was kappa = .90; with 95% agreement for memory/elaborative questions, 97% for yes/no questions, 94% for context statements, and 92% for evaluations. In the specific event conversation, interrater agreement was kappa = .88; with 94% agreement for memory/elaborative questions, 95% for yes/no questions, 91% for context statements, and 94% for evaluations. Interrater reliability on the variable indexing children's memory responses in the chapter conversation was kappa = .91, with 97% agreement for memory responses and 94% agreement for non-memory responses; in the specific event conversation it was kappa = .89, with 98% agreement for memory responses and 96% agreement for non-memory responses.

Results

We first present results pertinent to the chapter conversations, followed by results pertinent to the specific event conversations, and finally comparisons of and correlations between variables in the two conversations. All reported statistics are based on analyses of transcriptions with off-topic and future talk removed. For examples of the chapter and specific event conversations, see Appendix B.

Chapter conversations

Chapter conversations ranged from 2 to 80 ($M = 30.11$, $SD = 18.69$) conversational turns for mothers and 5–86 ($M = 30.00$, $SD = 20.03$) conversational turns for children. All chapters focused on the child's kindergarten year, as per instructions. The majority of conversations contained references to people other than the child (83%), specific locations (83%), and activities (96%), and some also contained references to emotions (28%). In line with instructions to mothers to discuss chapters, on average 9.5 ($SD = 11.18$) or 31% of mothers' conversational turns and 7.11 ($SD = 8.34$) or 36% of children's memory responses referred to one-point-in-time events within chapters, while the majority (69% for mothers and 64% for children) referred to general chapter information. Although chapter conversations usually included some discussion of specific past events, several participants (4/28 or 14%) never referred to a specific event in their chapter conversation. Among those participants who did refer to a specific event during at least one conversational turn in the chapter conversation, the first mention of a specific event was on average at the 9th conversational turn ($M = 8.54$, $SD = 5.01$, range 1–18). In 62% of these transcriptions, it was the child who first mentioned the specific event, whereas in the remaining 38% it was the mother.

Turning to mother–child conversational variables, as in Study 1, mothers' speech in the chapter conversation ranged substantially in elaborativeness and its subcomponents. Children also varied substantially in the number of memory responses they gave. (See Table 4 for means, standard deviations and ranges of mother and child variables.)

The subcomponents of mothers' elaborativeness were all highly correlated with each other, suggesting an "elaborative style" in these chapter conversations. Each component of mothers' elaborativeness, as well as the composite elaborativeness variable, was also significantly positively correlated with children's memory responses (Table 5). These correlations remained highly significant in analyses partialling out the percentage of mothers' conversational turns that referred to specific events (all p's < .01).

We then examined whether this pattern of results would hold when controlling for number of words in the conversation. The number of words in the entire parent–child conversation about the kindergarten life chapter, including the speech of both mother and child, was calculated using Microsoft Word. Number of words was highly correlated with mothers' conversational turns ($r = .86$, $p < .001$), and also with mothers' elaborativeness ($r = .89$,

$p < .001$). Number of words was highly correlated with all subcomponents of elaborativeness, including: memory/elaborative questions ($r = .50$, $p = .007$), yes/no questions ($r = .75$, $p < .001$), context statements ($r = .89$, $p < .001$), and evaluations ($r = .77$, $p < .001$).

We ran a series of analyses examining correlations (in the kindergarten chapter conversation) between mothers' conversational variables and children's memory responses controlling for the total number of words in the conversation. Correlations between almost all mothers' conversational variables and children's memory responses remained significant, including: mothers' elaborativeness ($r = .56$, $p = .003$), memory/elaborative questions ($r = .60$, $p = .001$), yes/no questions ($r = .59$, $p = .001$) and evaluations ($r = .47$, $p = .01$). The only exception was context statements ($r = .05$, $p = .80$).

Specific event conversations

Specific event conversations ranged from 5 to 50 ($M = 19.89$, $SD = 12.02$) conversational turns for mothers and 4–52 ($M = 19.93$, $SD = 12.25$) conversational turns for children. Consistent with instructions given to participants, all conversations focused on a clearly identifiable specific past event (e.g., going to a birthday party, visiting the zoo), with the exception of one. Because this conversation did not meet the criteria for a specific event conversation, it was not coded, although the chapter conversation from the same dyad was included in the dataset. Thus, in all analyses that focus on the specific event conversation, the sample size was $N = 27$. In line with instructions to discuss specific events, on average 18.07 ($SD = 12.61$) or 91% of mothers' conversational turns and 11.67 ($SD = 8.24$) or 91% of children's memory responses referred to one-point-in-time events, while the remainder referred to general themes.

In terms of mother–child conversational variables, mothers' speech ranged substantially in overall elaborativeness and its subcomponents, in line with previous literature on mother–child discussions of past events (e.g., Leichtman et al., 2000). Children also varied substantially in the degree to which they provided memory responses. (See Table 4 for means, standard deviations and ranges of mother and child variables.)

The subcomponents of mothers' elaborativeness were almost all significantly correlated with each other, also consistent with previous findings. Each component of mothers' elaborativeness, as well as the composite elaborativeness variable, were again significantly positively correlated with children's memory responses, similar to the pattern in the chapter conversation (Table 5).

We then examined whether this pattern of results would hold when controlling for number of words in the conversation. The number of words in the entire parent–child conversation about the specific event, including the speech of both mother and child, was calculated using Microsoft Word. The number of words was highly correlated with mothers' conversational turns ($r = .74$, $p < .001$),

Table 4. Means, standard deviations and ranges of mothers' and children's main conversational variables in the life story chapter and specific event conversations (Study 2), $N = 28$.

Variable	Mean	SD	Range
Chapter conversation mothers' variables			
Memory/elaborative questions	10.00	6.03	2–28
Yes/no questions	19.71	10.68	3–43
Context statements	20.57	20.24	2–94
Evaluations	7.04	6.86	0–31
Elaborativeness[a]	57.32	38.69	9–182
Children's variable			
Memory responses	19.54	15.16	4–65
Specific event conversation mothers' variables			
Memory/elaborative questions	7.41	5.66	1–25
Yes/no questions	13.74	8.42	2–37
Context statements	13.56	9.50	1–45
Evaluations	4.37	4.25	0–18
Elaborativeness[a]	39.07	22.02	8–101
Children's variable			
Memory responses	12.89	8.80	3–41

[a]Elaborativeness is a composite variable equal to the sum of memory/elaborative questions, yes/no questions, context statements and evaluations.

Table 5. Correlations between mothers' conversational variables and children's memory responses in chapter and specific event conversations (labelled SpEv), N = 28.

		1	2	3	4	5	6	7	8	9	10	11
1	Memory/elaborative questions											
2	Yes/no questions	.69**										
3	Context statements	.40*	.77**									
4	Evaluations	.50**	.67**	.82**								
5	Elaborativeness	.65**	.91**	.95**	.87**							
6	Memory responses	.67**	.85**	.82**	.82**	.91**						
7	Memory/elaborative questions SpEv	.77**	.51**	.34	.40*	.51**	.57**					
8	Yes/no questions SpEv	.80**	.69**	.36	.41*	.58**	.64**	.73**				
9	Context statements SpEv	.32	.60**	.85**	.71**	.78**	.64**	.42*	.39*			
10	Evaluations SpEv	.35	.49**	.61**	.67**	.63**	.67**	.33	.38*	.65**		
11	Elaborativeness SpEv	.71**	.75**	.71**	.69**	.81**	.80**	.78**	.81**	.82**	.71**	
12	Memory responses SpEv	.60**	.72**	.66**	.65**	.75**	.80**	.70**	.76**	.70**	.68**	.91**

*$p < .05$, **$p < .01$.

and also with mothers' elaborativeness ($r = .85$, $p < .001$). Number of words was highly correlated with all subcomponents of elaborativeness, including: memory/elaborative questions ($r = .62$, $p = .001$), yes/no questions ($r = .56$, $p = .003$), context statements ($r = .76$, $p < .001$), and evaluations ($r = .74$, $p < .001$).

We conducted a series of analyses examining correlations between mothers' conversational variables and children's specific event memory responses controlling for the total number of words in the conversation. The relationship between mothers' elaborativeness and children's memory responses remained significant ($r = .66$, $p < .001$), as did the relationship between mothers' yes/no questions and children's memory responses ($r = .64$, $p < .001$). Relationships between mothers' memory/elaborative questions and children's memory responses ($r = .40$, $p = .055$), mothers' context statements and children's memory responses ($r = .16$, $p = .44$), and mothers' evaluations and children's memory responses ($r = .12$, $p = .57$) were no longer significant at the $p < .05$ level.

Comparison and relationship between conversations

To directly compare the chapter and specific event conversations, paired samples t-tests were run contrasting the same variables in each, including mothers' elaborativeness and its subcomponents and children's memory responses. Measured in conversational turns for mother and child combined, chapter conversations ($M = 61.22$, $SD = 38.68$) contained approximately one-third more turns than specific event conversations ($M = 39.81$, $SD = 24.15$), $t(26) = 4.28$, $p < .001$. Consistent with this difference, all elements of the conversations were significantly greater in the chapter conversation; see means in Table 4 (all p's < .01). However, these differences all became non-significant when the same analyses were conducted using the ratio of each variable over conversational turns, all p's > .10. For example, when elaborativeness/mother's total conversational turns in the chapter conversation was contrasted with elaborativeness/mother's total conversational turns in the specific event conversation, $t(26) = -.43$, $p = .67$, and when memory responses/children's total conversational turns in the chapter conversation were contrasted with memory responses/children's total conversational turns in the specific event conversation, $t(26) = -1.22$, $p = .23$, differences between the conversations were no longer apparent.

Correlations between identical variables in the chapter and specific event conversations were assessed and are displayed in Table 5. Mothers' memory/elaborative questions, yes/no questions, evaluations, context statements and overall elaborativeness were all highly correlated across the two conversations (all p's < .01). Children's memory responses in the chapter and specific event conversations were also correlated ($r = .80$, $p < .001$), indicating high levels of consistency in the style of both conversational partners in the two conversational contexts.

Discussion

Results of Study 2 confirmed the pattern of findings established in Study 1, and provided further insight into the comparison between mother–child reminiscing conversations about chapters and specific events. Here, mothers and children again engaged in detailed chapter conversations, this time focusing on the child's kindergarten year, which on average contained more conversational turns than specific event conversations. Similar to chapter conversations in Study 1, dyads typically discussed the people, locations and activities that were part of the chapter, and the majority of conversational turns focused on general chapter information. In contrast, the majority of conversational turns in the specific event conversations focused on specific one-point-in-time memories, confirming that the focus of the two conversations was different.

Comparisons between the conversations indicated that once the number of conversational turns was taken into account, the mean levels of identical variables in the two conversations were similar. The components of mother's elaborativeness were closely associated with children's memory responses in both the chapter and specific event conversations. Further, mothers' elaborativeness was positively correlated in the chapter and specific event conversations, and children's memory responses also were positively correlated across the conversations.

General discussion

Previous research has convincingly shown that parents differ in the degree to which they use an elaborative questioning strategy when talking with their preschool and kindergarten children about events that occurred in the child's personal past, and that parents' conversational style is a consistent predictor of children's memory performance (Fivush et al., 2006; Fivush & Nelson, 2004; Wang, 2013). This work has focused almost exclusively on parent–child talk about circumscribed, one-moment-in-time events, but recent research on temporally extended past experiences reported by older children and adults indicates that life story chapters are also a familiar and integral component of autobiographical memory (Thomsen, 2015; Thomsen et al., 2016). Yet research on the development of autobiographical memory in early childhood has not targeted parent–child conversations about chapters in the child's life. Accordingly, the present two studies were designed as a first effort to describe the quality of parent–child talk about chapters, to examine correlations between parents' conversational styles and children's chapter memory performance, and to compare findings for chapters to findings when the conversational topic is memories of specific events.

When asked to discuss life story chapters in any way that seemed natural to them, mother–child pairs in Study 1 engaged in lengthy and detailed conversations where the focus was primarily on general chapter information rather than on specific events that had occurred within the chapter, and children readily provided new information about chapter content. Consistent with literature on adults' chapters (Thomsen, 2015; Thomsen et al., 2016), children's chapters frequently included information about locations, people, activities, and emotions. Components of parents' conversational styles identified in studies of specific memories (e.g., memory/elaborative questions, yes/no questions) could be reliably coded in chapter conversations. Consistent with our expectations, parental elaborativeness was strongly and positively associated with children's independent contributions to chapter memory discussions. This finding is consistent with the idea that children learn to think about the past as extended time periods through conversations with parents. Such conversations may also play a role in structuring children's memory, such that temporally extended chapters come to provide an organisational structure for specific recollections (Conway & Pleydell-Pearce, 2000; Thomsen, 2015).

Study 2 included direct within-participant comparisons between conversations about a particular life story chapter (the kindergarten year) and a specific event (an event identified by the parent as special or fun for the child) that took place during that same period of the child's life. As in Study 1, parents and children engaged in extended conversations about the kindergarten life chapters. Indeed, conversations about life chapters contained more conversational turns than conversations about specific events, perhaps because life chapters by definition span a longer time period and have the potential to refer to multiple specific events and extensive general information. Correlations between parental elaborativeness and children's memory production were positive and highly significant for both the chapter and specific event conversations. In addition, parents who were highly elaborative when talking with their children about chapters also tended to be highly elaborative when talking with their children about specific events, and children's memory production was strongly and positively correlated across the chapter and specific event conversations.

In both Study 1 and Study 2, indices of parental elaboration were strongly correlated with the number of words spoken in parent–child chapter and memory conversations. This raises the question of whether associations between parental elaboration and children's memory responses are attributable primarily to the fact that high elaborative parent–child pairs simply talk more expansively than low elaborative parent–child pairs. The high correlations between parental elaboration and number of words is entirely consistent with the defining qualities of high elaborative parents, who "talk a great deal about past events, asking many questions and providing a great deal of embellished detail"; in contrast, low elaborative parents engage in less expansive memory talk, "discussing the past in less detail and asking fewer and more redundant questions" (Fivush & Nelson, 2004, pp. 574–575). Because expansiveness is a defining feature of an elaborative parental conversational style, it is problematic conceptually to separate quality from quantity of talk in analyses of parent–child conversations about the past. Nevertheless, positive correlations between indices of parental elaboration and children's memory responses remained significant when controlling for the total number of words spoken, suggesting that amount of memory talk does not fully explain the observed correlations; particular qualities of an elaborative style, such as asking memory/elaborative questions and providing evaluations, also appear to be associated with children's more detailed and extensive memory responses.

The strikingly similar patterns of results for parent–child talk about life story chapters and talk about specific events have potentially important consequences for both memory theory and new research. Because prior research has focused on conversations about memories of pinpointed episodes in the child's personal life, parental elaborativeness has been portrayed as a way to promote in the child a conception of the self as "having a unique perspective, thus creating a truly personal past" (Fivush & Nelson, 2004, p. 576). In contrast, general memories, which do not target particular moments, "often imply social conventions and an individual's relation to significant others and the community, thus contributing to a sense of relatedness and belonging" (Wang, 2013, p. 77). By this reasoning, in the current studies a general memory of kindergarten, such as the daily activity of playing outside on school grounds, would not be expected to promote the same sense of uniqueness as would a specific memory of a particular occurrence, such as the child winning a race or finally mastering the fear of going down the big slide.

Despite these apparent differences in underlying goals or functions of reminiscing about specific versus general experiences, Study 2 showed that relationships between parental elaborativeness and children's memory performance when talking about specific events were strikingly similar to relationships when talking about chapters: indeed, the correlation between the composite parental elaboration index for chapters and specific memories was a robust .81, and the correlation between children's memory responses, in which the child added new information to the conversation, across the chapter and specific event conversations was .80. These findings would seem to call into question the idea that the primary and distinctive function of elaborative parent–child memory talk is to promote specific autobiographical memories and a unique sense of self, since they demonstrate that this kind of talk also occurs in the context of more general reflections on a life chapter. However, another possibility is that reminiscing about specific events is not the only form of parent–child memory talk that serves the function of highlighting for children what is unique and special about themselves and their own histories. Chapters are a form of general memory that may also be important to forming a distinct and eventually mature sense of individual identity.

Cross-cultural studies have identified an association between elaborative parent–child conversations about specific past events and the degree to which a culture embraces individualistic versus collectivist values (Leichtman, Wang, & Pillemer, 2003; Pillemer, 1998; Sahin-Acar & Leichtman, 2015; Wang, 2001, 2013). Parents in individualistic cultures tend to engage in more elaborative questioning of their children during reminiscing, and the children's personal memories are more detailed and self-focused, promoting the goal of independence. In contrast, parents' memory questioning in more collectivist cultures focuses less on specific details of the child's particular circumstances, instead emphasising group processes, promoting the goal of interdependence. Our findings call into question the idea that cultural differences in parent–child memory talk are evident primarily because the focus is on unique personal episodes. They suggest that reminiscing about particular events may be only one component of a broader interactive style that encompasses memory talk about the self—whether the topic is a one-time occurrence or a broader description of the temporally extended events that comprise life story chapters. Although research has shown that individual differences in parents' elaboration do not extend across all conversational contexts (e.g., Fivush et al., 2006; Haden & Fivush, 1996), they may extend across more varied forms of reminiscing than researchers have typically considered. New cross-cultural studies could compare relationships between parental memory styles and children's memory performance when the discussions focus on life story chapters versus specific events. If cultural differences are still evident when the focus is on general rather than specific information, this would question the privileged status of specific memories in theories of autobiographical memory in general and cross-cultural differences in particular.

Another research strategy would involve comparing parent–child talk about specific events and temporally extended experiences that occurred in academic settings. Prior research has shown that when parents engage their preschool children in after school conversations about particular school activities that the child experienced firsthand, such as a surprise visit of a teacher and her newborn baby (Leichtman et al., 2000) or a special science demonstration about properties of light (Leichtman et al., 2017), high maternal elaborativeness is positively associated children's memory for the event. Children could also be queried about temporally extended activities or "chapters" in the school year, such as a month-long ecology project in which seeds are planted and flowers are tended. Our findings suggest that an elaborative maternal conversational style will be positively associated with the richness of children's memory reports even when the focus is on temporally-extended learning activities in a group setting.

One potential limitation of the present studies is the use of homogeneous samples: most of the participating parents were white and college educated. In light of prior research showing cultural differences in maternal elaborativeness and in the detail and quality of self-representations in children's memories (Wang, 2013), further work with diverse populations is desirable. Although prior research has failed to find a relationship between maternal education and maternal elaborativeness (Fivush et al., 2006; Leichtman et al., 2017), the scope of future studies should also be broadened to include more socioeconomically diverse samples.

In conclusion, theories of autobiographical memory assign a key role to temporally extended lifetime periods or chapters (Barsalou, 1988; Brown et al., 2012; Conway & Pleydell-Pearce, 2000; Thomsen et al., 2016), yet prior developmental research and theory has focused almost exclusively on memories of specific past episodes. The present studies were designed as a starting point for new work on the origins and early development of life story chapter memories, especially as they are facilitated by conversations with parents. In light of recent research with adults showing that the emotional tone of life story chapters is more predictive of personality and self esteem than the emotional tone of specific memories (Steiner et al.,

2017; Thomsen & Pillemer, 2017), deepening our understanding of how chapters develop could provide new insights into how they contribute to both a coherent and continuous sense of self and psychological well being.

Disclosure statement

No potential conflict of interest was reported by the authors.

Funding

This work was supported by Velux Fonden [grant number 33266].

References

Barsalou, L. W. (1988). The content and organization of autobiographical memories. In U. Neisser, & E. Winograd (Eds.), *Remembering reconsidered: Ecological and traditional approaches to the study of memory* (pp. 193–243). New York: Cambridge University Press.

Bauer, P. J. (2007). *Remembering the times of our lives: Memory in infancy and beyond*. Mahwah, NJ: LEA.

Bauer, P. J., & Larkina, M. (2016). Predicting remembering and forgetting of autobiographical memories in children and adults: A 4-year prospective study. *Memory, 24*, 1345–1368.

Bohn, A., & Berntsen, D. (2008). Life story development in childhood: The development of life story abilities and the acquisition of cultural life scripts from late middle childhood to adolescence. *Developmental Psychology, 44*(4), 1135–1147.

Brown, N. R., Hansen, T. G. B., Lee, P. J., Vanderveen, S. A., & Conrad, F. G. (2012). Historically defined autobiographical periods: Their origins and implications. In D. Berntsen, & D. C. Rubin (Eds.), *Understanding autobiographical memory. Theories and approaches* (pp. 160–180). New York: Cambridge University Press.

Chen, Y., McAnally, H. M., & Reese, E. (2013). Development in the organization of episodic memories in middle childhood and adolescence. *Frontiers in Behavioral Neuroscience, 7*, 1–9.

Conway, M. A., & Pleydell-Pearce, C. W. (2000). The construction of autobiographical memories in the self-memory system. *Psychological Review, 107*(2), 261–288.

Farrant, K., & Reese, E. (2000). Maternal style and children's participation in reminiscing: Stepping stones in children's autobiographical memory development. *Journal of Cognition and Development, 1*, 193–225.

Fivush, R., & Fromhoff, F. A. (1988). Style and structure in mother–child conversations about the past. *Discourse Processes, 11*, 337–355.

Fivush, R., Haden, C. A., & Reese, E. (2006). Elaborating on elaborations: Role of maternal reminiscing style in cognitive and socioemotional development. *Child Development, 77*(6), 1568–1588.

Fivush, R., & Nelson, K. (2004). Culture and language in the emergence of autobiographical memory. *Psychological Science, 15*(9), 573–577.

Freud, S. (1953). Three essays on the theory of sexuality. In J. Strachey (Ed.), *The standard edition of the complete psychological works of Sigmund Freud* (Vol. 7, pp. 135–243). London: Hogarth Press. [Original work published 1905].

Habermas, T., & Bluck, S. (2000). Getting a life: The emergence of the life story in adolescence. *Psychological Bulletin, 126*(5), 748–769.

Habermas, T., & de Silveira, C. (2008). The development of global coherence in life narratives across adolescence: Temporal, causal, and thematic aspects. *Developmental Psychology, 44*, 707–721.

Habermas, T., Ehlert-Lerche, S., & de Silveira, C. (2009). The development of the temporal macrostructure of life narratives across adolescence: Beginnings, linear narrative form, and endings. *Journal of Personality, 77*(2), 527–560.

Habermas, T., & Paha, C. (2001). The development of coherence in adolescents' life narratives. *Narrative Inquiry, 11*, 35–54.

Haden, C. A., & Fivush, R. (1996). Contextual variation in maternal conversational styles. *Merrill-Palmer Quarterly, 42*, 200–227.

Jack, F., MacDonald, S., Reese, E., & Hayne, H. (2009). Maternal reminiscing style during early childhood predicts the age of adolescents' earliest memories. *Child Development, 80*(2), 496–505.

Leichtman, M., Camilleri, K. A., Pillemer, B. D., Amato-Wierda, C., Hogan, J. E., & Dongo, M. D. (2017). Talking after school: Parents' conversational styles and children's memory for a science lesson. *Journal of Experimental Child Psychology, 156*, 1–15.

Leichtman, M. D., Pillemer, D. B., Wang, Q., Koreishi, A., & Han, J. J. (2000). When baby Maisy came to school: Mothers' interview styles and preschoolers' event memories. *Cognitive Development, 15*(1), 99–114.

Leichtman, M. D., Wang, Q., & Pillemer, D. B. (2003). Cultural variations in interdependence and autobiographical memory: Lessons from Korea, China, and the United States. In R. Fivush, & C. Haden (Eds.), *Autobiographical memory and the construction of a narrative self: Developmental and cultural perspectives* (pp. 73–97). Mahwah, NJ: Erlbaum.

Neisser, U. (1982). *Memory observed: Remembering in natural contexts*. San Francisco: W.H. Freeman.

Nelson, K., & Fivush, R. (2004). The emergence of autobiographical memory: A social cultural developmental theory. *Psychological Review, 111*(2), 486–511.

Newcombe, R., & Reese, E. (2004). Evaluations and orientations in mother–child narratives as a function of attachment security: A longitudinal inves-tigation. *International Journal of Behavioral Development, 28*, 230–245.

Pillemer, D. B. (1998). *Momentous events, vivid memories*. Cambridge, MA: Harvard University Press.

Pillemer, D. B., Goldsmith, L. R., Panter, A. T., & White, S. H. (1988). Very long-term memories of the first year in college. *Journal of Experimental Psychology: Learning, Memory and Cognition, 14*(4), 709–715.

Pillemer, D. B., Krensky, L., Kleinman, S. N., Goldsmith, L. R., & White, S. H. (1991). Chapters in narratives: Evidence from oral histories of the first year in college. *Journal of Narrative and Life History, 1*, 3–14.

Pillemer, D. B., Picariello, M. L., & Pruitt, J. C. (1994). Very long-term memories of a salient preschool event. *Applied Cognitive Psychology, 8*(2), 95–106.

Pillemer, D. B., & White, S. H. (1989). Childhood events recalled by children and adults. In H. W. Reese (Ed.), *Advances in child development and behavior* (Vol. 21, pp. 297–340). New York: Academic Press.

Reese, E., & Fivush, R. (1993). Parental styles of talking about the past. *Developmental Psychology, 29*(3), 596–606.

Reese, E., Haden, C. A., & Fivush, R. (1993). Mother-child conversations about the past: Relationships of style and memory over time. *Cognitive Development, 8*, 403–430.

Reese, E., Levya, D., Sparks, A., & Grolnick, W. (2010). Maternal elaborative reminiscing increases low-income children's narrative skills relative to dialogic reading. *Early Education and Development, 21* (3), 318–342.

Sahin-Acar, B., & Leichtman, M. D. (2015). Mother–child memory conversations and self-construal in Eastern Turkey, Western Turkey and the USA. *Memory, 23*(1), 69–82.

Steiner, K. L., & Pillemer, D. B. (2018). Development of the life story in early adolescence. *Journal of Early Adolescence, 38*, 125–138.

Steiner, K. L., Pillemer, D. B., & Thomsen, D. K. (2017). Life story chapters, specific memories, and conceptions of the self. *Applied Cognitive Psychology, 31*, 478–487.

Steiner, K. L., Pillemer, D. B., Thomsen, D. K., & Minigan, A. P. (2014). The reminiscence bump in older adults' life story transitions. *Memory, 22*, 1002–1009.

Thomsen, D. K. (2009). There is more to life stories than memories. *Memory, 17*, 445–457.

Thomsen, D. K. (2015). Autobiographical periods: A review and central components of a theory. *Review of General Psychology, 19*, 294–310.

Thomsen, D. K., & Berntsen, D. (2008). The cultural life script and life story chapters contribute to the reminiscence bump. *Memory, 16*, 420–435.

Thomsen, D. K., & Pillemer, D. B. (2017). I know my story and I know your story: Developing a conceptual framework for vicarious life stories. *Journal of Personality, 85*(4), 464–480.

Thomsen, D. K., Steiner, K. L., & Pillemer, D. B. (2016). Life story chapters: Past and future, you and me. *Journal of Applied Research in Memory and Cognition, 5*, 143–149.

Wang, Q. (2001). "Did you have fun?" American and Chinese mother–child conversations about shared emotional experiences. *Cognitive Development, 16*(2), 693–715.

Wang, Q. (2013). *The autobiographical self in time and culture.* New York: Oxford University Press.

Wang, Q., Leichtman, M. D., & Davies, K. I. (2000). Sharing memories and telling stories: American and Chinese mothers and their 3-year-olds. *Memory, 8*, 159–177.

White, S. H., & Pillemer, D. B. (1979). Childhood amnesia and the development of a socially accessible memory system. In J. F. Kihlstrom, & F. J. Evans (Eds.), *Functional disorders of memory* (pp. 29–73). Hillsdale, NJ: Erlbaum. Experimental psychology series.

Appendix A

Conversation Instructions for Parents

Instructions for the life story chapter conversation:

We would like you to have a conversation with your child about **a chapter in your child's life.** A chapter is an extended period of time in a person's life that lasts weeks, months or even years. The chapter we would like you to talk about today is: **the child's kindergarten year.** Take your time and discuss this chapter in any way you would naturally or normally talk with your child. There is no time limit and how you discuss the chapter is totally up to you.

Instructions for the specific event conversation:

We would like you to have a conversation with your child about a specific memory. A specific memory takes place on a particular occasion and lasts less than a day. Please select a specific event that your child experienced **during his or her kindergarten year.** The specific memory we would like you to talk about today is: **A particular event that was special or fun for your child.** Take your time and discuss this specific memory in any way you would naturally or normally talk with your child. There is no time limit and how you discuss the memory is totally up to you.

Appendix B

Sample Chapter and Specific Event Conversations

Chapter Conversation (Topic: The kindergarten year)

Mother: What were your favorite things about it?
Child: Well, about kindergarten, um, we, we did at, lots of activities together. Um, we, we had um, lots of animals that we have seen, like a butterfly, little chicks.
Mother: Yeah. I remember you talking about the little chicks.
Child: And we had play, like plants that we planted. And, and kindergarten was so cool.
Mother: It was so cool. Do you remember your friends in your class?
Child: Yeah. Sam, Katherine, um, Spencer, Lisa, Jack, um, I think that's all I can remember.
Mother: So I remember, I remember you talking a lot about "centers." What was centers?
Child: Well, we were building. There's a building blocks. We played games.
Mother: Did you do centers every day?
Child: Not always every day but some days.

Specific Event Conversation (Topic: A day at the beach)

Mother: What do you remember seeing?
Child: Um, we saw lots of seagulls and one almost stole my potato chips. And, well, he did steal my potato chip.
Mother: What did you do when we were on the beach? Did you guys boogie board or anything?
Child: We took our boogie boards and we rode on them. And then, and then when I didn't want to go on my boogie board anymore we dried off and then I played in the sand a little bit. And then my dad took me out in the water. And um, I didn't have my floaty on ... well, I think I did have my floaty on. And he took me way into um, he took me like where the deep water was. Uh, but I had my floaty on. And, and I couldn't touch the ground. But I was floating and it was really deep.
Mother: Wow. So do you remember anything else that you saw or ... ?
Child: Well, another thing was that we were at the beach and it was going to start to rain ... and then all of a sudden it brightened. The sun came out again.

Predictors of age-related and individual variability in autobiographical memory in childhood

Patricia J. Bauer and Marina Larkina

ABSTRACT
Development of autobiographical memory is as a gradual process beginning in early childhood and continuing through late adolescence. Substantial attention has been paid to early childhood when first personal memories are formed; less attention has been focused on the flourishing of memories from the late preschool years onward. We addressed this void with a three-year cohort-sequential study of age-related changes in the length, completeness, and coherence of autobiographical narratives by children 4–10 years. We also examined the unique and combined variance in autobiographical narrative explained by children's own language, maternal narrative style, domain-general cognitive abilities, non-autobiographical story recall, and memory-specific skills. There was substantial growth in autobiographical narrative skill across the 4–10-year period. Non-autobiographical story recall was a strong concurrent and cross-lagged predictor for all autobiographical narrative measures. Memory-specific and domain-general cognitive abilities systematically predicted narrative completeness and coherence but not length. Children's language and maternal narrative style did not contribute additional variance when these predictors were considered. The findings highlight that age-related changes in autobiographical memory are the results of combined contributions of a variety of domain-general and domain-specific predictors.

The fates of memories of events from childhood have been a focus of research attention since the 1890s (Miles, 1895) when it was found that among Western adults, the average age of earliest memory was age 3.5 years. The "remarkable amnesia of childhood" was noted and named by Sigmund Freud in 1905 (Freud, 1905/1953). In the century-plus since these markers of the beginning of the study of earliest memories from childhood, there has been a great deal of attention paid to whether adults remember their childhoods (Bauer, Tasdemir-Ozdes, & Larkina, 2014; Jack & Hayne, 2010; Pillemer & White, 1989). Interest in whether children also experience so-called *childhood amnesia* – and the factors that determine increases in the density of autobiographical memories – is a more recent phenomenon, however (see Bauer, 2015, for a review). Perhaps because so much research attention has been directed at the phase of childhood from which few memories survive, less attention has been focused on the flourishing of memory from the late preschool years onward. In the present research, we addressed this void with a 3-year cohort-sequential study of age-related changes in autobiographical memory reports by children ages 4–10 years. We also measured potential correlates of developmental changes in the reports, including children's own language skills, maternal narrative style, domain-general cognitive abilities, children's memories for non-autobiographical stories, and memory-specific abilities.

As noted by the guest editors of this special issue (Wang & Gülgöz, this issue), numerous previous studies have investigated the neurological, cognitive, linguistic, social, and cultural mechanisms that contribute to developmental changes in autobiographical memory across childhood. The studies have tended to be of one of two sorts. First, there have been longitudinal studies of the individual and joint contributions of subsets of these factors to early developments in autobiographical memory skill. For example, Reese and colleagues (e.g., Harley & Reese, 1999; see Reese, 2014, for a summary), conducted a longitudinal examination of changes in memory for specific past events beginning at 19 months of age, and followed children through to 32 months of age. They identified changes in self-concept and language as important determinants of both age-related and individual variability in memory skill (see also Haden, Ornstein, Rudek, & Cameron, 2009; Wang, 2007, for similar approaches). When at 16 years of age, some of the same children were tested for their earliest memories, maternal narrative style (whether more or less elaborative; e.g., Reese, Haden, & Fivush, 1993) was found to be a unique predictor of the age of earliest memory.

The second type of study in the existing literature is cross-sectional examination of age-related differences in memory ability or narrative skill. Some studies also include measures of performance in one or another non-narrative domain, and examine relations with memory or narrative. For example, Bauer et al. (2012), reported age-related increases in the accuracy of location memory across 4-, 6-, and 8-year-old children. In terms of narrative skill, Reese et al. (2011) reported age-related increases in the coherence of narrative reports across childhood to adulthood (with coherence measured in terms of context, chronology, and theme). In this area of the literature, links to childhood amnesia tend to come in the form of cross-sectional investigations of potential correlates of age-related changes in either memory or narrative. Studies of this type have revealed the importance of a variety of memory-specific and domain-general correlates of memory, narrative, or both, including self-concept (Harley & Reese, 1999; Howe & Courage, 1993, 1997), understanding of time and place (Friedman, Reese, & Dai, 2011), subjective sense of self (Fivush, 2014), mental time travel (Suddendorf, Nielsen, & von Gehlen, 2011; Tulving, 2005; Wheeler, 2000), and autonoetic consciousness (Perner & Ruffman, 1995). Relations between memory and narrative and the measured correlate are taken as evidence that the later is a determinant of autobiographical memory, licensing speculation that it plays a role in the explanation of childhood amnesia.

The extant literatures provide rich pictures of the variety of correlates of the emergence of autobiographical memory in infancy and early childhood, and of relations between individual memory-specific or domain-general cognitive abilities and age-related differences in memory or narrative in the late preschool and early school years. Largely absent from the literature are longitudinal studies of multiple potential correlates of changes in autobiographical narrative across the period that marks the onset of childhood amnesia (Bauer & Larkina, 2014b) and the emergence of an adult-like distribution of autobiographical memories (Bauer & Larkina, 2014a). The present research was such an investigation.

The present research was a cohort-sequential examination of autobiographical narratives produced by children in each of three cohorts, namely, 4-year-olds, 6-year-olds, and 8-year-olds, over a 3-year period. At each time point, spaced one-year apart, children were asked to provide narratives of a number of events that had taken place within the past four months. We characterised the narratives in terms of their length, breadth or completeness, and their coherence (Reese et al., 2011). One major purpose of the research was to chart age-related changes in autobiographical narrative production over the period of the study, encompassing ages 4–10 years. At each time point, we also assessed a number of potential correlates of developmental changes in autobiographical narrative including domain-general abilities of speed of processing, working memory, and sustained attention; non-autobiographical story recall; deliberate and strategic remembering and metamemory; and source memory. In addition, we estimated children's own language abilities and obtained measures of maternal narrative style. We used these measures to accomplish the second major purpose of the study, which was to examine the unique and combined variance in autobiographical narrative explained by a range of potential correlates.

The motivation for focus on 4–10 years was as noted above: the period marks the onset of childhood amnesia (Bauer & Larkina, 2014b) and the emergence of an adult-like distribution of autobiographical memories (Bauer & Larkina, 2014a). We estimated children's language skills under the assumption that they would be related to narrative abilities. We obtained measures of maternal narrative style because it has been shown to be a predictor of children's contributions to co-constructed autobiographical narratives in early childhood (e.g., Larkina & Bauer, 2010; Reese et al., 1993) as well as older children's independently produced narratives (Reese, Jack, & White, 2010; although see Larkina & Bauer, 2012; Peterson, Sales, Reese, & Fivush, 2007, for exceptions).

We assessed children's non-autobiographical story recall following the logic that the ability to recall the basic elements of a story, either in verbatim or gist, is part-and-parcel of producing a "story" about a personal past event. To our knowledge, with the exception of Han, Leichtman, and Wang (1998), who used non-autobiographical story recall as a control variable, there has not been a study of relations between autobiographical and non-autobiographical story narrative production. We assessed deliberate and strategic remembering and metamemory following the logic that memory-specific skills and abilities come into play in the course of event reconstruction and recall (see Güler, Larkina, Kleinknecht, & Bauer, 2010; Larkina, Güler, Kleinknecht, & Bauer, 2008, for discussion). We assessed memory for the source of information for newly learned facts following the logic that the ability to remember the context of events and experiences is an essential element of episodic memory (e.g., Newcombe, Lloyd, & Balcomb, 2012). We expected that all three of these domains of ability (non-autobiographical story recall, deliberate and strategic remembering and metamemory, source) would predict variance in children's autobiographical narrative reports, especially at the earlier time points, which we expected to be characterised by substantial variability in episodic recall (see Ghetti & Lee, 2014, for a review of age-related changes in episodic memory), deliberate and strategic remembering and metamemory (see Roebers, 2014, for a review), and source memory (Riggins, 2014).

Finally, we assessed domain-general cognitive abilities with the expectation that they would contribute to encoding, consolidation, and subsequent retrieval of memories across the age range. Considering that these capacities undergird more domain-specific skills and abilities, we entertained competing hypothesis that they either would

Table 1. Sample characteristics (Panel a) and average delays between assessment points (Panel b).

Variable	Overall	4-year-olds	6-year-olds	8-year-olds
Panel a: sample characteristics				
Number of participants	101	37	34	30
Participant gender (F/M)	53/48	16/21	19/15	18/12
Age at initial assessment (in years, M, SD, range)	n/a	4.18 (0.06)	6.19 (0.05)	8.20 (0.04)
		4.07–4.40	6.10–6.28	8.12–8.28
Panel b: average delay between assessment points				
Initial assessment to 2nd-year assessment	364 (34)	369 (34)	360 (37)	364 (34)
	270–442	308–442	270–440	300–440
2nd-year assessment to 3rd-year assessment	329 (26)	326 (24)	330 (24)	331 (29)
	264–403	264–366	278–365	292–403

(a) account for the majority of variance at all time points, relative to non-autobiographical story recall and memory-specific skills; or (b) come into predictive play at the later time points, under the assumption that variability in specific domains would begin to resolve with increasing age, allowing individual differences in domain-general cognitive abilities to ascend in importance. The source of the data for the present research was the same cohort-sequential study as reported in Bauer and Larkina (2014b). The questions posed in the present research were unique and all analyses are unique to this report.

Method

Participants

Participants were 101 children (53 girls, 48 boys). At the beginning of the study, children were ages 4, 6, and 8 years (Table 1, Panel a). Families were drawn from a voluntary participant pool maintained by the Institute of Child Development, University of Minnesota, USA. The families were primarily Caucasian (94%); none was of Hispanic descent. Based on parental report, the families were of middle to upper-middle socio-economic status (at the beginning of the study, 84% of mothers and 85% of fathers had a technical degree or more). At the inception of the study, the sample was reflective of the community from which it was drawn.

There were four assessment points or phases, each approximately one year apart (Table 1, Panel b). Because not all potential predictors were measured at the final phase, the present analyses focus on the first three phases only. At each of the first three phases, children took part in two test sessions, spaced one week apart. The University of Minnesota institutional review board approved the protocol prior to the start of the study. At each phase, written parental consent was obtained for children; children 7 years and older provided written assent; children younger than 7 gave verbal assent. At the end of the second session of each phase, children received a toy, and parents were given a gift certificate to a local merchant.

An additional 30 families were enrolled but did not complete all phases and thus are not included in the analyses. Attrition was roughly evenly distributed across the age groups (23%, 23%, and 30% from the 4-, 6-, and 8-year-old groups, respectively). The demographic characteristics of families lost to attrition did not differ from those of families retained.

Materials and procedure

Testing took place in a university laboratory outfitted with table and chairs and a small couch. At each phase, children took part in two 1–1.5 hour sessions, approximately 1 week apart. Over the course of data collection, nine female experimenters administered the tasks. The two sessions within a phase were conducted by the same experimenter; children were tested by different experimenters at each phase. Task procedures were outlined in a written protocol, and the experimenters regularly reviewed and discussed videotaped sessions to ensure protocol fidelity.

Event narratives

Approximately four months prior to each phase of testing, children's parents were sent a blank calendar. They were instructed to note on the calendar at least one unique event per week in which their children participated. Parents were asked to select events of interest to their children (e.g., family outings, special school or afterschool events, celebrations) and to avoid routine events unless something unique happened (e.g., while making cookies, the cookies burned and set off the smoke alarm). The calendar entries were brief titles of events; narrative descriptions of the events were not elicited or provided. Families brought the completed calendars to the lab at their first of two visits at each phase.

At the first visit of each phase, we used the calendars to select events for the memory interviews. Specifically, calendars typically featured 16 events: one for each of 4 weeks for 4 months. The events were numbered sequentially and a random-number generator was used to select the subset of events that would be queried in the interviews. At each phase, the target number of events was 5: 3 events for experimenter–child interviews and 2 events for mother–child interviews (see below). The experimenter–child interviews were conducted across two sessions to avoid fatigue; mother–child interviews were conducted early in the first lab visit of each phase. Once the target events were selected, the experimenter engaged the child in a task during which time the child's parent recorded two to three unique details of each event (e.g., who else participated in the event). To generate the details, parents were prompted by the event title recorded on the calendar. The titles and details were used by the experimenter in the interview with the child.

For the mother–child interviews, mothers were provided the titles of the two events they were to discuss, along with the instruction to "Talk about the events normally, as you would in the car or at the dinner table, for as long as you like" (instructions as in, e.g., Larkina & Bauer, 2010; Reese et al., 1993). The experimenter–child interviews were initiated with general prompts in the form of titles for the events (taken from the calendars): "What can you tell me about X?" If this prompt failed to elicit a report, the experimenter provided additional cues, taken from the parents' descriptions of the events (e.g., "Your brother was there"). The experimenter encouraged children to continue their reports using generic prompts ("Tell me more," "Do you remember anything else?"). After the unstructured report had been exhausted, the experimenter asked a series of seven direct *wh-* memory probes about the event: who was there, what else did you do, where did you X, when did you X, why did you X, how did you X, and how did you feel about X?

Potential correlates

Table 2 provides a description of the tasks and procedures to assess children's (a) domain-general cognitive abilities (Woodcock–Johnson Tests of Cognitive Abilities; Woodcock, McGrew, & Mather, 2001: speed of processing (Test 6 Visual Matching), working memory (Test 7 Number Reserved), and attention (Test 20 Pair Cancellation); (b) language comprehension (Tests 1A-D); (c) non-autobiographical story recall; (d) use of memory strategies (Coyle & Bjorklund, 1997), and metamemory understanding (e.g., Cavanaugh & Perlmutter, 1982); and (e) memory for items and source of new factual knowledge (Riggins, 2014). Other tasks also were administered (Test of Nonverbal Intelligence [TONI]; 9-step picture sequencing; primacy/recency of items in 9-step sequences; recognition of items in 9-step sequences; tapping as a measure of executive function). Because they did not load on any of the factors of cognitive ability (see below) and were not correlated with autobiographical narrative performance, they are not discussed.

Coding and reliability and data reduction

The memory interviews were videotaped and later transcribed verbatim and reviewed for accuracy of transcription. Coding was from the transcripts. For the experimenter–child interviews, only children's contributions to the conversations were coded (not the experimenters'). For the mother–child interviews, only the mothers' contributions were coded (not the children's). For each measure described below, for each phase of the study, we calculated the average across the three events discussed in the experimenter–child interviews and the two events in the mother–child interviews. The averages were used in analyses.

Child contributions to experimenter–child interviews

One individual parsed all on-task contributions into propositional units (i.e., unit of meaning that included subject-verb construction). To estimate the reliability of parsing, 25% of the transcripts were parsed by an independent rater. Interrater agreement was 94% (range 92–99%). The primary coders' judgments were used in all analyses.

Events were considered to be recalled if the child provided at least two unique pieces of information about the event (see Bauer & Larkina, 2014b; Fivush & Schwarzmueller, 1998; Reese et al., 1993, for a similar criterion). Experimenters made on-line judgments of this criterion during the interviews. When it seemed that a child failed to meet the criterion, additional events were sampled from the calendars. For analysis, we used off-line judgments based on the transcripts. A master coder trained two individuals each of whom then coded 50% of all transcripts. To assess reliability, the master coder independently re-coded a randomly selected 20% of the transcripts with roughly equal proportional representation of age groups. Reliability was 98% (range 90–100%).

For events that met the criterion for recall, the narrative reports were coded for length, breadth, and coherence. For length and breadth, the entire memory interview was coded. Separate scores were calculated for the open-ended portion of the interview and for the entire report, including responses following additional cues and the *wh-* questions (i.e., length-free recall, breadth-free recall; length-total recall, breadth-total recall, respectively). The measure of length was the total number of propositions (reliability of coding indicated above). The measure of breadth reflects narrative completeness in terms of the number of different narrative categories included in the report: who, what-action, what-object, when, where, why, how-description, and how-evaluation (see for e.g., Bauer & Larkina, 2014a, 2014b). For each event, children received one point for a token reflective of the category, regardless of the number of tokens provided (max breadth score = 8). All transcripts were coded by one individual. For reliability, 25% of the transcripts were coded by an independent rater. Interrater agreement was 95% (range 91–99%). The primary coders' judgments were used in all analyses.

To assess the coherence of the narrative reports, we used the Narrative Coherence Coding Scheme (NaCCs) developed by Reese et al. (2011). Coherence is the overall quality of the narrative in terms of how well the story can be understood by a naive listener. The full NaCCs coding scheme assesses three dimensions: context,

Table 2. Descriptions of measures of children's language (Panel a), Domain-general cognition functions (Panel b), non-autobiographical story recall (Panel c), deliberate and strategic remembering and metamemory (Panel d), and memory for source (Panel e).

Domain/task		Description/data reduction & coding/dependent measure(s)
Panel a: language (obtained at Phase 1 only)		
WJ language	Description	Four subscales of the test of verbal comprehension: Picture vocabulary, synonyms, antonyms, and verbal analogy.
	Data reduction/coding	The number of correct responses was recorded
	Dependent measure(s)	The four subscales were combined into a total score
Panel b: domain-general cognitive functions		
WJ visual matching (VM)	Description	VM1 at 4 years; VM2 at 5 years and older. Instruction: "Look at these rows of numbers (VM1–pictures). Draw circles around (VM1–point to) the 2 numbers that are alike in each row. Do them as fast as you can."
	Data reduction/coding	Number of correct circles (VM1 = points) was recorded
	Dependent measure(s)	Total score = number of rows (VM1–items) correctly completed in 3 minutes (VM1–2 mn)
WJ numbers reversed	Description	Children given a series of numbers (2–9) and instructed to repeat the numbers in reverse order.
	Data reduction/coding	The number of correct items was recorded
	Dependent measure(s)	Total score (max = 30)
WJ pair cancellation	Description	Children asked to circle a pair of objects (ball and dog) when they appear in a certain order on the response sheet.
	Data reduction/coding	The number of correct pairs was recorded
	Dependent measure(s)	The number of correct pairs completed in 3 minutes (max = 69)
Panel c: non-autobiographical story recall		
Story recall: encoding	Description: encoding (Session 1)	Experimenter read a story to the child using an illustrated book: "I'm going to tell you a story and show you some pictures. Next time you come, I'm going to see if you can tell the story back to me without looking at the pictures." Different stories were used at each wave.
	Data reduction/coding	NA – no child response at Session 1
	Dependent measure(s)	NA—no measures obtained at Session 1
Story recall: retrieval	Description: retrieval (Session 2)	Child was shown the cover of the story book: "Last week, we read the story about_____. Tell me what happened in the story." If child did not respond in free recall, prompted by reading 1st page of story.
	Data reduction/coding	Children's responses were transcribed and coded for 1) total number of parses (proposition units centered around a verb); 2) verbatim units (recall of specific story information); and 3) gist units (statements not explicit in but derived from the story, such as inferences that encompassed the essence of multiple elements/points, that merged multiple lines, or that summarised the main point of the story)
	Dependentmeasures	Number of parses, verbatim units, and gist units
Panel d: deliberate and strategic remembering and metamemory		
Sort-recall	Description	E presented 18 picture cards (6 from each of 3 categories; 15 at age 4: 5 from each of 3 categories), labelling and arranging them on the table. Instruction: "Study the cards and do whatever you want with them so you can remember them later." After a 2 mn study period, the cards were removed; child was engaged in a 30 mn buffer activity, and then asked to "Recall as many cards in any order."
	Data reduction/coding	Experimenter recorded items recalled. From videotape, encoding behaviour was coded for organisational strategies: *sorting* (arranging cards into categorical groups), and *category naming*. Recall was coded for clustering (i.e., ARC score 0.5 and above)
	Dependent measure(s)	Proportion of items recalled. Strategic behaviour: total number of organisational strategies (sorting, category naming, clustering)
Metamemory	Description	Children asked 8 metamemory questions regarding the sort-recall task (e.g., *Did you do anything to help you remember?*).
	Data reduction/coding	One point for each correctly answered question (or mnemonically facilitative response)
	Dependent measure(s)	Total metamemory score (max = 8)
Panel e: memory for source		
Source memory: encoding	Description: encoding (Session 1)	Children were presented with 12 novel facts by either a person or a puppet (on a computer monitor). E instructed children to watch the videos and learn the new facts because they would be asked about them later.
	Data reduction/coding	Number of already known facts was recorded. These facts were excluded from the analysis.
	Dependent measure(s)	NA – no measures obtained at Session 1
Source memory: retrieval	Description: retrieval (Session 2)	Children were asked to recall (a) what they learned (items), and (b) the source (person/puppet) that presented the item.
	Data reduction/coding	Items mentioned and sources to which they were attributed were recorded
	Dependent measure(s)	Proportion of correctly recalled items and for correct items, proportion of correctly recalled sources

Notes: WJ: Woodcock–Johnson tests of cognitive abilities (Woodcock et al., 2001); ARC: adjusted ratio of clustering (Roenker, Thompson, & Brown, 1971).

chronology, and theme. In the current research, the context dimension (orienting in time and space) was not coded because the experimenters often provided this information in their prompts for recall. The chronology dimension (relating event components along a timeline) was not used because for 61% of the events, the dimension either could not be coded or was coded a 0. This was the case because experimenter prompts interrupted the reports (e.g., "Was there anything else?" or "Tell me more"), resulting in interview segments that were too brief for valid coding of chronology.

For the final narrative coherence dimension of theme, we used children's responses following the open-ended prompt; because they are external to the participants' own narrative, responses to *wh-* questions were not coded. The dimension was coded on a 4-point scale.

A rating of 0 indicated that the narrative was substantially off-topic; a score of 1 was assigned to minimally developed narratives; and narratives rated as 2 were substantially developed through evaluations, interpretations, or causal links. Narratives coded as 3 included all of the previous characteristics with additional links to other autobiographical experiences and/or self-concept. Coding reliability originally was established in Morris, Baker-Ward, and Bauer (2010), based on approximately 10% of the children's transcripts. For present purposes, we recalculated reliability on the subset of the children included in the current research. The intraclass correlation was .90.

Maternal narrative style

Maternal contributions to conversations about recalled events were coded for *elaborations* (providing or requesting new information) and *repetitions* (repeating previously provided or requested information). Two individuals each coded approximately 50% of the transcripts plus 25% of the transcripts coded by the other individual. Coding reliability was 91% (range 88–93%). Maternal elaboration ratio (elaborations divided by repetitions) was used in all analyses.

Results

The primary purposes of the present research were to determine (a) age-related changes in narrative production across the age range 4–10 years, and (b) relations between narrative production and potential correlates of developmental changes in autobiographical memory.

Age-related changes in autobiographical narratives

Depictions of children's autobiographical narrative competence across the span of the study are provided in Figure 1. To examine age-related changes in narrative production, for each dependent variable, we conducted a 3 (Cohort: 4, 6, 8 years) × 3 (Phase: 1, 2, 3) mixed linear model. Mixed linear models are an extension of generalised linear models that take into consideration the repeated measures design and interdependency across observations. In the models, we specified an unstructured correlation matrix and conducted significance tests using the Type III tests of fixed effects. The output of the analysis consists of F values for main effects and interactions within a given model and estimated marginal means that can then be examined with pairwise comparisons, using the Tukey–Kramer adjustment method. Because maximum likelihood estimations were used in the mixed models, effect sizes were calculated through an *ad-hoc* approach using predicted residuals and the F values from the models (Tippey & Longnecker, 2016). Importantly, the resulting pseudo-effect sizes should only be compared with other effect sizes produced using the same *ad-hoc* method. All participants had complete narrative data. Data were analysed using PROC MIXED procedure in SAS 9.4.

As suggested by Figure 1, there were significant cohort effects for all 5 dependent measures: $Fs(2, 98) = 20.32$, 16.19, 50.79, 35.89, and 20.71, $ps < .001$, for length-free recall (in propositions; $\eta_p^2 = 0.12$), length-total recall ($\eta_p^2 = 0.10$); breadth-free recall ($\eta_p^2 = 0.25$); breadth-total recall ($\eta_p^2 = 0.19$); and theme ($\eta_p^2 = 0.12$), respectively. For the length measures, 8-year-olds differed from both 6- and 4-year-olds, which did not differ from one another. For the breadth measures and theme, pairwise comparison indicated significant differences between all three age groups.

There also were significant phase effects: $Fs(2, 98) = 16.31$, 38.14, 5.37, 6.81, and 22.72, $ps < .01$, for length-free recall ($\eta_p^2 = 0.10$), length-total recall ($\eta_p^2 = 0.20$); breadth-free recall ($\eta_p^2 = 0.03$); breadth-total recall ($\eta_p^2 = 0.04$); and theme ($\eta_p^2 = 0.15$), respectively. For length-free recall and breadth-free recall, pairwise comparisons indicated differences between Phases 1 and 3; Phase 2 was intermediate and did not differ from either Phase 1 or Phase 3. For length-total recall and breadth-total recall, Phase 1 differed from Phases 2 and 3 which did not differ from each other. For the measure of thematic coherence, pairwise comparisons indicated that Phases 1 and 3 did not differ and that both were lower than Phase 2.

The interaction effects were not significant for length-free recall ($\eta_p^2 = 0.01$); breadth-free recall ($\eta_p^2 = 0.01$); breath-total recall ($\eta_p^2 = 0.01$); or theme ($\eta_p^2 = 0.02$), $ps > .14$; for length-total recall, the interaction reached significance, $p = .09$, $\eta_p^2 = 0.03$.

Because on breadth-total recall, performance approached ceiling, the measure will not be analysed further. Also, because patterns of performance and relations for length-free and total recall were the same, in the interest of space, we present the analyses for length-free recall only.

Correlates of developmental change in autobiographical narratives

Descriptive statistics on the potential predictor variables are provided in Table 3. To assess potential correlates of autobiographical memory narratives, we first imputed missing data for specific measures using maximum-likelihood estimation (a technique recommended for handling missing data in longitudinal studies; see Jeličić, Phelps, & Lerner, 2009) based on children's age, gender, and available data from other tasks for each phase separately (PROC MI procedure in SAS 9.4). Children had missing data because they did not complete a task due to time constraints. The overall percent of missing data range from 1% (sort-recall) to 21% (pair cancellation).

After imputing data, to reduce the number of potential predictors, for each phase, we conducted factor analyses using principal components extraction and Varimax rotation. The measures considered in the factor analyses were indices of domain-general cognitive functions, non-

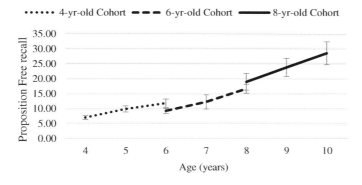

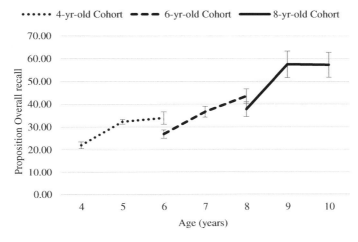

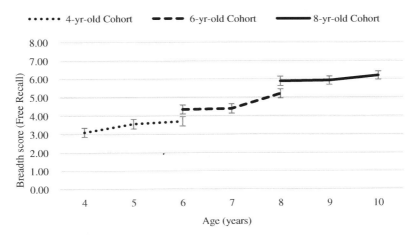

Figure 1. Graphic representations of changes over time for three cohorts of children (4-, 6-, and 8-year-olds) over three time points, for narrative measures of length (in propositions) in free recall and total recall (Panel a), breadth in free recall and total recall (Panel b), and thematic coherence in free recall (Panel c).

autobiographical story recall, deliberate and strategic remembering and metamemory, and memory for source. For all three phases, 3 factors with Eigenvalues above 1.0 emerged and were retained for interpretation; loadings less than .30 were deleted (Kaiser, 1960). We then examined correlations between each of the factors and the autobiographical narrative measures of interest, and between each of the potential predictor variables. Finally, we conducted regression analyses to examine concurrent and cross-lagged (Phases 2 and 3 only) contributions of each of the factor scores, above and beyond the variance explained by children's own language ability and maternal

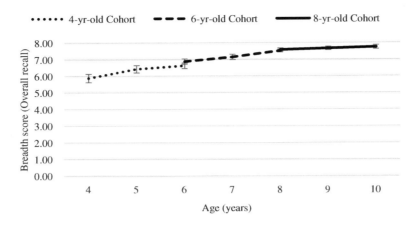

Panel d: Narrative Breadth-Total Recall

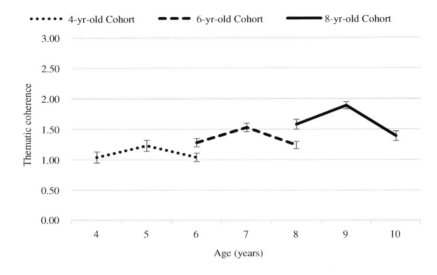

Panel e: Thematic Coherence-Free Recall

Figure 1. Continued.

narrative style, which were entered as Steps 1 and 2, respectively.

Factor analyses

As reflected in Table 4, the factors that emerged from the analyses were largely consistent across the phases. Specifically, at all three phases, the factors that emerged were reflective of non-autobiographical story recall, of domain-general cognitive abilities and item memory, and of deliberate and strategic remembering and metamemory.

At Phases 1 and 2 (ages 4, 6, 8 and 5, 7, 9, respectively), the same factors accounted for the most variance, whereas at Phase 3, the relative strength of the factors changed. That is, at Phases 1 and 2, non-autobiographical story recall emerged as the strongest factor, accounting for almost 50% of the variance in the measures. Domain-general cognitive abilities and item memory were a distant second, accounting for between 12% and 17% of the variance. Deliberate and strategic remembering and metamemory were the weakest factors, accounting for roughly 10% of the variance. At Phase 3 (ages 6, 8, and 10), whereas the composition of the factors remained the same, the relative positions of non-autobiographical story recall and domain-general cognitive abilities and item memory reversed, such that domain-general cognitive abilities and item memory accounted for roughly 50% of the variance in the measures, and non-autobiographical story recall accounted for only 15%. As at Phases 1 and 2, deliberate and strategic remembering and metamemory were the weakest factors, accounting for roughly 10% of the variance.

Correlations between factors and autobiographical narrative measures

As reflected in Table 5, with the exception of the relation between thematic coherence and Factor 2 at Phase 3, all

Table 3. Descriptive statistics for potential predictors of narrative competence (raw data before imputation).

Measure	Study phase								
	Phase 1			Phase 2			Phase 3		
Cohort	4-year-olds	6-year-olds	8-year-olds	4-year-olds	6-year-olds	8-year-olds	4-year-olds	6-year-olds	8-year-olds
Age	4 years	6 years	8 years	5 years	7 years	9 years	6 years	8 years	10 years
	M (SD)	M (SD)	M (SD)	M (SD)	M (SD)	M (SD)	M (SD)	M (SD)	M (SD)
Children's language	18.68 (5.22)	28.48 (6.72)	38.55 (3.32)	n/a	n/a	n/a	n/a	n/a	n/a
Maternal elaboration ratio	5.33 (3.63)	6.17 (2.62)	10.26 (7.38)	5.25 (2.32)	12.12 (12.30)	14.75 (11.12)	7.90 (6.99)	11.49 (13.10)	13.43 (12.45)
Domain-general cognitive functions (Woodcock–Johnson)									
Visual matching[a]	21.65 (4.52)	19.97 (3.87)	30.77 (6.07)	12.41 (6.58)	27.38 (4.34)	36.63 (3.83)	18.49 (4.17)	31.03 (5.81)	39.97 (6.32)
Number reversed	4.71 (1.69)	7.91 (2.14)	10.70 (3.03)	5.80 (2.14)	9.62 (2.84)	12.60 (3.19)	7.06 (1.98)	10.35 (2.96)	13.86 (3.50)
Pair cancellation	15.69 (7.24)	26.76 (7.72)	44.97 (11.96)	19.15 (7.86)	37.50 (6.72)	55.90 (8.21)	25.46 (8.36)	48.06 (7.90)	61.73 (6.39)
Non-autobiographical story recall									
Story parse	3.96 (4.50)	3.48 (2.71)	12.67 (6.47)	6.08 (5.88)	9.16 (5.80)	13.73 (6.29)	6.68 (5.27)	12.04 (6.07)	15.57 (5.26)
Story verbatim	2.60 (2.86)	2.28 (2.26)	10.46 (6.81)	4.40 (4.97)	6.68 (5.31)	10.81 (7.23)	4.72 (4.61)	8.80 (6.37)	14.09 (6.13)
Story gist	2.72 (2.78)	3.00 (2.35)	10.88 (5.49)	4.56 (4.65)	7.64 (4.99)	10.31 (4.76)	5.84 (5.08)	9.40 (4.69)	12.70 (3.89)
Deliberate and strategic remembering and metamemory									
Sort-recall item (proportion)	0.29 (0.16)	0.42 (0.12)	0.56 (0.14)	0.29 (0.11)	0.51 (0.15)	0.70 (0.16)	0.38 (0.15)	0.62 (0.16)	0.76 (0.16)
Sort-recall strategies	0.42 (0.50)	0.62 (0.70)	0.90 (0.88)	0.54 (0.65)	0.94 (0.85)	1.27 (0.94)	0.78 (0.90)	0.91 (0.82)	1.30 (1.12)
Metamemory	3.13 (1.16)	4.29 (1.49)	5.37 (1.65)	3.75 (1.16)	5.41 (1.08)	5.87 (1.46)	4.20 (1.49)	5.88 (1.66)	5.83 (1.44)
Memory for source									
Source fact (proportion)	0.03 (0.05)	0.15 (0.11)	0.29 (0.14)	0.11 (0.12)	0.21 (0.14)	0.34 (0.19)	0.17 (0.12)	0.27 (0.14)	0.37 (0.15)
Source/source	0.14 (0.24)	0.12 (0.18)	0.25 (0.22)	0.14 (0.22)	0.23 (0.26)	0.29 (0.25)	0.21 (0.24)	0.31 (0.23)	0.28 (0.20)

Note. [a]Means for visual matching I is reported for 4-year-olds at Phase 1.

Table 4. Results of factor analyses for each of Phases 1, 2, and 3.

Phase/predictor	Factor		
	Factor 1	Factor 2	Factor 3
Phase 1 (72% variance)			
WJ visual matching		**.68**	
WJ numbers reversed		**.75**	
WJ pair cancellation	.31	**.66**	.43
Story parse	**.92**		
Story verbatim	**.87**	.32	
Story gist	**.91**		
Number recalled	.33	.35	**.61**
Deliberate strategies			**.39**
Metamemory		.38	**.44**
Source item memory		**.70**	
Memory for source			.48
Eigenvalue	5.65	1.39	1.14
% Variance	48.5	12.6	10.4
Phase 2 (76% variance)			
WJ visual matching	.30	**.81**	.36
WJ numbers reversed		**.79**	
WJ pair cancellation		**.83**	.32
Story parse	**.92**		
Story verbatim	**.92**		
Story gist	**.94**		
Number recalled		**.64**	**.52**
Deliberate strategies			**.53**
Metamemory		.37	**.58**
Source item memory		**.58**	
Memory for source	.39		
Eigenvalue	5.47	1.89	1.01
% Variance	49.7	17.2	9.14
Phase 3 (74% variance)			
WJ visual matching	**.88**		
WJ numbers reversed	**.74**		
WJ pair cancellation	**.82**	.33	
Story parse		**.89**	
Story verbatim		**.86**	
Story gist	.31	**.90**	
Number recalled	**.60**		**.55**
Deliberate strategies			**.64**
Metamemory	.54		**.39**
Source item memory	**.60**	.30	
Memory for source			
Eigenvalue	5.52	1.61	1.04
% Variance	50.2	14.6	9.5

of the correlations were statistically significant and tended to be moderate in magnitude. Thus the factors related to the outcome variables of interest, across the age range of the study.

Table 5. Correlations between factors and autobiographical narrative measures.

Phase/factor		Autobiographical narrative measure		
		Length-free recall	Breadth-free recall	Thematic coherence
Phase 1	Factor 1	.30***	.43***	.31**
	Factor 2	.33**	.37***	.20*
	Factor 3	.26**	.37***	.38***
Phase 2	Factor 1	.31**	.28**	.40***
	Factor 2	.34***	.43***	.40***
	Factor 3	.24*	.39***	.26**
Phase 3	Factor 1	.31**	.51***	.31**
	Factor 2	.30**	.30**	.13
	Factor 3	.23*	.32**	.25*

Note: *p < .05; **p < .01; ***p < .001.

Correlations between each of the potential predictor variables

As reflected in Table 6, children's own language abilities (assessed at Phase 1) and maternal narrative style were correlated at all phases. As well, with the exception of Factor 1 at Phase 2, children's language was moderately to strongly correlated with all three factors. Maternal narrative style also correlated with the factors, though the correlations were small and by Phase 3, not statistically significant. The only statistically significant correlations among the factors themselves were at Phases 1 and 2, between Factors 2 and 3 (domain-general cognitive abilities and item memory, and deliberate and strategic remembering and metamemory, respectively).

Regression analyses

Results of the regression analyses are provided in Table 7. Both when it was the only variable in the equation, and when maternal narrative style was entered as a second step, children's own language (assessed at Phase 1) predicted all three measures of autobiographical narrative. In contrast, maternal narrative style accounted for significant variance only in prediction of thematic coherence at Phases 1 and 2. Upon entry of the factor scores into the equations, neither children's language nor maternal narrative style explained significant variance.

At both Phases 1 and 2, the length of children's free recall was predicted by Factor 1 (non-autobiographical story recall), both concurrently and over time (i.e., Factor 1 from Phase 1 explained significant variance in Phase 2 narrative length-free recall). The maximum total variance explained at Phases 1 and 2 was 19% and 22%, respectively. None of the factors explained significant variance in the length of free recall at Phase 3.

At Phase 1, the breadth of children's free recall was predicted by Factors 1 and 3 (non-autobiographical story

Table 6. Correlations between each of the potential predictor variables/factors.

Phase/measure		Measure			
		Maternal narrative style	Factor 1	Factor 2	Factor 3
Phase 1	Child language	.35***	.38***	.70***	.41***
	Maternal narrative style		.26**	.31**	.20*
	Factor 1			.05	.09
	Factor 2				.22*
Phase 2	Child language	.27**	.15	.81***	.43***
	Maternal narrative style		.27**	.18	.23*
	Factor 1			.01	.06
	Factor 2				.23*
Phase 3	Child language	.27**	.76***	.37***	.20*
	Maternal narrative style		.19	.07	.11
	Factor 1			.04	.15
	Factor 2				.02

Note: *p < .05; **p < .01; ***p < .001.

Table 7. Results of regression analyses for length-free recall (Panel a), breadth-free recall (Panel b), and thematic coherence (Panel c).

Phase/step/predictor	Test statistic				
	B	SE	t(predictor)	F(model)	R^2 (R^2 adj)
Panel a: length-free recall					
Phase 1					
Step 1				$F(1, 98) = 16.50$***	.14 (.14)
Child's language	0.42***	0.102	4.06***		
Step 2				$F(2, 97) = 8.51$***	.15 (.13)
Child's language	0.39***	0.109	3.55***		
Maternal style	0.15	0.199	0.77		
Step 3				$F(5, 93) = 5.59$***	.23 (.19)
Child's language	−0.02	0.179	−0.13		
Maternal style	0.04	0.197	0.20		
Factor 1 Ph1	3.31**	1.19	2.78**		
Factor 2 Ph1	3.27^	1.65	1.98		
Factor 3 Ph1	2.49^	1.48	1.68		
Phase 2					
Step 1				$F(1, 99) = 18.74$***	.16 (.15)
Child's language	0.50***	0.115	4.33***		
Step 2				$F(2, 96) = 9.21$***	.16 (.14)
Child's language	0.50***	0.122	4.06***		
Maternal style	0.03	0.115	0.25		
Step 3				$F(5, 93) = 5.90$***	.24 (.20)
Child's language	0.22	0.222	0.98		
Maternal style	−0.06	0.116	−0.54		
Factor 1 Ph2	3.53**	1.19	2.96**		
Factor 2 Ph2	2.29	2.11	1.09		
Factor 3 Ph2	1.96	1.70	1.15		
Step 4				$F(8, 90) = 4.36$***	.28 (.22)
Child's language	0.02	0.241	0.07		
Maternal style	−0.09	0.116	−0.76		
Factor 1 Ph2	2.04	1.42	1.43		
Factor 2 Ph2	2.50	2.79	0.90		
Factor 3 Ph2	1.82	1.85	0.99		
Factor 1 Ph1	3.21*	1.49	2.15*		
Factor 2 Ph1	0.79	2.37	0.33		
Factor 3 Ph1	1.43	1.92	0.74		
Phase 3					
Step 1				$F(1, 99) = 22.07$***	.18 (.17)
Child's language	0.67***	0.142	4.70***		
Step 2				$F(2, 96) = 10.43$***	.18 (.16)
Child's language	0.66**	0.152	4.31***		
Maternal style	0.043	0.132	0.27		
Step 3				$F(5, 93) = 5.59$***	.23 (.19)
Child's language	0.40	0.268	1.48		
Maternal style	0.03	0.129	0.27		
Factor 1 Ph3	1.07	2.46	0.43		
Factor 2 Ph3	3.20^	1.69	1.89		
Factor 3 Ph3	3.31^	1.86	1.79		
Step 4				$F(8, 90) = 3.69$***	.25 (.18)
Child's language	0.44	0.297	1.48		
Maternal style	0.03	0.132	0.21		
Factor 1 Ph3	−1.32	5.03	−0.26		
Factor 2 Ph3	2.05	2.29	0.90		
Factor 3 Ph3	3.34	2.44	1.37		
Factor 1 Ph2	2.38	2.16	1.10		
Factor 2 Ph2	2.00	5.06	0.39		
Factor 3 Ph2	−.58	3.16	−0.18		
Panel b: breadth-free recall					
Phase 1					
Step 1				$F(1, 98) = 39.24$***	.29 (.28)
Child's language	0.10***	0.016	6.26***		
Step 2				$F(2, 97) = 18.64$***	.29 (.28)
Child's language	0.09***	0.017	5.52***		
Maternal style	0.03	0.032	1.04		
Step 3				$F(5, 94) = 12.48$***	.40 (.38)
Child's language	0.04	0.016	1.50		
Maternal style	0.01	0.031	0.24		
Factor 1 Ph1	0.62***	0.176	3.49***		
Factor 2 Ph1	0.33	0.253	1.29		
Factor 3 Ph1	0.56*	0.218	2.55*		

(Continued)

Table 7. Continued.

Phase/step/predictor	Test statistic				
	B	SE	t(predictor)	F(model)	R^2 (R^2 adj)
Phase 2					
Step 1				$F(1, 99) = 29.14^{***}$	.23 (.22)
Child's language	0.08***	0.16	5.40***		
Step 2				$F(2, 96) = 13.88^{***}$	.29 (.28)
Child's language	0.08***	0.17	4.96***		
Maternal style	0.01	0.015	0.40		
Step 3				$F(5, 93) = 9.83^{***}$	.35 (.31)
Child's language	0.01	0.029	0.33		
Maternal style	−0.01	0.015	−0.55		
Factor 1 Ph2	0.47**	0.157	2.97**		
Factor 2 Ph2	0.61*	0.279	2.19*		
Factor 3 Ph2	0.64**	0.224	2.88**		
Step 4				$F(8, 90) = 6.98^{***}$	.38 (.33)
Child's language	−0.02	0.032	−0.48		
Maternal style	−0.01	0.015	−0.70		
Factor 1 Ph2	0.24	0.187	1.28		
Factor 2 Ph2	0.61^	0.368	1.67		
Factor 3 Ph2	0.59*	0.243	2.41*		
Factor 1 Ph1	0.42*	0.197	2.14*		
Factor 2 Ph1	0.08	0.312	0.26		
Factor 3 Ph1	0.31	0.253	1.21		
Phase 3					
Step 1				$F(1, 99) = 44.67^{***}$	.31 (.30)
Child's language	0.10***	0.15	6.68***		
Step 2				$F(2, 96) = 20.86^{***}$	.30 (.29)
Child's language	0.10***	0.16	6.02***		
Maternal style	0.01	0.14	0.62		
Step 3				$F(5, 93) = 12.93^{***}$	.41 (.38)
Child's language	0.02	0.026	0.90		
Maternal style	0.01	0.012	0.67		
Factor 1 Ph3	0.61*	0.243	2.53*		
Factor 2 Ph3	0.42*	0.167	2.52*		
Factor 3 Ph3	0.55**	0.183	2.98**		
Step 4				$F(8, 90) = 8.83^{***}$	.44 (.39)
Child's language	0.01	0.028	0.35		
Maternal style	0.01	0.013	0.24		
Factor 1 Ph3	0.12	0.489	0.24		
Factor 2 Ph3	0.27	0.223	1.30		
Factor 3 Ph3	0.22	0.238	0.93		
Factor 1 Ph2	0.16	0.210	0.77		
Factor 2 Ph2	0.46	0.492	0.94		
Factor 3 Ph2	0.66*	0.308	2.14*		
Panel c: thematic coherence					
Phase 1					
Step 1				$F(1, 98) = 19.36^{***}$	.16 (.16)
Child's language	0.02***	0.005	4.40***		
Step 2				$F(2, 97) = 12.35^{***}$	.20 (.19)
Child's language	0.02***	0.005	3.46**		
Maternal style	0.02*	0.010	2.15*		
Step 3				$F(5, 94) = 7.51^{***}$	.29 (.25)
Child's language	0.012^	0.008	1.67		
Maternal style	0.02^	0.010	1.84		
Factor 1 Ph1	0.08	0.056	1.50		
Factor 2 Ph1	−0.06	0.080	−0.69		
Factor 3 Ph1	0.28**	0.069	2.66*		
Phase 2					
Step 1				$F(1, 99) = 25.08^{***}$	.20 (.19)
Child's language	0.02***	0.005	5.01***		
Step 2				$F(2, 96) = 14.31^{***}$	.23 (.21)
Child's language	0.02***	0.005	4.26**		
Maternal style	0.01*	0.004	1.99*		
Step 3				$F(5, 93) = 10.12^{***}$	.35 (.32)
Child's language	0.004	0.009	0.45		
Maternal style	0.005	0.005	1.09		
Factor 1 Ph2	0.19***	0.047	3.99***		
Factor 2 Ph2	0.17*	0.083	1.98^		
Factor 3 Ph2	0.07	0.067	1.08		
Step 4				$F(8, 90) = 7.27^{***}$	.39 (.34)
Child's language	−0.002	0.010	−0.19		
Maternal style	0.005	0.005	0.99		

(Continued)

Table 7. Continued.

Phase/step/predictor	Test statistic				
	B	SE	t(predictor)	F(model)	R^2 (R^2 adj)
Factor 1 Ph2	0.13*	0.056	2.32*		
Factor 2 Ph2	0.23*	0.110	2.13*		
Factor 3 Ph2	0.07	0.072	0.97		
Factor 1 Ph1	0.11^	0.056	1.82		
Factor 2 Ph1	−0.07	0.093	−0.79		
Factor 3 Ph1	0.07	0.076	0.94		
Phase 3					
Step 1				$F(1, 99) = 17.52$***	.15 (.14)
Child's language	0.02***	0.004	4.19***		
Step 2				$F(2, 96) = 8.52$***	.15 (.13)
Child's language	0.01***	0.004	3.59***		
Maternal style	0.004	0.004	0.99		
Step 3				$F(5, 93) = 4.19$**	.18 (.14)
Child's language	0.01	0.007	1.47		
Maternal style	0.003	0.004	0.91		
Factor 1 Ph3	0.03	0.068	0.40		
Factor 2 Ph3	0.01	0.047	0.22		
Factor 3 Ph3	0.10^	0.051	1.91		
Step 4				$F(8, 90) = 3.92$***	.26 (.19)
Child's language	0.004	0.008	0.48		
Maternal style	0.005	0.004	1.30		
Factor 1 Ph3	−0.28*	0.134	−2.11*		
Factor 2 Ph3	−0.09	0.061	−1.54		
Factor 3 Ph3	−0.02	0.065	−0.30		
Factor 1 Ph2	0.12*	0.058	2.10*		
Factor 2 Ph2	0.32*	0.135	2.41*		
Factor 3 Ph2	0.24**	0.084	2.84**		

Note: Children's language was measured at Phase 1 only. The Phase 1 score was used in all analyses.

recall and deliberate and strategic remembering and metamemory, respectively), with 38% of variance explained. At Phases 2 and 3, all three factors contributed explanatory variance in the breadth of free recall. Additionally, at Phase 2, Phase 1 Factor 1 contributed significant variance (maximum total variance explained 33%), and at Phase 3, Phase 2 Factor 3 contributed significant variance (maximum total variance explained 39%).

Finally, at Phase 1, the thematic coherence of children's autobiographical narratives was predicted only by Factor 3 (deliberate and strategic remembering and metamemory; maximum total variance explained 25%). At Phase 2, significant variance was contributed by both Factors 1 and 2 (non-autobiographical story recall and domain-general cognitive abilities and item memory). There were no cross-lagged predictors and the maximum total variance explained was 32%. At Phase 3, none of the concurrent measures explained significant variance in thematic coherence. However, measures of all three factors from Phase 2 explained significant variance (maximum total variance explained 19%).

Discussion

The primary purposes of the present research were to determine age-related changes in autobiographical narrative production across the age range 4–10 years, and relations between autobiographical narrative production and potential domain-general and memory-specific correlates of change. The study complements and extends the existing literature in that it is a relatively rare longitudinal investigation of autobiographical memory narrative production in the period surrounding the onset of childhood amnesia (Bauer & Larkina, 2014b) and the achievement of an adult-like distribution of autobiographical memory (Bauer & Larkina, 2014a). The number and combination of domain-general and domain-specific predictor variables included allowed a unique perspective on the determinants of autobiographical narrative competence in this important developmental period.

As reflected in Figure 1, there were steady increases in the qualities of children's autobiographical memory reports across the age range included in the study. The most striking change was in the length of narratives produced in free recall, which increased from roughly 5 propositions at age 5 years to almost 30 at age 10 years. The breadth of the narratives produced in free recall, as reflected in the number of different elements that children included in their narratives (e.g., *who, what, where*), roughly doubled over the period of the study, from 3 to 6 (of 8 possible). The slowest rate of change was observed in the thematic coherence of narratives produced. Over the course of the study, the average thematic coherence scores increased from 1 to 2. Taking all three variables into account, at the close of the study, the children were substantially more narratively competent than at its inception. Yet notably, even by the time they were 10 years of age, children's autobiographical narratives were not as long, nor as complete, nor as thematically coherent as those of adult women tested in the same protocol. As reported in Bauer and Larkina (2014b), at Phase 1 of the study, adult women (the mothers of some of the children) included an average of 80 propositions in their autobiographical memory reports. They also tended to include all of the narrative elements that lend breadth to the report ($M = 7.92$ of 8.00). The thematic coherence of their narratives averaged 2.06 (of 3.0 possible). Interestingly, as reflected in Figure 1, Panel e, the 8-year-old cohort approached this level of thematic coherence at Phase 2, but did not sustain it at Phase 3. Thus the present research documented substantial growth in autobiographical narrative skill across the 4- to 10-year period. Even at 10 years, autobiographical narratives were not yet adult-like (see Reese et al., 2011, for similar conclusions based on cross-sectional data). This finding compels additional research on changes in autobiographical narrative throughout middle childhood and into early adolescence, a period relatively neglected in the existing literature (although see Bauer, Hättenschwiler, & Larkina, 2016, and Larkina, Merrill, & Bauer, 2016).

With respect to the second purpose of the research, the results shed new light on the correlates of developmental changes in autobiographical narrative. Consistent with expectations, children's own language abilities predicted significant variance in their narrative reports. This was the case even when maternal narrative style also was considered as a predictor. Yet once the other potential predictor variables were entered into the equation, neither children's own language nor maternal narrative style contributed added variance. The finding that maternal narrative style contributed little in the way of explanatory variance was not entirely unexpected. Although it is a consistent determinant of children's contributions to co-constructed autobiographical narratives in early childhood (e.g., Larkina & Bauer, 2010; Reese et al., 1993), it does not always emerge as a predictor of older children's independently produced narratives (contrast Reese et al., 2010; and Larkina & Bauer, 2012; and Peterson et al., 2007, for example).

We included in the present research measures of a range of cognitive and specifically memory abilities as potential predictors. The factors that emerged from factor analyses were consistent across the period of the study. Specifically, at all three phases, three factors emerged: non-autobiographical story recall, domain-general cognitive abilities and item memory, and deliberate and strategic remembering and metamemory. At Phases 1 and 2, non-autobiographical story recall explained the most variance in the measures, whereas at Phase 3, domain-general cognitive abilities and item memories took pride of place. To our knowledge, non-autobiographical story recall has not been considered in prior related research. The present research indicates that it should be considered in future research. Non-autobiographical story recall contributed variance to prediction of autobiographical narrative length in free recall at Phases 1 and 2. As well, Phase 1 variance in the factor explained variance in narrative length at Phase 2. Non-autobiographical story recall contributed to prediction of the breadth of autobiographical narratives in free recall at all three phase, as well as cross-lagged prediction from Phase 1 to Phase 2. It also contributed to prediction of the thematic coherence of autobiographical narratives in free recall at Phase 2, and provided cross-lagged prediction from Phase 2 to Phase 3. Clearly, individual and age-related variance in the ability to recall over a delay who did what to whom in the context of a non-autobiographical story overlaps with that in personal or autobiographical narrative production. This finding is logically consistent and to our knowledge, represents a novel contribution to the literature.

The measures of domain-general cognitive abilities (speed of processing, working memory, and sustained attention) as well as item memory also formed a factor at all three phases. The factor contributed both concurrent and cross-lagged variance in prediction of the breadth of autobiographical narratives in free recall at Phases 2 and 3. It also contributed to the prediction of thematic coherence in free recall at Phase 2, as well as cross-lagged prediction to the same variable at Phase 3. The fact that the factor contributed variance to prediction of narrative breadth and thematic coherence, but not to narrative length, suggests that its importance lies not in supporting engagement in the memory interviews, or even talkativeness. Rather, it lends to the skills necessary to produce a complete narrative that is understandable to a naïve listener and which links the event to others in the child's personal history (see Larkina et al., 2016 for discussion). The observation that domain-general cognitive abilities (and item memory) was more predictive at the later phases is consistent with expectation that the importance of domain-general abilities might ascend as variability in more domain-specific skills and abilities begins to resolve with development.

Measures of deliberate and strategic remembering and metamemory also formed a factor at all three phases. The factor contributed explanatory variance to prediction of narrative breadth in free recall at all three phases. It also contributed explanatory variance to prediction of thematic coherence in free recall at Phase 1, as well as cross-lagged prediction from Phase 2 to Phase 3. As noted regarding domain-general cognitive abilities, the fact that the factor did not contribute variance to narrative length suggests that its importance lies in supporting the skills necessary to produce a complete and comprehensible narrative that relates the event within the child's autobiography.

Even as we highlight the explanatory power of the measures obtained in the present research, we note that even when they were combined, they did not explain substantial amounts of variance in children's autobiographical narrative reports. Rather, the total variance explained ranged from 19% (length) to 33–39% (breadth). This finding implies that there is still work to be done to fully account for autobiographical narrative development across the childhood years. Another interesting finding is that memory for the source of events and experiences did not exhibit a consistent pattern of factor loading. At Phase 1, it loaded with measures of deliberate and strategic remembering and metamemory; at Phase 2, it loaded with measures of non-autobiographical story recall; at Phase 3, it loaded with domain-general cognitive abilities and item memory. This was an unexpected finding that escapes ready explanation (see Riggins, 2014, for details on performance in the memory for source task).

Even as we celebrate the strengths of the present research, we also note some of its limitations. One limitation is the sample on which the research was conducted – the sample was homogeneous in terms of is racial and ethnic makeup, as well as the socio-economic status of the families of the children. Although the homogeneity did not restrict the range of behaviour (see Table 3, which indicates variability across the measures obtained), in future research, it will be important to increase the diversity of the participants. A second limitation is that the potential correlates that we entertained were all cognitive in nature. Previous research has revealed the importance of more self-referent variables, such as self-concept (Harley & Reese, 1999; Howe & Courage, 1993, 1997) and subjective perspective (Fivush, 2014), for example, as important determinants of autobiographical memory. In future research, it would be ideal to measure self-referent as well as cognitive factors, to gain a more complete understanding of the contributors to autobiographical narrative competence.

In conclusion, the present research provides a unique, longitudinal perspective on age-related changes in autobiographical narrative production across the period of 4 to 10 years. It indicates that a number of domain-general and domain-specific cognitive abilities contribute to the changes, including speed of processing, working memory, and sustained attention (domain-general abilities); the ability to recall the elements of a non-autobiographical story after a 1-week delay; and the ability to marshall resources to engage in deliberate remembering, and to reflect on how memory works. Each of these abilities related to children's language throughout the period of the study (with the exception of Factor 1 at Phase 2). At the inception of the study, they also related to maternal narrative style, though the relations weakened across the phases. Together, the measures explained between approximately 20% and 40% of the variance in children's autobiographical narratives across the 4- to 10-year age range. The results indicate that these elements of the "profile" of the rememberer are important throughout this period of development of autobiographical competence. They simultaneously highlight the importance of other skills and abilities not measured here and thus the familiar refrain that more research is needed to fully elucidate the development of autobiographical memory in childhood.

Acknowledgements

The authors thank Melissa Burch, Evren Güler, and Tracy Riggins, for their assistance with aspects of the research, as well as members of the Cognition in the Transition laboratory (University of Minnesota) and Memory at Emory laboratory (Emory University) for their help at various stages of the research. They also express their deep and abiding gratitude to the children and families who took part in the longitudinal study, data from which are reported in this manuscript.

Disclosure statement

No potential conflict of interest was reported by the authors.

Funding

The research reported in this manuscript was supported by the NIH HD28425 to Patricia J. Bauer.

References

Bauer, P. J., Doydum, A. O., Pathman, T., Larkina, M., Güler, O. E., & Burch, M. (2012). It's all about location, location, location: Children's memory for the "where" of personally experienced events. *Journal of Experimental Child Psychology*, *113*, 510–522. doi:10.1016/j.jecp.2012.06.007

Bauer, P. J., Hättenschwiler, N., & Larkina, M. (2016). "Owning" the personal past: Adolescents' and adults' autobiographical narratives and ratings of memories of recent and distant events. *Memory (Hove, England)*, *24*, 165–183. doi:10.1080/09658211.2014.995673

Bauer, P. J., & Larkina, M. (2014a). Childhood amnesia in the making: Different distributions of autobiographical memories in children and adults. *Journal of Experimental Psychology: General*, *143*, 597–611. doi:10.1037/a0033307

Bauer, P. J., & Larkina, M. (2014b). The onset of childhood amnesia in childhood: A prospective investigation of the course and determinants of forgetting of early-life events. *Memory (Hove, England)*, *22*, 907–924. doi:10.1080/09658211.2013.854806

Bauer, P. J. (2015). A complementary processes account of the development of childhood amnesia and a personal past. *Psychological Review*, *122*, 204–231. doi:10.1037/a0038939

Bauer, P. J., Tasdemir-Ozdes, A., & Larkina, M. (2014). Adults' reports of their earliest memories: Consistency in events, ages, and narrative characteristics over time. *Consciousness and Cognition*, *27*, 76–88. doi:10.1016/j.concog.2014.04.008

Cavanaugh, J. C., & Perlmutter, M. (1982). Metamemory: A critical examination. *Child Development*, *53*, 11–28. doi:10.2307/1129635

Coyle, T. R., & Bjorklund, D. F. (1997). Age differences in, and consequences of, multiple- and variable-strategy use on a multitrial sort-recall task. *Developmental Psychology*, *33*, 372–380. doi:10.1037/0012-1649.33.2.372

Fivush, R. (2014). Maternal reminiscing style: The sociocultural construction of autobiographical memory across childhood and adolescence. In P. J. Bauer & R. Fivush (Eds.), *The Wiley-Blackwell handbook on the development of children's memory* (pp. 568–585). West Sussex: Wiley-Blackwell.

Fivush, R., & Schwarzmueller, A. (1998). Children remember childhood: Implications for childhood amnesia. *Applied Cognitive Psychology*, *12*, 455–473. doi:10.1002/(SICI)1099-0720(199810)12:5<455::AID-ACP534>3.0.CO;2-H

Freud, S. (1905/1953). Childhood and concealing memories. In A. A. Brill (Trans. & Ed.), *The basic writings of Sigmund Freud* (pp. 62–68). New York, NY: The Modern Library.

Friedman, W. J., Reese, E., & Dai, J. (2011). Children's memory for the times of events from the past years. *Applied Cognitive Psychology*, *25*, 156–165. doi:10.1002/acp.1656

Ghetti, S., & Lee, J. K. (2014). The development of recollection and familiarity during childhood: Insight from studies of behavior and brain. In P. J. Bauer & R. Fivush (Eds.), *The Wiley-Blackwell handbook on the development of children's memory* (pp. 309–335). West Sussex: Wiley-Blackwell.

Güler, O. E., Larkina, M., Kleinknecht, E., & Bauer, P. J. (2010). Memory strategies and retrieval success in preschool children: Relations to maternal behavior over time. *Journal of Cognition and Development*, 11, 159–184. doi:10.1080/15248371003699910

Haden, C. A., Ornstein, P. A., Rudek, D. J., & Cameron, D. (2009). Reminiscing in the early years: Patterns of maternal elaborativeness and children's remembering. *International Journal of Behavioral Development*, 33, 118–130. doi:10.1177/0165025408098038

Han, J. J., Leichtman, M. D., & Wang, Q. (1998). Autobiographical memory in Korean, Chinese, and American children. *Developmental Psychology*, 34, 701–713. doi:10.1037/0012-1649.34.4.701

Harley, K., & Reese, E. (1999). Origins of autobiographical memory. *Developmental Psychology*, 35, 1338–1348. doi:10.1037/0012-1649.35.5.1338

Howe, M. L., & Courage, M. L. (1993). On resolving the enigma of infantile amnesia. *Psychological Bulletin*, 113, 305–326. doi:10.1037/0033-2909.113.2.305

Howe, M. L., & Courage, M. L. (1997). The emergence and early development of autobiographical memory. *Psychological Review*, 104, 499–523. doi:10.1037/0033-295X.104.3.499

Jack, F., & Hayne, H. (2010). Childhood amnesia: Empirical evidence for a two-stage phenomenon. *Memory (Hove, England)*, 18, 831–844. doi:10.1080/09658211.2010.510476

Jeličić, H., Phelps, E., & Lerner, R. M. (2009). Use of missing data methods in longitudinal studies: The persistence of bad practices in developmental psychology. *Developmental Psychology*, 45, 1195–1199. doi:10.1037/a0015665

Kaiser, H. F. (1960). The application of electronic computers to factor analysis. *Educational and Psychological Measurement*, 20, 141–151. doi:10.1177/001316446002000116

Larkina, M., & Bauer, P. J. (2010). The role of maternal verbal, affective, and behavioral support in preschool children's independent and collaborative autobiographical memory reports. *Cognitive Development*, 25, 309–324. doi:10.1016/j.cogdev.2010.08.008

Larkina, M., & Bauer, P. J. (2012). "Family stories" and their implications for preschoolers' memories of personal events. *Journal of Cognition and Development*, 13, 473–504. doi:10.1080/15248372.2011.591295

Larkina, M., Güler, O. E., Kleinknecht, E., & Bauer, P. J. (2008). Maternal provision of structure in a deliberate memory task in relation to their preschool children's recall. *Journal of Experimental Child Psychology*, 100, 235–251. (Ms. ID# NIHMS65165). doi:10.1016/j.jecp.2008.03.002

Larkina, M., Merrill, N. A., & Bauer, P. J. (2016). Developmental changes in consistency of autobiographical memories: Adolescents' and young adults' repeated recall of recent and distance events. *Memory (Hove, England)*, 25, 1036–1051. Advance online publication. doi:10.1080/09658211.2016.1253750

Miles, C. (1895). A study of individual psychology. *The American Journal of Psychology*, 6, 534–558. doi:10.2307/1411191

Morris, G., Baker-Ward, L., & Bauer, P. J. (2010). What remains of that day: The survival of children's autobiographical memories across time. *Applied Cognitive Psychology*, 24, 527–544.

Newcombe, N. S., Lloyd, M. E., & Balcomb, F. (2012). Contextualizing the development of recollection: Episodic memory and binding in young children. In S. Ghetti & P. J. Bauer (Eds.), *Origins and development of recollection: Perspectives from psychology and neuroscience* (pp. 73–100). Oxford: Oxford University Press. doi:10.1093/acprof:oso/9780195340792.003.0004

Perner, J., & Ruffman, T. (1995). Episodic memory and autonoetic conciousness: Developmental evidence and a theory of childhood amnesia. *Journal of Experimental Child Psychology*, 59, 516–548. doi:10.1006/jecp.1995.1024

Peterson, C., Sales, J. M., Rees, M., & Fivush, R. (2007). Parent–child talk and children' memory for stressful events. *Applied Cognitive Psychology*, 21, 1057–1075. doi:10.1002/acp.1314

Pillemer, D. B., & White, S. H. (1989). Childhood events recalled by children and adults. In H. W. Reese (Ed.), *Advances in child development and behavior* (Vol. 21, pp. 297–340). Orlando, FL: Academic Press.

Reese, E. (2014). Taking the long way: Longitudinal approaches to autobiographical memory development. In P. J. Bauer & R. Fivush (Eds.), *The Wiley-Blackwell handbook on the development of children's memory* (pp. 972–995). West Sussex: Wiley-Blackwell.

Reese, E., Haden, C. A., Baker-Ward, L., Bauer, P. J., Fivush, R., & Ornstein, P. A. (2011). Coherence of personal narratives across the lifespan: A multidimensional model and coding method. *Journal of Cognition and Development*, 12, 424–462. doi:10.1080/15248372.2011.587854

Reese, E., Haden, C. A., & Fivush, R. (1993). Mother-child conversations about the past: Relationships of style and memory over time. *Cognitive Development*, 8, 403–430. doi:10.1016/S0885-2014(05)80002-4

Reese, E., Jack, F., & White, N. (2010). Origins of adolescents' autobiographical memories. *Cognitive Development*, 25, 352–367. doi:10.1016/j.cogdev.2010.08.006

Riggins, T. (2014). Longitudinal investigation of source memory reveals different developmental trajectories for item memory and binding. *Developmental Psychology*, 50, 449–459. doi:10.1037/a0033622

Roebers, C. (2014). Children's deliberate memory development: The contribution of strategies and metacognitive processes. In P. J. Bauer & R. Fivush (Eds.), *The Wiley-Blackwell handbook on the development of children's memory* (pp. 865–894). West Sussex: Wiley-Blackwell.

Roenker, D. L., Thompson, C. P., & Brown, S. C. (1971). Comparison of measures for the estimation of clustering in free recall. *Psychological Bulletin*, 76, 45–48. doi:10.1037/h0031355

Suddendorf, T., Nielsen, M., & von Gehlen, R. (2011). Children's capacity to remember a novel problem and to secure its future solution. *Developmental Science*, 14, 26–33. doi:10.1111/j.1467-7687.2010.00950.x

Tippey, K., & Longnecker, M. (2016). *An Ad Hoc method for computing pseudo-effect size for mixed models*. Proceedings of 2016 south central SAS users group conference. Retrieved from http://www.scsug.org/proceedings/2016-papers/

Tulving, E. (2005). Episodic memory and autonoesis: Uniquely human? In H. S. Terrace & J. Metcalfe (Eds.), *The missing link in cognition* (pp. 3–56). Oxford: Oxford University Press.

Wang, Q. (2007). "Remember when you got the big, big bulldozer?" Mother-child reminiscing over time and across cultures. *Social Cognition*, 25, 455–471. doi:10.1521/soco.2007.25.4.455

Wheeler, M. A. (2000). Episodic memory and autonoetic awareness. In E. Tulving & F. I. M. Craik (Eds.), *The Oxford handbook of memory* (pp. 597–608). New York, NY: Oxford University Press.

Woodcock, R. W., McGrew, K. S., & Mather, N. (2001). *Woodcock–Johnson-III test of cognitive abilities*. Itasca, IL: Riverside.

Origins of adolescents' earliest memories

Elaine Reese and Sarah-Jane Robertson

ABSTRACT
This prospective longitudinal study traced changes and individual differences in childhood amnesia over adolescence. A sample of 58 adolescents were followed from age 1-1/2 to age 16 years across 8 timepoints. At ages 12 ($n = 46$) and 16 ($n = 51$), adolescents completed an early memory interview. Early childhood measures included children's self-awareness, attachment security, nonverbal memory, verbal memory, language, theory of mind, narrative, and the early reminiscing environment (mothers' elaborative reminiscing). Adolescents continued to forget their earliest memories over adolescence, such that the age of first memory increased from 40 to 52 months from ages 12 to 16. The sole unique contributor to individual differences in age of earliest memory at both 12 and 16 years was mothers' elaborative reminiscing, with adolescents recalling earlier memories if their mothers had reminisced more elaboratively with them during early childhood. At age 16, the role of maternal reminiscing was moderated by self-awareness at age 1-1/2. Mothers' elaborative reminiscing mattered for the age of adolescents' earliest memories only for children who showed lower levels of self-awareness as toddlers. This pattern suggests a buffering effect for the role of maternal reminiscing in children's earliest memories, and supports integrated theories of childhood amnesia.

Why can't we recall our earliest experiences? Freud (1901/1960) was one of the first to note the phenomenon of childhood amnesia, which is adults' inability to remember personally experienced events from early childhood. Freud (p. 46) opined that "we take the fact of infantile amnesia –the loss, that is of the memories of the first years of our life – much too easily; and we fail to look upon it as a strange riddle." The phenomenon is still apparent in contemporary society, despite the massive technological changes over the past century in documenting early childhood experiences through photos and videos. Adults cannot recall any experiences before ages 3 to 4 years, on average, and can recall only isolated events from the next several years of childhood (e.g., Bauer & Larkina, 2014a; Peterson, 2002; Rubin, 1982, 2000; but see MacDonald, Uesiliana, & Hayne, 2000; Wang, 2006, for cultural differences in earliest memories; for reviews see Bauer, 2007; Hayne, Imuta, & Scarf, 2015; Reese, 2009; Wang, 2013).

Critically, childhood amnesia begins in childhood. Prospective longitudinal studies reveal the offset of childhood amnesia continues to move forward throughout early childhood and into adolescence, with the age of earliest memory becoming progressively later until stabilising in adolescence (Bauer & Larkina, 2014b; Cleveland & Reese, 2008; Peterson, Grant, & Boland, 2005; Tustin & Hayne, 2010; Wang & Peterson, 2014, 2016). The main aim of the present study is to address existing theories of childhood amnesia through the longest running prospective study to date of earliest memories in a sample of children followed from age 1-1/2 to 16 years of age.

Theories of childhood amnesia

The main theories of childhood amnesia can be grouped into several types (see Reese, 2002a, 2002b, 2009 for reviews; cf. Bauer, 2015 for a different typology). All of these theories focus primarily on memories of personally experienced events that can be recalled verbally (see Pillemer & White, 1989). The first type of theory posits a single critical influence that enables autobiographical (self-relevant) memories in early childhood. Two prominent theories of this type are Howe and Courage's (1993, 1997) self-recognition theory of autobiographical memory, and Perner and colleagues' (Perner, 2000, 2001; Perner & Ruffman, 1995) autonoetic theory of autobiographical memory. For instance, Howe and Courage (1993, 1997) proposed that the advent of self-awareness in the second year of life was the critical prerequisite for the onset of autobiographical memory; with self-awareness, they argued, children have a self-concept upon which to attach memories such that they can become autobiographical. After achieving that milestone, individual differences in elaboration of the self-concept would be associated with the rate of acquisition of autobiographical memories. Perner and colleagues (Perner, 2000; Perner & Ruffman, 1995) proposed a much later age of onset, between ages 4 and 6 years, for true autobiographical memory – which they argued must entail autonoesis or a sense of personal recollection – and a different prerequisite: the advent of meta-representation and specifically the knowledge that autobiographical memory can result only from direct experience. Neural explanations of childhood amnesia emphasise development of the hippocampus and cortex during early childhood as the primary factor enabling long-term retention of event memories in human and non-human species. For instance, Josselyn and Frankland (2012) proposed that rapid neurogenesis in the dentate gyrus of the hippocampus in early childhood paradoxically disrupts already formed early memories, thus leading to forgetting. In non-human species, as neurogenesis in the dentate gyrus slows, memories are retained for longer periods (Akers et al., 2014). In their account of the onset of autobiographical memory, Olson and Newcombe (2014) focused instead on the advent in the first two years of life of binding processes linking the various features of events and leading to more durable memories. Finally, other critical-influence theories proposed that lack of language skill is the main delimiting factor in preventing early childhood events from being encoded in verbal form, and later from being retrieved and reported verbally (Neisser, 1962; Simcock & Hayne, 2002; but see Jack, Simcock, & Hayne, 2012).

In contrast to these critical-influence theories, other theories propose a host of factors over early childhood that contribute to the offset of childhood amnesia and the onset of autobiographical memory. These integrated theories posit a complex interplay among neural, cognitive, linguistic, and social factors that together leads to the gradual emergence of more durable memories in childhood (e.g., Bauer, 2007; Fivush & Nelson, 2004; Nelson & Fivush, 2004). In these theories, multiple influences come online at different ages to strengthen children's autobiographical memories and to protect against forgetting. The social environment of reminiscing is prominent in these theories, and in particular the level of detail (elaboration) with which parents discuss events with their children as they are occurring or shortly afterwards (see Fivush, Haden, & Reese, 2006; Ornstein, Haden, & Hedrick, 2004; Reese, 2018). In a novel twist, Bauer (2015) proposed a complementary set of processes to account for the enigma of childhood amnesia, incorporating interactions between the factors that work to enable young children to form and retain memories in the long-term and the factors that protect children and adolescents from forgetting those early memories once formed.

A final set of contemporary theories that is particularly relevant for the present paper focuses on the processes of selecting and dating early childhood memories. In terms of selecting memories to report, Tustin and Hayne (2010) argued that individuals may have different thresholds for what counts as a memory, thus affecting reporting of early memories, and that these thresholds may vary as a function of gender and culture. In terms of dating processes, Wang, Peterson, and colleagues (Wang & Peterson, 2014, 2016; Wang, Peterson, & Hou, 2010) noted that dating errors could affect the age of earliest memories. They discovered that children tended to "telescope" their early memories over time by dating them to an older age – closer to their current age – than their earlier estimates of the dates of the events. Their age estimates were later than their parents' age estimates of the same events, especially for events that parents dated as occurring prior to the time the child was 48 months old.

Finally, the first author (Reese, 2009, 2018) proposed an emergent remembering theory of childhood amnesia – developed in concert with results from a prospective study of autobiographical memory that began in the late 1990s – in which the primary factors in determining the age of earliest memory are the child's early reminiscing environment (which varies by culture and as a function of the child's attachment security with the primary caregiver), the child's early self-awareness, and their language development (cf. Reese, 1999, 2002a, 2002b; Reese, Jack, & White, 2010). Each of these factors is proposed to interact in complex ways with each other and with features of the event to jump-start autobiographical memory and to end childhood amnesia. In this theory, the advent of autobiographical memory is probabilistic and additive: possession of advanced forms of any one of these factors in early childhood will increase the likelihood that early memories will survive into adolescence and adulthood, and possessing multiple factors should result in an eventual store of earlier memories.

The evidence

The complexity of factors relating to the onset of autobiographical memory is now apparent across several prospective longitudinal studies from different countries and cultures (e.g., Bauer & Larkina, 2014b; Haden, Ornstein, Rudek, & Cameron, 2009; Jack, MacDonald, Reese, & Hayne, 2009; Peterson, Hallett, & Compton-Gillingham, 2017; Peterson, Warren, & Short, 2011; Reese, Jack, et al., 2010; Wang, 2007, 2008; Wang, Hutt, Kulkofsky, McDermott, & Wei, 2006; Welch-Ross, 1995). When multiple factors are measured, the extant evidence always points to a complex mix of those factors in accounting for individual differences in autobiographical memory, with mothers' elaborative reminiscing a prominent feature. For instance, Reese (2002a) showed that self-recognition at age 1-1/2 years was important for the volume of children's later autobiographical memory at 2-1/2 and 3-1/2 years, but only in concert with their mothers' elaborative reminiscing style and their language development. Mothers become more elaborative in their reminiscing with children who achieved self-recognition earlier in development, and it was this elaborative reminiscing style that was the best predictor of children's autobiographical memory. Self-recognition itself was moderated by children's language skill, in that self-recognition only mattered for later autobiographical memory for children with less advanced language levels. In an experimental extension with a different sample of families, when mothers were coached in elaborative reminiscing when their children were toddlers, the effect on the volume of accurate autobiographical memories children produced two years later, at age 3-1/2, was stronger if children had achieved self-recognition milestones prior to the coaching period (Reese & Newcombe, 2007). Children's self-recognition itself is supported by developing connections between the prefrontal and other brain structures and is linked to children's symbolic capacity (Herschkowitz, 2000; see Prebble, Addis, & Tippett, 2013). Thus, children with advanced symbolic capacity may be better able to utilise their mothers' enriched narratives about the event to strengthen their own memories and to later recall more details (see Ornstein et al., 2004). Indeed, children's language skill is the other main factor identified across studies in the onset of autobiographical memory, especially given that autobiographical memory is almost always tested verbally (see Hayne, Scarf, & Imuta, 2015; Jack et al., 2012; Morris & Baker-Ward, 2007; Simcock & Hayne, 2002, 2003). For instance, in Jack et al. (2012), the nine 8- to 10-year-old children who recalled a novel event (the Magic Shrinking Machine) from early childhood after a 6-year delay did not differ from children who later forgot the event in their earlier nonverbal recall of the event or in their language skills, but they did differ in how often they had verbally brought up the event in conversation with their mothers soon after it had occurred. In contrast, individual differences in nonverbal memory skills and theory of mind do not appear to act as major contributors or prerequisites for autobiographical memory during childhood or early adolescence (see Reese, 2009 for a review; Reese, Jack, et al., 2010), although individual differences in theory of mind may contribute to the quality of the memories retained after the offset (in richness and in recollective detail) (see Reese & Cleveland, 2006; Welch-Ross, 1997).

Features of the event itself and its representation are also critical in the survival of individual memories. For instance, young children (4- to 8-years old at encoding) were more likely to retain memories of novel events after one year when they were able to report on the event in coherent narrative form soon after its occurrence (Morris, Baker-Ward, & Bauer, 2010). For 4- to 13-year-olds reporting their earliest memories, Peterson, Morris, Baker-Ward, and Flynn (2014) found that the coherence of the memory narrative at the first timepoint was the best predictor of children recalling that memory two years later. Representing an event through narrative in the consolidation phase appears to promote the durability of the memory. Children's ability to create a coherent narrative about an event is itself a product of their early reminiscing environment (e.g., Cleveland, Reese, & Grolnick, 2007; Reese & Newcombe, 2007), but is also influenced by the nature of the event itself. Some events with an underlying high point or goal-directed structure lend themselves to more coherent accounts than others, and some events are simply more distinctive than others (see Reese et al., 2011). In the present study, we did not have a measure of the coherence of children's earliest memories from early childhood, but we did include a measure of their narrative skill in retelling a fictional story as a predictor of the age of their earliest memories.

Highly relevant for the present study, only one other study to our knowledge has followed children's earliest memories prospectively from childhood to adolescence. Peterson and colleagues tracked the earliest memories of a sample of 140 children aged 4 to 13 years at outset across a 2-year delay (Peterson et al., 2011) and an 8-year delay ($n = 37$; Peterson et al., 2017). The first strong pattern was for children's earliest memories to grow later over time (from 32 to 39 months on average after a 2-year delay). The second strong pattern was for younger children to nominate different earliest memories at later timepoints, indicating greater forgetting of their earliest memories compared to older children and adolescents. For instance, only 7% of the youngest children (age 4–5 years at outset) nominated the same earliest memory 2 years later, compared to 39% of the adolescents (age 12–13 years at outset) over the same delay. After 8 years, 46% of the youngest children (age 4–5 years at outset) could not recall their previous earliest memory even after verbal cueing, whereas only 17% of the older children (age 8–9 years at outset) completely forgot their earliest memory over the same delay. (Note that the adolescents aged 12–13 years from the original sample were not followed up at the 8-year delay). Older adolescent samples with much shorter delays provide further evidence of the instability of earliest memories. For instance, Jack and Hayne (2010) found that 17% of the 19-year-olds in their sample provided a different earliest memory over a 1-week delay, and 42% of a sample of high-school students provided a different earliest memory over a 3-month delay (Kihlstrom & Harackiewicz, 1982).

This pattern of instability in earliest memories for young children and adolescents stands in contrast to a study following adults' earliest memories over several years. Adults showed strong consistency in their earliest memories across a 4-year period, with 82% of adults nominating the same earliest memory at each of four timepoints (Bauer, Tasdemir-Ozdes, & Larkina, 2014).

A second robust finding across this small body of research on consistency of earliest memories across time is that children who did recall the same events over time often dated the same event to an older age at the second timepoint (telescoping), particularly for events that occurred prior to 48 months (Wang & Peterson, 2014, 2016). In contrast, the age of earliest memory appears to be more reliable across time for older adolescents (Kihlstrom & Harackiewicz, 1982) and adults (Bauer et al., 2014).

The present study

The present study evaluated contemporary theories of childhood amnesia by analysing the continued progression of childhood amnesia in a sample of 16-year-olds we have followed since age 1-1/2 years. In addition to measures of earliest memories at ages 12 and 16, the early childhood phase of the study (from 1-1/2 to 5-1/2 years) contained measures of self-awareness, attachment security, nonverbal memory, verbal memory, language, theory of mind, narrative, and the reminiscing environment (mothers' elaborative reminiscing) (see Reese, Jack, et al., 2010 for a description up to the age 12 timepoint). Research questions were: 1) Did the age of earliest memory stabilise between 12 and 16 years, or did the age of earliest memory continue to shift over adolescence?; 2) What were the main early childhood contributors to the age of earliest memories at 12 and 16 years? In Reese, Jack, et al. (2010), we explored in this same sample the contributors in early childhood to early memories and life narratives at age 12, but the present analysis is the first to explore contributors to adolescents' earliest memories at ages 12 and 16.

Method

Participants

With their mothers, the participants in this study have been part of a longitudinal study of autobiographical memory from the age of 1-1/2 years. Mother–child dyads were recruited in 1996 from a database compiled from birth records in a small city in New Zealand. At the start of the study, mothers were all primary caregivers for the children. Timepoints on the study occurred at 19, 25, 32, 40, 51, and 65 months, and again at ages 12 and 16 years. A total of 58 dyads participated in the early childhood timepoints from 19 to 40 months. Of these original 58 dyads, 52 participated at 51 months, 50 at 65 months, and 46 at age 12. At age 16, 51 of the original 58 child participants took part as adolescents ($M = 16.49$, $SD = 0.25$; 26 males). All early childhood measures were collected in the children's homes, and the adolescent timepoints in a family study lab at the university (although a researcher visited four adolescents at home at age 12 and six adolescents at home at age 16 because their families had moved to a different city or country). Of the original 58 children, 52 were of New Zealand European descent, five had one or both parents of New Zealand Māori descent, and one child had one parent of Chinese descent. Children received small gifts at each early childhood timepoint, and adolescents received vouchers to local shops to recognise their contribution.

Previous publications from this sample describe in depth the measures collected in early childhood (e.g., Cleveland & Reese, 2005; Farrant & Reese, 2000; Harley & Reese, 1999; Newcombe & Reese, 2004; Reese & Cleveland, 2006) and early adolescence (Reese, Jack, et al., 2010). In the following, we refer to these earlier published measures but focus primarily on the adolescent timepoints, particularly at age 16.

Adolescent memory interview

At the start of the interview at ages 12 and 16, a female researcher asked the adolescents about their life stories using the Emerging Life Story Interview (Reese, Yan, Jack, & Hayne, 2010; see Jack et al., 2009; Reese, Jack, et al., 2010 for more details). Then the researcher asked the adolescent to provide and date their very earliest memory using the following prompt: *First, I'd like you to think back to your early childhood, as far back as you can go, and try to identify your very earliest memory. I want to know about the very first thing in your life that you remember doing or that you remember happening; your earliest memory of a specific moment or event in your life story. There will be some things from when you were very young that you'll know about because you've seen photos or because you've been told about what happened, but I want to know what's the very earliest thing in your life that you actually have your <u>own memory</u> of.* After the adolescent had freely recalled as much as possible about the earliest memory, the researcher asked specific questions about people, places, and feelings, followed by the dating questions: How old were you when [the event] happened? and "How do you know you were that old?" If the adolescent gave an age range (e.g., 3 or 4 years old), the researcher asked the adolescent to try to narrow the estimate to one year if possible. The researcher then prompted the adolescent for their next earliest memory and for previously recalled memories from earlier timepoints on the study. At age 16, for instance, participants were then asked to recall and date their two earliest memories that they had previously recalled at the age 12 timepoint, if different to the two earliest memories they had just supplied. The following analyses focus primarily on the adolescents' responses to the dating question for the earliest memory they spontaneously supplied at each age (12 and 16 years). We note below any exceptions to this decision. The ages of the earliest memories adolescents reported were scored using Jack and Hayne's (2010) procedure, in which ages were converted to months. For instance, when an adolescent dated a memory to "3 years old", the memory was dated to 42 months as midway between 3 and 4 years. If an adolescent could not narrow down to a specific age the midpoint of that range was the final score (e.g., for the range of 3–4 years, the midpoint was scored as 48 months).

At the age 12 timepoint, mothers attended the lab session and completed demographic questionnaires while a researcher conducted the life story interview with the adolescent in a separate room. Then the adolescent completed questionnaires on a computer while the researcher listened to the audiofile of the earliest memories and transcribed each utterance and the adolescent's age estimates onto a scoresheet for mothers to check.

Mothers then checked the adolescents' age estimates and content of all memories from the scoresheet (adapted from Jack & Hayne, 2010). We acknowledge that this procedure may lead to a tendency for mothers to confirm their children's age estimate unless it is extremely discrepant, and that the results may have been different if we had asked mothers for an independent age estimate. At age 16, mothers did not attend the lab session so we transcribed the earliest memory interview in full and posted the transcripts out afterward for checking using the same procedure (with the exception that seven adolescents indicated they didn't want their mothers to see the transcripts). Only 25 of the remaining 44 mothers (57%) checked and returned the transcripts for this timepoint.

Early childhood phase

The early childhood measures for this sample are described in detail in earlier publications. Table 1 provides an overview of the measures included in the present analyses, which tap children's self-awareness (see Harley & Reese, 1999; Reese, Jack, et al., 2010), attachment security (see Newcombe & Reese, 2004), nonverbal memory (see Harley & Reese, 1999), verbal memory (see Cleveland & Reese, 2005, 2008; Farrant & Reese, 2000; Harley & Reese, 1999), vocabulary (see Farrant & Reese, 2000), theory of mind (see Reese & Cleveland, 2006), narrative (see Suggate, Schaughency, McAnally, & Reese, 2018), and their mothers' elaborative reminiscing (see Cleveland & Reese, 2005; Farrant & Reese, 2000). Table 2 shows the descriptive statistics for the final scores for early childhood measures included in analyses.

Results

The two main research questions were: 1) Did adolescents' age of earliest memory change over time?; and 2) What were the predictors of the age of earliest memory across adolescence? Analyses were performed with bootstrapping when noted; below we report both the significance levels and the confidence intervals for those analyses. We interpret as significant all results that either reached traditional levels of significance ($p < .05$) or for which the 95% confidence interval did not include zero (Field, 2013), noted in bold-faced type on tables.

Preliminary analyses

At the age 12 timepoint, three participants' earliest memories were not specific, so their second earliest memories were used in analyses instead. Mothers confirmed their adolescents' age estimates for 31 out of the 46 memories (67%). Of the 15 disagreements, 10 were within one year (from 5 years for adolescent to 6th birthday for mother; 5 years to 4 years; two from 1 year to 2 years; 3 years to 4 years; 3 years to 2.5 years; 1.5 years to 11 months; 1.5 years to 1.75 years; 1.5 years to 1 year; and 4–5 months to 8 months 3 weeks). The remaining five disagreements were from 5 years for adolescent to 29 months for mother; 4 years to 2.75 years, 4 years to 2.5 years, 4 years to 1.5 years, and 1 year to 3 years. At the age 16 timepoint, five participants' earliest memories were not specific. Three of those participants gave a specific second earliest memory which was used in analyses; however, the remaining two participants' second earliest memories were also not specific, so they were excluded from analyses. For the 24 adolescents at age 16 who had at least one specific memory and whose mothers checked their ages of earliest memories, 20 of the mothers (83%) judged the adolescents' ages to be accurate. Of the 4 disagreements, three were within one year (from 71 months for adolescent to 73 months for mother; 4 to 3 years; and 3 to 4 years). One adolescent claimed an event had occurred at 4 years but the mother said it was instead at 18 months. These rates of agreement between mothers and adolescents at both ages are in line with rates of agreement for age of

Table 1. Overview and source of early childhood measures (see Reese, Jack, et al., 2010).

Measure	Timepoint (months)	Source
Self-awareness	19	Lewis and Brooks-Gunn (1979)
• Mirror self-recognition task		
• Photo self-recognition task		
Attachment security	19	Waters (1987)
• Attachment q-set (maternal sort)		
Nonverbal memory	25	Bauer and Fivush (1992)
• Deferred imitation (total actions)		
Verbal memory	25, 32, 40, 51, 65	Fivush, Haden, and Adam (1995)
• Researcher-child interview		
Vocabulary	32, 40, 51, 65	
• Peabody Picture Vocabulary Test-III (Forms A, B)		Dunn & Dunn (1997)
• Expressive Vocabulary Test		Williams (1997)
Theory of mind	51	Welch-Ross (1997)
• False belief (mistaken location; unexpected contents; appearance-reality tasks)		
• Origins of knowledge (see-know; see-tell; informative view tasks)		
Narrative	51	Reese (1995)
• Fictional story retell (memory units)		
• Fictional story quality (narrative devices)		
Maternal elaborative reminiscing	19, 25, 32,	Fivush and Fromhoff (1988)
• Mother-child reminiscing about shared past events	40, 51, 65	Reese, Haden, and Fivush (1993), Haden (1998)

Table 2. Descriptive statistics for early childhood variables.

Measure	Range	M (SD)	Missing scores (%)
Self-awareness			
Self-recognition (mirror, 19 months)	0–1	0.48 (0.50)	0
Self-recognition (photo, 19 months)	0–1	0.49 (0.50)	1 (1.7%)
Attachment security (q-set, 19 months)	−0.11–0.67	0.38 (0.19)	0
Nonverbal memory (total actions, 25 months)	0–9	4.77 (2.44)	5 (8.6%)
Verbal memory (memory units per event)			
25 months	0–8.50	1.35 (1.91)	0
32 months	0–24.50	3.11 (4.50)	0
40 months	0–12.00	1.96 (2.80)	0
51 months	0–22.67	4.20 (3.92)	7 (12.1%)
65 months	0–28.67	6.69 (5.67)	8 (13.8%)
Vocabulary			
32–40 months (receptive standard score)	74–119	98.79 (11.10)	0
32–40 months (expressive standard score)	74–122	100.92 (11.80)	0
51–65 months (receptive standard score)	78–124	104.74 (10.85)	10 (17.2%)
51–65 months (expressive standard score)	80–126	107.41 (11.26)	12 (20.7%)
Theory of mind (51 months)			
False belief (correct trials)	0–6	2.44 (2.11)	6 (10.3%)
Origins of knowledge (correct trials)	2–12	7.08 (2.53)	6 (10.3%)
Narrative (51 months)			
Fictional story memory (# units)	0–26	6.25 (6.01)	6 (10.3%)
Fictional story quality (# devices)	0–9	1.52 (2.08)	6 (10.3%)
Maternal reminiscing (open-ended elaborative questions per event)			
19 months	0–8.5	1.96 (1.70)	0
25 months	0.67–8.67	3.69 (2.18)	0
32 months	0–11.0	4.90 (2.26)	0
40 months	1–12.0	4.30 (2.32)	0
51 months	1.33–15.67	4.99 (2.90)	6 (10.3%)
65 months	1.33–13.33	5.19 (2.48)	8 (13.8%)

earliest memories between mothers and offspring in previous research (e.g., 68% of the 5- to 20-year-olds in Tustin & Hayne, 2010; 85% of the university students in Usher & Neisser, 1993).

We tested for differences between adolescents' and mothers' age estimates at each timepoint using paired t-tests (see Figure 1). Adolescents' and mothers' age estimates did not differ significantly at age 12 ($t(45) = 1.21$, $p = .23$, 95% CI [−0.91, 4.88]) or at age 16 ($t(23) = 1.11$, $p = .28$, 95% CI [−1.00, 5.42]). Adolescents' and mothers' age estimates were also strongly correlated at both age 12 ($r = .85$, $p < .001$) and age 16 ($r = .87$, $p < .001$). Therefore, the following analyses focus on adolescents' age estimates to maintain the sample size.

Age of earliest memories at 12 and 16 years

The first research question addressed changes in the adolescents' age of earliest memories from 12 to 16 years. This analysis was conducted only on those adolescents who reported specific earliest memories at both timepoints at ages 12 and 16 ($n = 40$). A paired t-test showed that adolescents' earliest memories in this sample became significantly later from age 12 ($M = 40$ months) to age

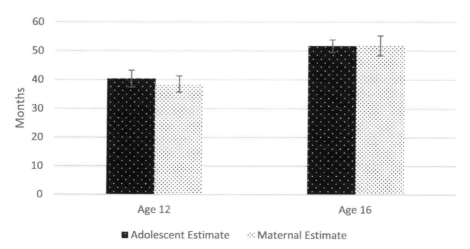

Figure 1. Age of adolescents' earliest memories.

16 ($M = 52$ months) ($t(39) = -3.26$, $p = .002$, 95% CI [−17.82, −4.62]).[1] According to unpaired t-tests, there were no significant effects of gender at age 12 or 16 ($ps > .48$). Nor was there a significant correlation in the age of earliest memory from 12 to 16 years ($r = .24$, $p = .08$, 95% CI [−0.004, 0.54]). Thus, adolescents' earliest memories were still shifting to older ages over this 4-year period, and individual differences in ages of earliest memories were not yet stable.

To address theories of forgetting and telescoping of earliest memories (e.g., Wang et al., 2010), the next analysis focused on how many of the earliest memories were the same at ages 12 and 16 for this subset of the sample. Only eight adolescents (20%) recalled the same earliest memory at ages 12 and 16; however, an additional three adolescents (7.5%) recalled an earliest memory at age 16 that was the same as their second earliest memory at age 12. The remaining 29 adolescents (72.5%) recalled a different earliest memory at age 16 to either of their age 12 earliest memories. For the 11 adolescents who recalled one of the same earliest memories at ages 12 and 16, all of their age estimates could be compared to their age estimates for the same memory at age 12. Six dated the memory back to exactly the same age at both timepoints (two each to 18 months, 42 months, and 54 months); three dated the memory at age 16 as occurring earlier than they had estimated at age 12 (one from 66 to 60 months; one from 66 to 54 months; and one from 54 to 42 months), and two dated the memory at age 16 as occurring later than they had estimated at age 12 (one from 48 to 69 months, and one from 54 to 78 months). Next, because Wang and Peterson (2014, 2016) found that children's telescoping was particularly prevalent for events that mothers had dated as prior to 48 months, we computed how many of these twice-recalled earliest memories were for events that had occurred before 48 months according to mothers. Maternal estimates were available for all 11 memories, of which 5 were for events that mothers stated had occurred prior to 48 months. For only one of these 5 events did an adolescent date to a later age over time (the earliest memory above from 54 to 78 months, which the mother had instead estimated at 30 months). Thus, the majority of adolescents recalled different earliest memories across this 4-year period, and for those few adolescents who did recall the same earliest memory over time, there was no consistent evidence of telescoping the date to a later age.

Contributors to earliest memories at ages 12 and 16

Table 2 contains the descriptive information for the predictor variables from early childhood. Although there was some missing data from the early childhood variables due to participants missing individual tasks or dropping out, the overall rate was low (6.06% missing across all early childhood variables). Analyses were thus conducted on available data without imputation of the missing scores (see Graham, 2009). The second research question regards the unique contributors to the age of earliest memories in adolescence, both at ages 12 and 16. To address this question, we first performed correlational analyses between the early childhood variables and the age of earliest memory at the age 12 and 16 timepoints. Notably, adolescents' age of earliest memories did not correlate significantly with demographic variables such as maternal education or paternal occupation (at age 12, $rs = -.14$ and $-.10$, n.s.; at age 16, $rs = .14$ and $.18$, n.s.). Table 3 contains the correlations between the early childhood variables and adolescents' earliest memories at ages 12 and 16. We then included all significant correlates at each age in a separate regression analysis with bootstrapping. For the verbal memory tasks that were repeated across timepoints, when the same assessment task from different early childhood timepoints both correlated significantly with the adolescents' earliest memories, we selected only the most strongly correlated timepoint for the regression model to avoid multicollinearity (i.e., at age 16, children's verbal memory from 51–65 months over 25–40 months). Because the repeated vocabulary assessments were strongly intercorrelated (rs ranged from .74 to .81, $ps < .001$), we selected the task from 32 to 40 months that was most strongly correlated with the earliest memory variable because that composite had complete data (i.e., expressive vocabulary at 32–40 months for predicting age 12 earliest memories and receptive vocabulary at 32–40 months for predicting age 16 earliest memories).

Table 3. Correlations between early childhood variables and adolescents' earliest memories.

Early childhood variables	Timepoint	Age 12 earliest memory, adolescent estimate	Age 16 earliest memory, adolescent estimate
Mirror self-recognition	19 months	−.10	−.17
Photo self-recognition	19 months	−.24	−.06
Attachment security	19 months	.19	−.04
Nonverbal memory	25 months	−.06	−.34*
Verbal memory	25–40 months	−.15	−.36*
	51–65 months	−.26	−.47**
Receptive vocabulary	32–40 months	−.22	−.43**
Expressive vocabulary	32–40 months	−.34*	−.41**
False belief	51 months	−.31*	−.38**
Origins of knowledge	51 months	−.28	−.18
Story memory	51 months	−.10	−.12
Story quality	51 months	−.31*	−.24
Maternal elaborative reminiscing	19–40 months	−.25	−.24
	51–65 months	−.38*	−.34*

*$p < .05$; **$p < .01$.

Table 4. Bootstrapped multiple linear regression analyses of early childhood variables predicting age 12 earliest memories.

Predictor variables	B (SE)	95% CI
Constant	75.56 (27.11)*	[23.20, 130.31]
Expressive vocabulary (32–40 months)	−0.18 (−0.31)	[−0.81, 0.40]
False belief (51 months)	−1.80 (1.60)	[−4.71, 1.62]
Story quality (51 months)	−1.69 (1.47)	[−4.20, 1.65]
Mothers' elaborative reminiscing (51–65 months)	−2.17 (1.31)+	[−5.17, −0.06]
R^2	.25	
F	3.26*	

+p < .10; *p < .05.

Table 5. Bootstrapped multiple linear regression analyses of early childhood variables predicting age 16 earliest memories.

Predictor variables	B (SE)	95% CI
Constant	98.61 (22.36)**	[53.89, 145.94]
Nonverbal memory (25 months)	−0.93 (1.18)	[−3.37, 1.24]
Receptive language (32–40 months)	−0.27 (0.22)	[−0.71, 0.16]
Theory of mind (false belief 51 months)	−1.21 (1.03)	[−3.27, 0.86]
Verbal memory (51–65 months)	−1.01 (0.71)	[−2.39, 0.46]
Mothers' elaborative reminiscing (51–65 months)	−1.60 (0.79)*	[−3.22, −0.11]
R^2	.39	
F	4.31**	

*p < .05; **p < .01.

Integrated theories predict interactions between factors in producing autobiographical memory, and earlier analyses of this same sample in early childhood revealed interactions between self-awareness and language in autobiographical memory (Reese, 2000). Therefore, we tested for moderator effects using the PROCESS module for SPSS (Hayes, 2013).

Age 12 model of age of earliest memory

The predictor variables entered for adolescent estimates of age 12 earliest memory were children's expressive vocabulary (32–40 months), false belief (51 months), story quality (51 months), and mothers' elaborative reminiscing (51–65 months). Tolerance values were all > .65. The overall model was significant (see Table 4). The sole unique predictor of the age of earliest memory was mothers' elaborative reminiscing. Although this result did not reach traditional levels of significance (p < .10), the 95% confidence interval did not include zero. Thus, higher levels of maternal elaborative reminiscing in early childhood are uniquely associated with earlier memories. We tested for moderation of the role of maternal elaborative reminiscing by children's self-awareness and early language development, but neither moderator was significant (ps > .23).

Age 16 model of age of earliest memory

The predictor variables entered for adolescent estimates of Age 16 earliest memory were children's nonverbal memory (25 months), receptive vocabulary (32–40 months), false belief (51 months), verbal memory (51–65 months) and mothers' elaborative reminiscing (51–65 months). Tolerance values were all > 0.74. The overall model was significant (see Table 5). The sole unique predictor was mothers' elaborative reminiscing, with higher levels in early childhood associated with earlier memories. We tested for moderation of the role of mothers' elaborative reminiscing by self-awareness (photo recognition at 19 months), and the interaction term was significant, accounting for an additional 8% of the variance in the age of earliest memory ($F(1, 39) = 6.51$, p = .015. For children with lower levels of self-awareness at the outset of the study, there was a significant negative association between mothers' elaborative reminiscing and their age of earliest memories (b = −3.72, p = .001, 95% CI [−5.34, −2.09], indicating that for those children, more elaborative maternal reminiscing was associated with earlier memories. For children with higher levels of self-awareness at the start of the study, there was no significant association between mothers' elaborative reminiscing and the age of earliest memory (b = −.01, p = .99, 95% CI[−2.46, 2.44]. Children's language was not a significant moderator (p = .95).

Discussion

This study traced the age of earliest memory prospectively in a sample of children who have been followed from age 1-1/2 to 16 years. A main finding is that the age of earliest memory was still changing for these adolescents, becoming significantly later from age 12 to age 16, whether the age was estimated by adolescents or mothers. Most of the adolescents (73%) recalled a different earliest memory at age 16 than they had at age 12, even with our liberal rule of allowing either of their two earliest memories at age 12 to count as the "same" earliest memory at age 16. This finding extends earlier research showing that many adolescents (42%) did not nominate the same earliest memory even over a 3-month delay (Kihlstrom & Harackiewicz, 1982). The second main finding is that although a host of early childhood variables was associated with earlier memories at ages 12 and 16, only mothers' elaborative reminiscing emerged as a unique predictor of earlier memories at both ages. At age 16, that association was moderated by children's self-awareness, such that mothers' elaborative reminiscing was linked to earlier memories only for those children with lower levels of self-awareness at 19 months.

This is the first study to trace earliest memories for this long and with this wealth of early childhood contributors (but see Peterson et al., 2017; Wang & Peterson, 2016, for a study of earliest memories spanning 8 years). The pattern of findings supports multiple explanations for the demise of early memories. Most adolescents recalled different earliest memories at age 16 compared to age 12, which suggests either forgetting and/or retrieval difficulties of the memories they had been able to recall four years earlier. Although mothers' elaborative reminiscing was a unique predictor of earlier memories at both ages, it was moderated by self-awareness at age 16.

Replicated and new evidence about childhood amnesia

Our results fit with those of a different New Zealand sample in the literature (Tustin & Hayne, 2010) in that earliest memories of younger adolescents (around 29 months for 12- to 13-year-olds in Tustin & Hayne) were younger than the earliest memories of older adolescents (around 40 months for 18- to 20-year-olds in Tustin & Hayne). This replication is notable because the techniques for eliciting earliest memories differed across the two studies (a timeline method using family photos in Tustin and Hayne versus the standard oral interview), as did the design (cross-sectional in Tustin and Hayne versus longitudinal). Our method of asking mothers to check from transcripts the accuracy of the age that children provided for the memory was the same as in Tustin and Hayne, but when these estimates differed, they used mothers' instead of children's age estimates in analyses. We showed that the average age of earliest memory is similar whether adolescents or mothers are conducting the estimates. Our results also fit with one of the few other longitudinal studies of earliest memories in childhood and adolescence; Peterson et al. (2011) noted that over a 2-year gap, parent-corrected ages of children's earliest memories grew from 32 to 39 months in a sample of children initially aged from 4 years to 13 years. For both adolescent and maternal estimates in our sample, however, average estimates of earliest memories were later (3.25/3.33 years at age 12 and 4.33 years at age 16) compared to both Peterson et al. (2.67 years and 3.25 years) and Tustin and Hayne's cross-sectional sample (2.25 years at ages 12–13 and 3.40 years at ages 18–20). We believe that these later ages overall, albeit with similar growth over time, are due to our conservative method of relying only on self-nominated memories, and not on cued memories. Taken together with these other findings, it is clear that adolescents' earliest memories are still in flux, especially when compared to the robust consistency for adults' earliest memories over multiple timepoints (see Bauer et al., 2014).

Also consistent with most of the literature on earliest memories, the present study did not find gender differences in the age of earliest memories (e.g., Rubin, 2000; although cf. Tustin & Hayne, 2010). It is possible that gender differences will emerge in this sample when measuring the content of adolescents' earliest memories, for which most studies show a female advantage (e.g., MacDonald et al., 2000).

Theoretical implications

In terms of individual differences in the age of earliest memories, the theories that best fit the data at both ages are the integrated theories (Bauer, 2007; Fivush & Nelson, 2004; Nelson & Fivush, 2004; Reese, 2002a, 2002b, 2009, 2018). Children's nonverbal memory, verbal memory, language, narrative, and theory of mind were all associated with earlier memories in adolescence. Although these other predictors fell out once mothers' elaborative reminiscing was entered into the models, elaborative reminiscing itself was moderated by children's self-awareness for the age 16 earliest memories. This interaction at first blush appears to be similar to earlier findings from this same sample and another New Zealand sample that self-awareness and elaborative reminiscing interact to produce young children's autobiographical memory (Harley & Reese, 1999; Reese & Newcombe, 2007). Yet in those earlier findings, it was always the case that children with more *advanced* self-awareness benefited more from mothers' elaborative reminiscing, especially in shaping the volume and narrative detail of their autobiographical memories. These findings in early childhood led to the additive, probabilistic model proposed by Reese (2002a, 2002b, 2009, 2018). Yet these latest findings in adolescence do not fit the additive explanation. Instead, they fit best with a buffering model of autobiographical memory, in which adolescents develop earlier memories when they have *either* advanced self-awareness as young children, *or* a mother who is highly elaborative when reminiscing. In yet another longitudinal New Zealand sample that addressed only the role of mothers' elaborative reminiscing in young adolescents' age of earliest memories, it is apparent that maternal reminiscing cannot be the only factor, because some adolescents had very early memories yet did not have mothers who reminisced elaboratively (see the bottom left quadrant of Figure 1 in Jack et al., 2009, p. 501). Other factors must also be important for shaping the age of early memories, and our current findings add to the idea that self-awareness is a major force (see Howe & Courage, 1993, 1997).

With the present results focusing only on the age of the earliest memory, however, it is difficult to fully differentiate amongst the critical-influence and integrated theories. As Bauer (2007) noted, theories of childhood amnesia are analogous to the parable of the blind men describing an elephant – all of the contemporary explanations are partially correct. In future analyses of this dataset, we look forward to testing the nuances of the various theories when considering features of the events recalled, the content and volume of the recall, and the qualities of the memory narratives. We also look forward to charting changes in self-concept beyond early childhood that may be supported by early self-awareness, and that could in turn explain even more variance in adults' early memories.

Limitations and future directions

This analysis is constrained by our focus only on the age of earliest memories, and not the emotional content or narrative qualities of the memories or features of the events that are later remembered or forgotten (see Morris et al., 2010; Peterson et al., 2014). A future analysis of this dataset will assess these dimensions across the entire corpus of memories that children in this sample recalled from age 1-1/2 to a final timepoint at age 20 years.

The sample size was small, so the power to detect significant differences was limited; however, the bootstrapping procedures adopted in analyses increase the robustness of the findings (see Field, 2013). Moreover, the correlational design prevents any conclusions about causal factors in shaping the age of earliest memories. In a longitudinal experimental study of maternal reminiscing with a separate sample (Reese & Newcombe, 2007), we will be able to test the causal role of enhanced elaborative reminiscing in early childhood for adolescents' earliest memories.

Although adolescents' and mothers' estimates of the ages of the events did not differ overall, many of the events were ones that would be difficult even for mothers to date exactly. This limitation is true of most research on earliest memories, except for a few events that can be dated with certainty, such as the birth of a sibling (see Usher & Neisser, 1993).

Like all longitudinal research, this study is limited in the comprehensiveness and currency of the measures. One notable gap was the omission of children's emotion knowledge as a predictor of their autobiographical memory (see Wang, 2008; Wang et al., 2006); however, we hypothesise that this feature would be associated more strongly with the content and quality of the memories rather than with the age of the memories. Another gap in the design was for children's executive functioning, which predicts the specificity of their autobiographical memories in the preschool years (Nieto, Ros, Ricarte, & Latorre, 2017). Undoubtedly, future research will identify other unmeasured variables that could help account more fully for the age of adolescents' earliest memories than the 25–39% of the variance accounted for here. For instance, intriguing new evidence shows gene by environment interactions in young children's autobiographical memory, and specifically their recall of details of personal experiences (Tõugu, Vaht, Tulviste, Veidebaum, & Harro, 2016). Children with the COMT gene Val[158] Met polymorphism recalled more autobiographical details at age 4 if their mothers had achieved higher levels of education, but the moderating effect of maternal education had disappeared by the time these children were 6 years old.

In future analyses of this dataset, we will be able to establish if earliest memories have stabilised between 16 and 20. Ideally these results would eventually be replicated and extended with other samples and across cultures. Although longitudinal research of this sort is time-consuming and expensive, there is no substitute for establishing the very long-term contributors of adolescent accomplishments (see Reese, 2014a, 2014b).

Conclusions

In the longest-running longitudinal study to date of the course of childhood amnesia, adolescents continued to forget their very earliest memories from ages 12 to 16. In a partial answer to Freud's (1901/1960, p. 46) question – "But with what are these differences in retaining childhood memories connected?" – the best predictor of individual differences in the retention of earliest memories was mothers' elaborative reminiscing in early childhood, in concert with children's self-awareness. Childhood amnesia is a complex phenomenon, but we seem to be getting closer to mapping that complexity.

The practical importance of having earlier memories remains to be established. Many researchers (e.g., Bauer, 2015; Fivush, 2012; Habermas & Köber, 2014; Prebble et al., 2013; Reese, 1999) have proposed that possessing personal memories stretching farther back in time leads to a stronger sense of self-continuity that is vital for one's sense of personal identity. The value of this feat, however, may differ across cultures (see Wang, 2003, 2013).

Note

1. We also conducted a paired t-test on mothers' estimates over time for the 21 mothers who had checked the memories at both timepoints ($t(20) = -1.80$, $p = .09$, 95% CI [−**20.62**, −**.14**]). Although the difference was only marginally significant due to low power, the 95% CI did not cross zero, indicating that mothers also estimated a later age of adolescents' earliest memory at age 16 ($M = 51$ months) compared to 12 years ($M = 41$ months).

Acknowledgements

We thank the families who have participated in this longitudinal study, many of whom continue to offer us their time and their memories. Your memories are truly taonga (treasures). We are also extremely grateful to all of the students and researchers who have contributed to this project along the way, with special thanks to Helena McAnally, Bridget Forsyth, and Naomi White for their work on the adolescent datapoints, and to Harlene Hayne and Jacqueline Clearwater for their assistance in recruiting the initial sample. The Marsden Fund of the Royal Society of New Zealand funded the early childhood phase of the study, and two grants from the University of Otago Division of Sciences funded the adolescent phase. Please direct correspondence to Professor Elaine Reese, ereese@psy.otago.ac.nz, University of Otago, Department of Psychology, PO Box 56, Dunedin, New Zealand 9054.

Disclosure statement

No potential conflict of interest was reported by the authors.

Funding

This work was supported by Royal Society of New Zealand Marsden Fund [grant Number UOO520 and UOO809].

References

Akers, K. G., Martinez-Canabal, A., Restivo, L., Yiu, A. P., De Cristofaro, A., Hsiang, H. L. L., … Ohira, K. (2014). Hippocampal neurogenesis regulates forgetting during adulthood and infancy. *Science, 344*, 598–602. doi:10.1126/science.1248903

Bauer, P. J. (2007). *Remembering the times of our lives: Memory in infancy and beyond.* Mahwah, NJ: Lawrence Erlbaum Associates.

Bauer, P. J. (2015). A complementary processes account of the development of childhood amnesia and a personal past. *Psychological Review, 122,* 204–231. doi:10.1037/a0038939

Bauer, P. J., & Fivush, R. (1992). Constructing event representations: Building on a foundation of variation and enabling relations. *Cognitive Development, 7,* 381–401. doi:10.1016/0885-2014(92)90023-K

Bauer, P. J., & Larkina, M. (2014a). Childhood amnesia in the making: Different distributions of autobiographical memories in children and adults. *Journal of Experimental Psychology: General, 143,* 597–611. doi:10.1037/a0033307

Bauer, P. J., & Larkina, M. (2014b). The onset of childhood amnesia in childhood: A prospective investigation of the course and determinants of forgetting of early-life events. *Memory (Hove, England), 22,* 907–924. doi:10.1080/09658211.2013.854806

Bauer, P. J., Tasdemir-Ozdes, A., & Larkina, M. (2014). Adults' reports of their earliest memories: Consistency in events, ages, and narrative characteristics over time. *Consciousness and Cognition, 27,* 76–88. doi:10.1016/j.concog.2014.04.008

Cleveland, E. S., & Reese, E. (2005). Maternal structure and autonomy support in conversations about the past: Contributions to children's autobiographical memory. *Developmental Psychology, 41,* 376–388. doi:10.1037/0012-1649.41.2.376

Cleveland, E. S., & Reese, E. (2008). Children remember early childhood: Long-term recall across the offset of childhood amnesia. *Applied Cognitive Psychology, 22,* 127–142. doi:10.1002/acp.1359

Cleveland, E. S., Reese, E., & Grolnick, W. S. (2007). Children's engagement and competence in personal recollection: Effects of parents' reminiscing goals. *Journal of Experimental Child Psychology, 96,* 131–149. doi:10.1016/j.jecp.2006.09.003

Dunn, L. M., & Dunn, L. M. (1997). *PPVT-III: Peabody picture vocabulary test.* Circle Pines, MN: American Guidance Service.

Farrant, K., & Reese, E. (2000). Maternal style and children's participation in reminiscing: Stepping stones in children's autobiographical memory development. *Journal of Cognition and Development, 1,* 193–225. doi:10.1207/S15327647JCD010203

Field, A. (2013). *Discovering statistics using IBM SPSS statistics.* Los Angeles: Sage.

Fivush, R. (2012). Subjective perspective and personal timeline in the development of autobiographical memory. In D. Berntsen, & D. Rubin (Eds.), *Understanding autobiographical memory: Theories and approaches* (pp. 226–245). New York: Cambridge University Press.

Fivush, R., & Fromhoff, F. A. (1988). Style and structure in mother-child conversations about the past. *Discourse Processes, 11,* 337–355. doi:10.1080/01638538809544707

Fivush, R., Haden, C. A., & Adam, S. (1995). Structure and coherence of preschoolers' personal narratives over time: Implications for childhood amnesia. *Journal of Experimental Child Psychology, 60,* 32–56. doi:10.1006/jecp.1995.1030

Fivush, R., Haden, C. A., & Reese, E. (2006). Elaborating on elaborations: Role of maternal reminiscing style in cognitive and socioemotional development. *Child Development, 77,* 1568–1588. doi:10.1111/j.1467-8624.2006.00960.x

Fivush, R., & Nelson, K. (2004). Culture and language in the emergence of autobiographical memory. *Psychological Science, 15,* 573–577. Retrieved from http://www.jstor.org/stable/40064143

Freud, S. (1901/1960). *The psychopathology of everyday life* (J. Strachey, Transl.). New York: W. W. Norton & Co.

Graham, J. (2009). Missing data analysis: Making it work in the real world. *Annual Review of Psychology, 60,* 549–576. doi:10.1146/annurev.psych.58.110405.085530

Habermas, T., & Köber, C. (2014). Autobiographical reasoning is constitutive for narrative identity: The role of the life story for personal continuity. In K. McLean, & M. Syed (Eds.), *The Oxford handbook of identity development* (pp. 267–299). Oxford, UK: Oxford University Press.

Haden, C. A. (1998). Reminiscing with different children: Relating maternal stylistic consistency and sibling similarity in talk about the past. *Developmental Psychology, 34,* 99–114. doi:10.1037/0012-1649.34.1.99

Haden, C. A., Ornstein, P. A., Rudek, D. J., & Cameron, D. (2009). Reminiscing in the early years: Patterns of maternal elaborativeness and children's remembering. *International Journal of Behavioral Development, 33*(2), 118–130. doi:10.1177/0165025408098038

Harley, K., & Reese, E. (1999). Origins of autobiographical memory. *Developmental Psychology, 35,* 1338–1348. doi:10.1037/0012-1649.35.5.1338

Hayes, A. F. (2013). *Introduction to mediation, moderation, and conditional process analysis: A regression-based approach.* NY: Guilford Press.

Hayne, H., Imuta, K., & Scarf, A. D. (2015). Memory development during infancy and early childhood across cultures. *International Encyclopedia of the Social & Behavioral Sciences, 15,* 147–154. doi:10.1016/B978-0-08-097086-8.23062-6

Hayne, H., Scarf, D., & Imuta, K. (2015). Childhood memories. *International Encyclopedia of the Social & Behavioral Sciences, 15,* 465–470. doi:10.1016/B978-0-08-097086-8.51025-3

Herschkowitz, N. (2000). Neurological bases of behavioral development in infancy. *Brain and Development, 22,* 411–416. doi:10.1016/S0387-7604(00)00185-6

Howe, M. L., & Courage, M. L. (1993). On resolving the enigma of infantile amnesia. *Psychological Bulletin, 113,* 305–326. doi:10.1037/0033-2909.113.2.305

Howe, M. L., & Courage, M. L. (1997). The emergence and early development of autobiographical memory. *Psychological Review, 104,* 499–523. doi:10.1037/0033-295X.104.3.499

Jack, F., & Hayne, H. (2010). Childhood amnesia: Empirical evidence for a two-stage model. *Memory (Hove, England), 18,* 831–844. doi:10.1080/09658211.2010.510476

Jack, F., MacDonald, S., Reese, E., & Hayne, H. (2009). Maternal reminiscing style during early childhood predicts the age of adolescents' earliest memories. *Child Development, 80,* 496–505. doi:10.1111/j.1467-8624.2009.01274.x

Jack, F., Simcock, G., & Hayne, H. (2012). Magic memories: Young children's verbal recall after a 6-year delay. *Child Development, 83,* 159–172. doi:10.1111/j.1467-8624.2011.01699.x

Josselyn, S. A., & Frankland, P. W. (2012). Infantile amnesia: A neurogenic hypothesis. *Learning & Memory, 19,* 423–433. doi:10.1101/lm.021311.110

Kihlstrom, J., & Harackiewicz, J. (1982). The earliest recollection: A new survey. *Journal of Personality, 50,* 134–148. doi:10.1111/j.1467-6494.1982.tb01019.x

Lewis, M., & Brooks-Gunn, J. (1979). *Social cognition and the acquisition of self.* New York: Plenum Press.

MacDonald, S., Uesiliana, K., & Hayne, H. (2000). Cross-cultural and gender differences in childhood amnesia. *Memory (Hove, England), 8,* 365–376.

Morris, G., & Baker-Ward, L. (2007). Fragile but real: Children's capacity to use newly acquired words to convey preverbal memories. *Child Development, 78,* 448–458. doi:10.1111/j.1467-8624.2007.01008.x

Morris, G., Baker-Ward, L., & Bauer, P. J. (2010). What remains of that day: The survival of children's autobiographical memories across time. *Applied Cognitive Psychology, 24,* 527–544. doi:10.1002/acp.1567

Neisser, U. (1962). Cultural and cognitive discontinuity. In T. E. Gladwin, & W. Sturtevant (Eds.), *Anthropology and human behavior* (pp. 54–71). Washington, DC: Anthropological Society.

Nelson, K., & Fivush, R. (2004). The emergence of autobiographical memory: A social cultural developmental theory. *Psychological Review, 111,* 486–511. doi:10.1037/0033-295X.111.2.486

Newcombe, R., & Reese, E. (2004). Evaluations and orientations in mother–child narratives as a function of attachment security: A longitudinal investigation. *International Journal of Behavioral Development, 28,* 230–245. doi:10.1080/01650250344000460

Nieto, M., Ros, L., Ricarte, J. J., & Latorre, J. M. (2017). The role of executive functions in accessing specific autobiographical memories in 3- to 6-year-olds. *Early Childhood Research Quarterly, 43*, 23–32. doi:10.1016/j.ecresq.2017.11.004

Olson, I. R., & Newcombe, N. S. (2014). Binding together the elements of episodes: Relational memory and the developmental trajectory of the hippocampus. In P. J. Bauer, & R. Fivush (Eds.), *The wiley handbook on the development of children's memory* (pp. 285–308). West Sussex, UK: John Wiley & Sons, Ltd.

Ornstein, P. A., Haden, C. A., & Hedrick, A. M. (2004). Learning to remember: Social-communicative exchanges and the development of children's memory skills. *Developmental Review, 24*, 374–395. doi:10.1016/j.dr.2004.08.004

Perner, J. (2000). Memory and theory of mind. In E. Tulving, & F. I. M. Craik (Eds.), *The Oxford handbook of memory* (pp. 297–312). New York: Oxford University Press.

Perner, J. (2001). Episodic memory: Essential distinctions and developmental implications. In C. Moore, & K. Lemmon (Eds.), *The self in time: Developmental perspectives* (pp. 181–202). Mahwah, NJ: Lawrence Erlbaum Associates.

Perner, J., & Ruffman, T. (1995). Episodic memory and autonoetic conciousness: Developmental evidence and a theory of childhood amnesia. *Journal of Experimental Child Psychology, 59*, 516–548. doi:10.1006/jecp.1995.1024

Peterson, C. (2002). Children's long-term memory for autobiographical events. *Developmental Review, 22*, 370–402. doi:10.1016/S0273-2297(02)00007-2

Peterson, C., Grant, V., & Boland, L. (2005). Childhood amnesia in children and adolescents: Their earliest memories. *Memory (Hove, England), 13*, 622–637. doi:10.1080/09658210444000278

Peterson, C., Hallett, D., & Compton-Gillingham, C. (2017). Childhood amnesia in children: A prospective study across eight years. *Child Development*, doi:10.1111/cdev.12972

Peterson, C., Morris, G., Baker-Ward, L., & Flynn, S. (2014). Predicting which childhood memories persist: Contributions of memory characteristics. *Developmental Psychology, 50*, 439–448. doi:10.1037/a0033221

Peterson, C., Warren, K. L., & Short, M. M. (2011). Infantile amnesia across the years: A 2-year follow-up of children's earliest memories. *Child Development, 82*, 1092–1105. doi:10.1111/j.1467-8624.2011.01597.x

Pillemer, D. B., & White, S. H. (1989). Childhood events recalled by children and adults. *Advances in Child Development and Behavior, 21*, 297–340. doi; 10.1016/S0065-2407(08)60291-8

Prebble, S. C., Addis, D. R., & Tippett, L. J. (2013). Autobiographical memory and sense of self. *Psychological Bulletin, 139*, 815–840. doi:10.1037/a0030146

Reese, E. (1995). Predicting children's literacy from mother-child conversations. *Cognitive Development, 10*, 381–405. doi:10.1016/0885-2014(95)90003-9

Reese, E. (1999). What children say when they talk about the past. *Narrative Inquiry, 9*, 215–241. doi:10.1075/ni.9.2.02ree

Reese, E. (2002a). A model of the origins of autobiographical memory. In J. W. Fagen, & H. Hayne (Eds.), *Progress in infancy research, (Vol. 2,* pp. 215–260). Mahwah, NJ: Lawrence Erlbaum Associates.

Reese, E. (2002b). Social factors in the development of autobiographical memory: The state of the art. *Social Development, 11*, 124–142. doi:10.1111/1467-9507.00190

Reese, E. (2009). The development of autobiographical memory: Origins and consequences. *Advances in Child Development and Behavior, 37*, 145–200. doi:10.1016/S0065-2407(09)03704-5

Reese, E. (2014a). Taking the long way: Longitudinal approaches to autobiographical memory development. In P. J. Bauer, & R. Fivush (Eds.), *The wiley handbook on the development of children's memory* (pp. 972–995). West Sussex, UK: John Wiley & Sons, Ltd.

Reese, E. (2014b). Practical tips for conducting longitudinal studies of memory development. In P. J. Bauer, & R. Fivush (Eds.), *The wiley handbook on the development of children's memory* (pp. 1044–1050). West Sussex, UK: John Wiley & Sons, Ltd.

Reese, E. (2018). Encouraging collaborative remembering between young children and their caregivers. In M. Meade, C. Harris, P. van Bergen, J. Sutton, & A. Barnier (Eds.), *Collaborative remembering: Theories, research, and applications* (pp. 317–333). Oxford: Oxford University Press.

Reese, E., & Cleveland, E. S. (2006). Mother-child reminiscing and children's understanding of mind. *Merrill-Palmer Quarterly, 52*, 17–43. doi:10.1353/mpq.2006.0007

Reese, E., Haden, C. A., Baker-Ward, L., Bauer, P., Fivush, R., & Ornstein, P. A. (2011). Coherence of personal narratives across the lifespan: A multidimensional model and coding method. *Journal of Cognition and Development, 12*, 424–462. doi:10.1080/15248372.2011.587854

Reese, E., Haden, C. A., & Fivush, R. (1993). Mother-child conversations about the past: Relationships of style and memory over time. *Cognitive Development, 8*, 403–430. doi:10.1016/S0885-2014(05)80002-4

Reese, E., Jack, F., & White, N. (2010). Origins of adolescents' autobiographical memories. *Cognitive Development, 25*, 352–367. doi:10.1016/j.cogdev.2010.08.006

Reese, E., & Newcombe, R. (2007). Training mothers in elaborative reminiscing enhances children's autobiographical memory and narrative. *Child Development, 78*, 1153–1170. doi:10.1111/j.1467-8624.2007.01058.x

Reese, E., Yan, C., Jack, F., & Hayne, H. (2010). Emerging identities: Narrative and self from early childhood to early adolescence. In K. C. McLean, & M. Pasupathi (Eds.), *Narrative development in adolescence: Creating the storied self* (pp. 23–43). R. J. R. Levesque (Series Editor), *Advancing responsible adolescent development*. New York, NY: Springer Science.

Rubin, D. C. (1982). On the retention function for autobiographical memory. *Journal of Verbal Learning and Verbal Behavior, 21*, 21–38. doi:10.1016/S0022-5371(82)90423-6

Rubin, D. C. (2000). The distribution of early childhood memories. *Memory (Hove, England), 8*, 265–269. doi:10.1080/096582100406810

Simcock, G., & Hayne, H. (2002). Breaking the barrier? Children fail to translate their preverbal memories into language. *Psychological Science, 13*, 225–231. Retrieved from http://www.jstor.org/stable/40063711

Simcock, G., & Hayne, H. (2003). Age-related changes in verbal and nonverbal memory during early childhood. *Developmental Psychology, 39*, 805–814. doi:10.1037/0012-1649.39.5.805

Suggate, S. P., Schaughency, E. S., McAnally, H. M., & Reese, E. (2018). From infancy to adolescence: The longitudinal links between vocabulary, early reading, oral narrative, and reading comprehension. *Cognitive Development, 47*, 82–95. doi:10.1016/j.cogdev.2018.04.005

Tõugu, P., Vaht, M., Tulviste, T., Veidebaum, T., & Harro, J. (2016). The association between the COMT gene Val 158 Met polymorphism and preschoolers' autobiographical memory details and narrative cohesiveness. *Cognitive Development, 39*, 181–188. doi:10.1016/j.cogdev.2016.06.002

Tustin, K., & Hayne, H. (2010). Defining the boundary: Age-related changes in childhood amnesia. *Developmental Psychology, 46*, 1049–1061. doi:10.1037/a0020105

Usher, J. A., & Neisser, U. (1993). Childhood amnesia and the beginnings of memory for four early life events. *Journal of Experimental Psychology: General, 122*, 155–165. doi:10.1037/0096-3445.122.2.155

Wang, Q. (2003). Infantile amnesia reconsidered: A cross-cultural analysis. *Memory (Hove, England), 11*, 65–80. doi:10.1080/741938173

Wang, Q. (2006). Earliest recollections of self and others in European American and Taiwanese young adults. *Psychological Science, 17*, 708–714. doi:10.1111/j.1467-9280.2006.01770.x

Wang, Q. (2007). "Remember when you got the big, big bulldozer?" mother–child reminiscing over time and across cultures. *Social Cognition, 25*, 455–471. doi:10.1521/soco.2007.25.4.455

Wang, Q. (2008). Emotion knowledge and autobiographical memory across the preschool years: A cross-cultural longitudinal investigation. *Cognition, 108*, 117–135. doi:10.1016/j.cognition.2008.02.002

Wang, Q. (2013). *The autobiographical self in time and culture.* New York: Oxford University Press.

Wang, Q., Hutt, R., Kulkofsky, S., McDermott, M., & Wei, R. (2006). Emotion situation knowledge and autobiographical memory in Chinese, immigrant Chinese, and European American 3-year-olds. *Journal of Cognition and Development, 7,* 95–118. doi:10.1207/s15327647jcd0701_5

Wang, Q., & Peterson, C. (2014). Your earliest memory may be earlier than you think: Prospective studies of children's dating of earliest childhood memories. *Developmental Psychology, 50,* 1680–1686. doi:10.1037/a0036001

Wang, Q., & Peterson, C. (2016). The fate of childhood memories: Children postdated their earliest memories as they grew older. *Frontiers in Psychology, 6,* 597. doi:10.3389/fpsyg.2015.02038

Wang, Q., Peterson, C., & Hou, Y. (2010). Children dating childhood memories. *Memory (Hove, England), 18,* 754–762. doi:10.1080/09658211.2010.508749

Waters, E. (1987). *Attachment Q-set.* University of New York at Stony Brook. Unpublished instrument.

Welch-Ross, M. K. (1995). An integrative model of the development of autobiographical memory. *Developmental Review, 15,* 338–365. doi:10.1006/drev.1995.1013

Welch-Ross, M. K. (1997). Mother–child participation in conversation about the past: Relationships to preschoolers' theory of mind. *Developmental Psychology, 33,* 618–629. doi:10.1037/0012-1649.33.4.618

Williams, K. T. (1997). *EVT: Expressive vocabulary test.* Circle Pines, MN: American Guidance Service.

Recollection improves with age: children's and adults' accounts of their childhood experiences

Karen Tustin and Harlene Hayne

ABSTRACT
Since the time of Freud, psychologists have drawn conclusions about children's memory on the basis of retrospective research with adults. Here, we turn the tables by examining what prospective studies with children and adolescents can tell us about the retrospective memory accounts provided by adults. Adults were interviewed about recent events and events from different points during their childhood (Age 5, Age 10) and early adolescence (Age 13). Children (5- and 8- to 9-year-olds) and young adolescents (12- to 13-year-olds) were interviewed about recent events. When matched for age at the time of encoding, adults recalled more about the target events than did 5-year-olds, even though the retention interval for adults was substantially longer. We conclude that retrospective studies with adults may lead researchers to overestimate the content of the early childhood memories that survive. We discuss the theoretical implications of these findings for an understanding of memory development and the practical implications for the interpretation of adults' retrospective accounts in the courtroom.

Henri and Henri's (1898) seminal observation that adults experience virtually complete amnesia for events that occurred prior to the age of 2–4 years sparked empirical interest that has now spanned more than a century. This phenomenon, coined *infantile* or *childhood amnesia* by Freud (1905/1953), has been replicated time and again and the majority of researchers now agree that most adults' earliest memories are dated for events falling between the ages of 3 and 4 years (e.g., Bauer, 2007; Crovitz & Harvey, 1979; Dudycha & Dudycha, 1933a, 1933b; MacDonald, Uesiliana, & Hayne, 2000; Waldfogel, 1948; for a review see Rubin, 2000).

What is not so clear, and what remains the subject of considerable theory and research, is why childhood amnesia occurs in the first place. Freud (1905/1953) believed that our early childhood memories are not lost but that there is "a simple withholding of these impressions from consciousness, viz., in their repression" (p. 175). His theory has now largely been discounted in favour of a number of developmental theories, including explanations based on cognitive, social, and language development (for reviews see Bauer, 2007, 2014; Hayne & Jack, 2011), as well as explanations based on differential maturation of two or more functionally-distinct memory systems (for a review see Bachevalier, 2014). Each of these explanations supposes some form of encoding deficit; prior to the achievement of certain milestones (e.g., the ability to use language, the maturation of particular brain areas) children are unable commit the details of their personal experiences to memory. Although these theories differ in a number of important ways, they share the common assumption that a fundamental change takes place between the ages of 3 and 4, which accounts for the offset of childhood amnesia.

In contrast to traditional retrospective studies with adults, prospective studies with children demonstrate that the age of their earliest memories is significantly below the age of 3. For example, in a seminal study of childhood amnesia during childhood, Tustin and Hayne (2010) asked children and adults to report their earliest childhood memory. They found that children's single earliest memories were dated much earlier than were those of adults, falling well below the traditional 3–4-year-old boundary. A growing body of research has yielded this same basic finding (Jack, MacDonald, Reese, & Hayne, 2009; Peterson, Grant, & Boland, 2005; Peterson, Noel, Kippenhuck, Harmundal, & Vincent, 2009; Peterson, Wang, & Hou, 2009; Peterson, Warren, & Short, 2011; Reese, Jack, & White, 2010). Furthermore, recent research with adults has also shown that, when asked to recall their earliest personal memory, adults systematically postdate their memories by 6–12 months, a phenomenon that has been referred to as telescoping. When these telescoping errors are taken into account, estimates of the boundary of childhood amnesia in adults are much more consistent with those obtained in studies with children and adolescents (Wang, Peterson, Khuu, Reid, Maxwell & Vincent, 2017).

Taken together, studies on childhood amnesia in children and more recent studies of telescoping in adults are consistent with a wealth of prospective research showing that even very young children encode information about their past experiences and can retain and talk about them following delays of days, months, and even years (e.g., Fivush & Hamond, 1990; Fivush & Schwarzmueller, 1998; Fivush, Gray, & Fromhoff, 1987; Fivush, Haden, & Reese, 1996; Hayne, Gross, McNamee, Fitzgibbon, & Tustin, 2011; for a review see Reese, 2009). These data challenge explanations of childhood amnesia that rely on age-related changes in encoding alone, highlighting the important role that forgetting of previously-encoded memories must play in determining which memories survive into adulthood (Bauer, 2014; Bauer & Larkina, 2014; Hayne & Jack, 2011).

Historically, retrospective studies with adults have not only been used to estimate the boundary of childhood amnesia, but they have also been used to estimate the content of the childhood memories that survive (e.g., Bauer, Tasdemir-Ozdes, & Larkina, 2014; Henri & Henri, 1898; Howes, Siegel, & Brown, 1993; Johnson, Foley, Suengas, & Raye, 1988; MacDonald et al., 2000; Mullen, 1994; Wang, 2001). Among other things, these data have been used to draw inferences about the emotional content and perceptual detail of our childhood recollections. One major assumption of retrospective research of this kind is that participants' reports of their experiences reflect only what they remember of what they encoded about the events in the first place. Evidence from two experiments in our laboratory show that this may not be the case. In the first, Gross, Jack, Davis, and Hayne (2013) compared 2- to 5-year-old children's memories of the recent birth of a younger sibling with adults' memories of the birth of a sibling that had occurred when they were between 2 and 5 years old. For both the children and the adults, the older the participants were at the time that their sibling was born, the more detail they were able to recall about the birth and the events surrounding it – this finding is consistent with the view that age at the time of encoding plays an important role in what adults (or children) recall. Importantly, however, regardless of the age participants were when the birth happened, the adults reported more details about the event than did children. If anything, we would have expected the adults to report fewer details given that the retention interval was extremely long compared to that of the children (2 months at most for the children and more than a decade for the adults). On the basis of these findings, Gross et al. concluded that the adults supplemented their reports with details that they had gleaned from additional sources (e.g., talking to family, photographs), leading us to overestimate the content of their actual memory.

In a different experiment, Strange and Hayne (2013) examined the memory reports of 5–6-year-old and 9–10-year-old children who had experienced a unique event (a visit to the local fire station) two days earlier. Strange and Hayne coded the children's reports for the types of details that adults often report when they are asked for autobiographical accounts in the laboratory or in the courtroom (e.g., weather, time of day, clothing, emotion/thoughts of self/others, etc.). Children in both age groups rarely mentioned these details spontaneously. When explicitly asked to provide this information, the older children were able to answer some questions, but the younger children were not. Strange and Hayne concluded that young children do not notice or encode the types of details that adults often report when recounting their early experiences. They advised caution in evaluating adults' retrospective reports about childhood events that contain more information than a child of that age would be likely to encode at the time the event took place.

Taken together, the results reported by Gross et al. (2013) and Strange and Hayne (2013) indicate that what adults report may not reflect what they originally encoded as children. Instead, it is likely that adults, albeit without conscious intent, add details to their memories over time. These details may have been plucked from conversations with others, or from family photographs and videos, or they may have been inferred by the rememberer without additional external influence. In this way, relying on adults' retrospective reports of childhood events has led us to overestimate the content of those early memories.

Our aim here is to continue to explore the potential implications of retrospective studies with adults for our understanding of memory during childhood. Although there are some major advantages of comparing children's and adults' recollections of a common event like the birth of a sibling, there are also some disadvantages to this approach, including the fact that children and adults may not place the same weight on events of this kind (Fivush et al., 1987; Nelson, 1989). To circumvent this problem in the present experiment, children, young adolescents, and adults were interviewed about parent-nominated and self-nominated events from different points in their lives. In this way, we tried to capture recollections for events that were personally meaningful *at the time they took place*. We held the age at the time of the event constant and varied both the age of the rememberer and the retention interval. Based on our prior prospective research with children (Gross et al., 2013; Strange & Hayne, 2013), we hypothesised that adults would report more information about their childhood experiences than would children. Furthermore, given that females often (but not always) report more information than males in studies of autobiographical memory (for a recent review, see Gryson & Hudson, 2013), we also hypothesised that girls and women would report more information about their past experiences than would boys and men.

Method

Participants

Twelve adults (6 females) aged between 18 and 20 years ($M = 19.17$ years, $SD = .88$ years) were interviewed about recent events in their lives, as well as several events from their childhood and early adolescence. The adults were first- and second-year psychology undergraduate students at the University of Otago, Dunedin, New Zealand. In addition, three groups of children and young adolescents were interviewed about recent life events. There were six males and six females in each age group[1]: 5-year-old children ($M = 5.42$ years, $SD = .32$ years), 8- to 9-year-old children ($M = 8.99$ years, $SD = .40$ years), and 12- to 13-year-old adolescents ($M = 12.96$ years, $SD = .37$ years). The children and adolescents were recruited from an existing pool of participants enrolled in the Early Learning Project at the University of Otago. This participant pool was recruited via birth registrations of infants born in the Dunedin area. Consent for the children to participate was obtained from their parents, and independent consent was also obtained from the adolescents and the adults.

Materials

In the present experiment, we used the same Timeline procedure that has been described in detail previously (see Tustin & Hayne, 2010). In brief, we constructed a Timeline that marked each year of life on a large piece of coloured card (101.8 cm × 66.2 cm) for each participant. The participants' parents provided photographs of their child at various ages (see Tustin & Hayne, 2010 for more detail) and the experimenter also took a photo of the participant using a digital camera on the day of the interview. None of the photos that were used in the Timeline included additional cues (e.g., objects/locations) nor did the photos represent the memories that were subsequently discussed during the interview. Parents were specifically asked not to show their children the photos in advance of the interview. To the best of our knowledge, all parents adhered to these requests. For the 3 younger groups of participants, adding the photos to the Timeline was used as a warm-up activity. Photos for the adult participants were attached to their Timelines in advance of the interview by the experimenter. Participants were given the opportunity to decorate their Timelines with stickers and coloured markers during the memory interview. Sample Timelines for each age group are shown in Figure 1.

Procedure

All participants were tested in a quiet room in the Early Learning Project laboratory. The experimenter began each interview by explaining to the participant that he or she

Figure 1. Sample Timelines for (clockwise from top left) 5-year-olds, 8- to 9-year-olds, 18- to 20-year-olds, and 12- to 13-year-olds.

would be asked to describe some memories from the past. The participant was instructed to tell the experimenter only the details of his or her memories that he or she actually remembered, and not to fill in any blanks with details that he or she had obtained from family stories or photos and videos. Once the interview procedure had been explained, the experimenter reviewed the sequence of the Timeline with the participant (for more detail see Tustin & Hayne, 2010). All interviews were video- and audio-taped.

Adults' interviews

For each adult participant, the experimenter asked him or her to think of something that he or she remembered happening/doing during the past month. The experimenter pointed to the photo of the participant at their present age. Once the participant had nominated an event, the experimenter first gave him or her the opportunity for free recall by providing general prompts (e.g., "Tell me about [the event]", followed by "Can you remember anything else about [the event]") until the participant indicated that he or she did not have any more information to report. The experimenter then asked a set of four specific questions about the memory. The questions were: "Who else was there?," "Where were you?," "What did you do?," and "How did you feel?" The questions were followed by another opportunity for free recall, e.g., "Is there anything else that you can remember now that you would like to tell me about [the event]?," until the participant could recall no more. There was no time limit for either the free or directed recall portion of the interview.

After recalling this recent memory, the experimenter asked the participant to report one event (from most to least recent) for each of the following approximate target ages: 13 years old, 10 years old, and 5 years old. The recollection of all of the events took the same format as did recollection of the recent event (i.e., free recall followed by specific questions and ending with free recall).

Once the participant had recalled all of their self-nominated memories, the experimenter asked him or her whether s/he remembered four additional events (one per target age) that had been provided by his/her parent in advance of the interview. Parents had been asked to nominate two salient events per target age. Where the participant and parent had both nominated the same event, the experimenter asked about an event different to the self-nominated event. If the participant stated that he or she did not remember an event that his or her parent had nominated, the alternative was used (where it was different from what the participant had previously reported). The same interview structure was used for the parent-nominated events as for the self-nominated events.

Children's interviews[2]

Parents accompanied their children to the laboratory. Once the child felt comfortable, the parent went into another room with a second experimenter. As per the adults' interviews, the experimenter asked the participant to think of something that he or she remembered happening/doing during the past month. The same interview structure was used for the children as was used for the adults (i.e., free recall followed by specific questions and ending with free recall).

While the participant completed this portion of the interview, a second experimenter asked his or her parent to nominate two salient events in his or her child's life that had happened recently. The experimenter briefly transcribed these events (without specific detail) for the experimenter interviewing the participant.

Once the participant had recalled their self-nominated recent event, the experimenter asked him or her whether s/he remembered the recent event nominated by his/her parent. Where the participant and parent had both nominated the same event, the experimenter asked about an event different to the self-nominated event. If the participant stated that he or she did not remember an event that his or her parent had nominated, the alternative was used (where it was different from what the participant had previously reported). Once again, the same interview structure was used in recalling the parent-nominated events (i.e., free recall followed by specific questions and ending with free recall).

Accuracy

To determine the accuracy of participants' memories, the interviews were transcribed verbatim and the transcript of the interview was presented to one of the participant's parents. Parents were asked to first read over the memory and decide if the event had definitely happened, may have happened, or had definitely never happened. If the event had definitely happened, the parents were asked to indicate whether they had some first-hand knowledge of it. If the parents did have some first-hand knowledge, they were asked to consider each piece of information (i.e., each line of the transcript) and rate it as correct, possible, or incorrect. The parents were also asked to indicate whether their child's estimation of his or her age at the time of the event was correct or incorrect. If the age was incorrect, they were asked to note the correct age. This procedure was identical to that used in our prior research (Tustin & Hayne, 2010).

Coding

Participants' reports were parsed into clauses. A clause corresponded roughly to a simple sentence and was defined by the presence of a verb, such that there was one verb per clause (see Gross & Hayne, 1998). Any information that was unrelated to the description of the event was not included. Similarly, repetitions of the same information were not included (e.g., where the participant provided the same information in response to the specific questions as he or she had provided during free recall). The number of clauses provided by the participant during free recall and during directed recall was summed to produce a score for the total amount of information provided.

A second coder independently parsed 25% of each group's memories into clauses ($N = 41$ memories). Pearson product-moment correlations yielded inter-rater reliability coefficients of .91 for total recall, .95 for free recall, and .78 for directed recall.

Results

Recall that participants were asked to describe one self- and one parent-nominated memory for each of the target ages. Overall, participants reported 163 target memories. All participants in each of the four age groups reported one self- and one parent-nominated memory for the recent event. In addition, all adults reported at least one memory (self- or parent-nominated) from target ages 13 and 10, and all but one adult reported at least one memory from target age 5.

Accuracy

Of the 163 memories, parents were able to verify the ages of 151 memories (92.64%). In total, parents indicated that 2 of the memories (1.23%) had been dated incorrectly by their children. In one case, the incorrectly-dated memory by an 8–9-year-old fell within 6 months of the target age and was included in the final sample. In the other case, an incorrectly-dated memory by an 18–20-year-old fell 1 year from the target age of 10 and was excluded, yielding a final sample of 162 target memories.

Of the 162 target memories in the final sample, parents were able to verify the accuracy of the content of 103 memories (63.58%). As judged by their parents, the content of the participants' reports of these memories was largely accurate. On average, parents rated 76.34% ($SD = 24.57$%) of the details as correct, 21.02% ($SD = 23.41$%) of the details as possible, and only 2.65% ($SD = 9.34$%) of the details as incorrect. The 103 memories for which we had accuracy information (the proportion of details rated as correct or possible) were subjected to a 2 (Gender) × 4 (Age Group: 5-year-olds, 8–9-year-olds, 12–13-year-olds, 18–20-year-olds) Analysis of Variance (ANOVA). The proportion of details that parents rated as correct or possible did not vary as a function of gender, $F(1, 95) = 0.16$, $p = .69$, but there was a main effect of age group, $F(3, 95) = 5.66$, $p = .001$, $\eta_p^2 = 0.15$ (95% CI [0.03, 0.26]); although 5-year-olds' reports can still be regarded as accurate, the proportion of details that parents rated as correct or possible was lower for this group ($M = 90.30$%, $SD = 18.16$%) than for any other age group (8–9-year-olds: $M = 99.81$%, $SD = 0.87$%; 12–13-year-olds: $M = 100$%, $SD = 0$%; 18–20-year-olds: $M = 98.51$%, $SD = 4.62$%;) (Tukey, $ps < .01$). There was no interaction, $F(3, 95) = 0.47$, $p = .71$.

Amount of information reported

To determine the total amount of information that participants reported about each target memory they recalled, the number of free-recall clauses they reported was summed with the number of new clauses reported during directed recall (clauses which contained pieces of information that the participants had not reported during free recall). Because not all adults reported two memories from each target age, the amount of information reported was averaged across the self- and parent-nominated events for each target age (recent, 13 years, 10 years, 5 years) for all participants.[3]

The amount of information that participants reported during free and directed recall is shown in Table 1 and the total amount of unique information reported across both phases is shown in Figure 2. These data were analysed in three ways. First, we examined age-related changes in what participants reported about a recent event. To do this, the amount of information that participants reported about their recent experiences was subjected to a 2 (Gender) × 4 (Age Group: 5-year-olds, 8–9-year-olds, 12–13-year-olds, 18–20-year-olds) ANOVA. This analysis yielded main effects of age group, $F(3, 40) = 2.85$, $p = .049$, $\eta_p^2 = 0.18$ (95% CI [0, 0.33]), and gender, $F(1, 40) = 5.53$, $p = .02$, $\eta_p^2 = 0.12$ (95% CI [0.001, 0.31]), but no interaction, $F(3, 40) = 0.44$, $p = .73$. As shown in Figure 2, the adults reported more information about recent experiences than did 5-year-old children (Tukey, $p = .048$), but there were no further differences between the age groups (Tukey, $ps > .05$). With regard to gender, females reported more information ($M = 32.92$, $SD = 26.73$) than did males ($M = 19.63$, $SD = 10.82$). To determine whether participants' reports differed during free- and directed recall, we conducted an additional 2 (Gender) × 4 (Age Group) × 2 (Recall Type: free recall, directed recall) ANOVA with repeated measures over Recall Type. There was a main effect of Recall Type, $F(1, 40) = 16.22$, $p < .001$, $\eta_p^2 = 0.29$ (95% CI [0.08, 0.47]); overall, participants reported more information about a recent event during free recall than they did during directed recall (see Table 1). There were no interactions of Gender or Age Group with Recall Type, largest $F(3, 40) = 1.65$, $p = .19$.

Table 1. Mean (SE) number of clauses reported during free and directed recall for each target memory as a function of participant age.

Recall type	5-year-olds	8–9-year-olds	12–13-year-olds	18–20-year-olds
5-year target memory				
Free recall	8.71 (1.30)			16.18 (2.91)
Directed recall	4.54 (0.43)			9.36 (1.85)
10-year target memory				
Free recall		14.08 (2.21)		19.54 (2.09)
Directed recall		7.83 (1.23)		8.92 (0.88)
13-year target memory				
Free recall			21.88 (8.80)	17.08 (2.22)
Directed recall			8.63 (1.98)	10.75 (1.40)
18-year target memory				
Free recall				22.33 (2.43)
Directed recall				12.08 (2.92)

Note: $n = 12$ for each age group and target memory with the exception of the 5-year target memory for 18–20-year-olds ($n = 11$).

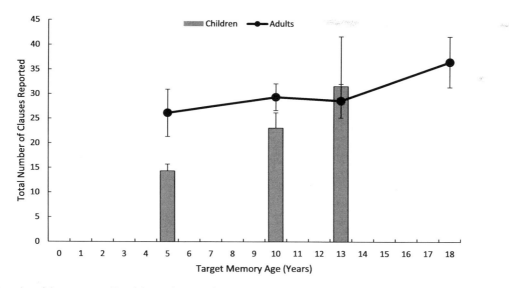

Figure 2. The total number of clauses reported by adults as a function of target memory age, with the corresponding number of clauses reported by children of each target age.

Next, in order to determine whether there were differences in the amount of information that adults reported about their memories as a function of the age at which the events occurred, we conducted a 2 (Gender) × 4 (Target Memory: 5 years, 10 years, 13 years, recent) ANOVA with repeated measures over Target Memory (Greenhouse-Geisser Correction Factor). As shown in Figure 2, adults reported the same amount of information, on average, about memories from each of the target ages, $F(1.73, 15.52) = 2.89$, $p = .09$. There was no effect of gender, $F(1, 9) = 3.89$, $p = .08$, and no Gender × Target Memory interaction, $F(1.73, 15.52) = 0.85$, $p = .43$. To determine whether adults' reports differed during free- and directed recall, we conducted an additional 2 (Gender) × 4 (Target Memory) × 2 (Recall Type) ANOVA with repeated measures over Target Memory and Recall Type. There was a main effect of Recall Type, $F(1, 9) = 33.07$, $p < .001$, $\eta_p^2 = 0.79$ (95% CI [0.33, 0.88]); as shown in Table 1, adults reported more information about their memories during free recall than they did during directed recall. There were no interactions of Gender or Target Memory with Recall Type, largest $F(3, 27) = 2.61$, $p = .07$.

Finally, we compared the amount of information reported by adults about memories at ages 5, 10, and 13 years with the recent memories reported by children of the corresponding age, in separate 2 (Gender) × 2 (Age Group: Adults vs Children) ANOVAs. In these analyses, recent memories reported by 5-year-olds were compared with adults' memories from age 5, recent memories reported by 8–9-year-olds were compared with adults' memories from age 10, and recent memories reported by 12–13-year-olds were compared with adults' memories from age 13.

Memories from age 13
The adults reported the same amount of total information about memories from the age of 13 years as did 12–13-year-olds about a recent event, $F(1, 20) = 0.08$, $p = .78$. There was no effect of gender, $F(1, 20) = 1.91$, $p = .18$, and no interaction, $F(1, 20) = 0.36$, $p = .56$. A separate 2 (Gender) × 2 (Age Group) × 2 (Recall Type) ANOVA with repeated measures over Recall Type yielded a main effect of Recall Type, $F(1, 20) = 6.31$, $p = .02$, $\eta_p^2 = 0.24$ (95% CI [0.004, 0.49]); participants reported more information during free recall ($M = 19.48$, $SD = 21.89$) than they did during directed recall ($M = 9.69$, $SD = 5.90$). There were no interactions of Gender or Age Group with Recall Type, largest $F(1, 20) = 1.43$, $p = .25$.

Memories from age 10
The adults reported the same amount of total information about memories from the age of 10 years as did 8–9-year-olds about a recent event, $F(1, 20) = 2.93$, $p = .10$. There was an effect of gender, $F(1, 20) = 7.10$, $p = .02$, $\eta_p^2 = 0.26$ (95% CI [0.01, 0.51]), – females reported more information ($M = 31.17$, $SD = 9.75$) than did males ($M = 21.38$, $SD = 8.89$) – but no interaction, $F(1, 20) = 0.72$, $p = .41$. A separate 2 (Gender) × 2 (Age Group) × 2 (Recall Type) ANOVA with repeated measures over Recall Type yielded a main effect of Recall Type, $F(1, 20) = 40.06$, $p < .001$, $\eta_p^2 = 0.67$ (95% CI [0.36, 0.78]); participants reported more information during free recall ($M = 16.81$, $SD = 7.82$) than they did during directed recall ($M = 8.38$, $SD = 3.67$). There were no interactions of Gender or Age Group with Recall Type, largest $F(1, 20) = 3.01$, $p = .10$.

Memories from age 5
The adults reported more total information about memories from the age of 5 years than did 5-year-olds about a recent event, $F(1, 19) = 6.43$, $p = .02$, $\eta_p^2 = 0.25$ (95% CI [0.004, 0.50]). There was an effect of gender, $F(1, 19) = 4.91$, $p = .04$, $\eta_p^2 = 0.25$ (95% CI [0, 0.46]), – females reported more information ($M = 24.75$, $SD = 15.25$) than did males

($M = 14.86$, $SD = 7.00$) – but no interaction, $F(1, 19) = 2.16$, $p = .16$. A separate 2 (Gender) × 2 (Age Group) × 2 (Recall Type) ANOVA with repeated measures over Recall Type yielded a main effect of Recall Type, $F(1, 19) = 26.03$, $p < .001$, $\eta_p^2 = 0.58$ (95% CI [0.23, 0.73]); participants reported more information during free recall ($M = 12.28$, $SD = 8.19$) than they did during directed recall ($M = 6.85$, $SD = 4.93$). There were no interactions of Gender or Age Group with Recall Type, largest $F(1, 19) = 1.42$, $p = .25$.

Given that adults reported more total information about an event that had taken place when they were 5 than did 5-year-olds who were describing a recent event, we next examined potential differences in the content of these reports. To do this, we determined the percentage of 5-year-olds recalling a recent event and the percentage of adults recalling an event from when they were 5 years old who provided information in each of 13 categories. The categories were based on those originally used by Strange and Hayne (2013) and reflect the kinds of information that adults often report when recounting childhood events in court. These data are shown in Table 2. Although only the layout of objects/furniture/places and reports regarding their own thoughts reached standard levels of statistical significance, a greater percentage of adults reported information from 11 of the 13 categories than did the 5-year-old children; none of the participants, irrespective of age, reported information about the date and day of the week.

Discussion

In the present experiment, children, young adolescents, and adults were interviewed about events from different points in their lives. Our aim was to explore the implications of prospective studies of memory development for our interpretation of adult's accounts of their earlier experiences. To achieve this aim, we held the age at the time of the event constant, but varied both the age of the rememberer and the retention interval. Three key findings emerged. First, adults reported the same amount of information about memories from different epochs in their lives, regardless of how long ago the event took place. Second, adults reported the same amount or more information about memories from the ages of 5, 10, and 13 years than did children of those ages recalling recent events, even though the retention intervals for adults were substantially longer (i.e., years vs. no more than a month). Although only the difference between the 5-year-olds and the adults reached conventional levels of statistical significance, we suspect that, given a larger sample, adults' accounts of their experiences as 10-year-olds would also be richer than those reported by children. Finally, consistent with a large body of prior research, we found that female participants reported more information than did male participants.

On the surface, the present data might lead to the conclusion that adults exhibited little, if any, forgetting over a 13+-year retention interval. The finding that adults reported the same amount of information about an event that happened when they were 5 as they did about an event that happened within the last month suggests that if an event is encoded and survives, it does so in its entirety, potentially indefinitely. Furthermore, the finding that adults reported at least as much (sometimes more) information about memories from the ages of 5, 10, and 13 years as did children of those ages would also lead to the conclusion that adults exhibited little or no forgetting over a retention interval that exceeded a decade – once the information is in, it's in, so to speak.

In contrast to this conclusion, decades of research on autobiographical and other kinds of memory has shown that all memory decays over time (Jack & Hayne, 2010; Rubin, 1982; Rubin & Wenzel, 1996; Rubin, Wetzler, & Nebes, 1986; Wetzler & Sweeney, 1986; White, 2001; Wickelgren, 1972, 1974, 1975). Accordingly, the content of the memories reported by adults and children should have reflected differences in the retention intervals. That is, the children (and young adolescents) were asked to report memories of events that took place no more than a month earlier whereas adults were also asked to report memories of events that occurred after delays of between 5 and 13+ years. Given these large differences in the retention intervals, we would have expected children to report more information about the recent event than did the adults about events from a similar age. They did not. In addition, we would have expected adults to report less information about earlier memories than about more recent memories. Clearly, this was also not the case.

How can we explain these results and what are the implications of these findings for the study of memory development? On the one hand, we might expect the accounts provided by the 5-year-olds to be lean. At the age of 5, children's ability to express their memories, along with their basic language skill, are undergoing a rapid period of development. The ability to use language

Table 2. Percent of 5-year-old children and adults who provided information in each of the 13 information categories for events that took place when they were 5 years old.

Category	Children	Adults	Chi-square*
Weather	0%	27.3%	$\chi^2(1, N = 23) = 3.76, p = .09$
Time of day	0%	18.2%	$\chi^2(1, N = 23) = 2.39, p = .22$
Date	0%	0%	–
Day of week	0%	0%	–
Duration of activity	0%	18.2%	$\chi^2(1, N = 23) = 2.39, p = .22$
Own clothing	8.3%	18.2%	$\chi^2(1, N = 23) = .49, p = .59$
Others' clothing	0%	9.1%	$\chi^2(1, N = 23) = 1.14, p = .48$
Layout	16.7%	63.6%	$\chi^2(1, N = 23) = 5.32, p = .04, V = .48$
Emotion (self)	83.3%	100.0%	$\chi^2(1, N = 23) = 2.01, p = .48$
Emotion (others)	16.7%	27.3%	$\chi^2(1, N = 23) = .38, p = .64$
Own thoughts	0%	72.7%	$\chi^2(1, N = 23) = 13.38, p < .001, V = .76$
Others' thoughts	8.3%	18.2%	$\chi^2(1, N = 23) = .49, p = .59$
Verbatim comments	16.7%	36.4%	$\chi^2(1, N = 23) = 1.16, p = .37$
n	12	11	

*Fisher's Exact Test probabilities reported when cells had expected counts < 5 (two-tailed).

in the service of memory, which develops in the context of shared conversations about the past, is a powerful way in which children learn to encode more details about an event and to organise those details in a coherent narrative (e.g., Fivush, 1991; Fivush, Haden, & Reese, 2006; Nelson, 1993a, 1993b; Nelson & Fivush, 2004; Reese, Haden, & Fivush, 1993; Tessler & Nelson, 1994). In this way, the youngest children in the present study were still learning how to use language in the service of memory, what is important to remember, and how to relate a coherent narrative to another listener.

While this explanation may account for the age-related increase in participants' accounts of a recent event, it does not explain why adults reported similar amounts of information about memories from the ages of 10 and 13 years as did same-aged children. Instead, our findings seem to mirror those of Gross et al. (2013). In their study, Gross et al. found that adults reported more information about the birth of a younger sibling that occurred many years earlier than did children about the birth of their younger sibling that occurred only a couple of months prior. Gross et al. concluded that the adults may have added details to their reports that they had gathered during the intervening years from talking to family, and seeing photographs or videos.

Similarly, the difference in the provision of information between the adults and children in our study could reflect additional information that the adults added to their original memories over time. If the amount of information that the children reported about recent events reflects the baseline level of information that children encode, then the adults should have reported less (or at least the same amount) about their memories of events that occurred during childhood. In the case of the 5-year-old target memories in particular, adults in the present study apparently added information gleaned from other sources to their memory reports. The present data are highly consistent with those reported by Strange and Hayne (2013) – children (especially young children) rarely report the kind of details that adults often report about their memories, even when explicitly asked. As such, adults' reports of events from childhood that contain more information than we would expect from a child of that age may have been supplemented with details that were not originally encoded but were picked up from other sources in the interim.

Taken together, our findings, along with those of Gross et al. (2013) and Strange and Hayne (2013), challenge the assumption that individuals' reports of their experiences reflect only what they have remembered of what they encoded about the events in the first place. Instead, we suggest that as children learn from those around them what is important to remember and how to "tell a good story," details from other sources (family members, photographs, videos, etc.) inadvertently become part of the narrative. This is unlikely to be a conscious process; rather, children's ability to distinguish between different sources of information in their memory representations (i.e., their own memory versus information from others) is still developing until the age of 9 or 10 years (Johnson, Hashtroudi, & Lindsay, 1993; Roberts, 2002; Robinson & Whitcombe, 2003; Ruffman, Rustin, Garnham, & Parkin, 2001) and all information (regardless of source) is likely to be attributed to genuine memory of the event. The fact that all participants in the present study were explicitly instructed to report only information that that they actually remembered but not information that they only knew about because they had seen photographs or heard family stories about it lends weight to the notion that they genuinely believed they actually encoded and remembered all of the information they reported. The accuracy of their memories (as indicated by their parents) also indicates that they were probably recounting details that actually took place, but that they may not have detected or encoded at the time of the original event.

The present data have both theoretical and practical implications for our understanding of memory development. From a theoretical perspective, these data add to a growing body of work demonstrating that although studies with adults can shed some light on memory development, we must also be cautious when taking their accounts of childhood experiences literally. The human adult's superior linguistic skills and greater breadth of experience gives them the remarkable ability to fill-in-the-blanks about events from their past. Irrespective of whether adults actually remember the information, whether it has been gleaned from another source, or whether it was added in an attempt to tell a better story, the information is readily incorporated into the representation and is recounted as if it was a genuine memory. The vast literature on children's and adults' performance in the Deese-Roediger-McDermott paradigm clearly illustrates that adults are much more likely to fill-in-the-blanks than are children and, once they do so, they feel as if the memory (and in this case, a false memory) is real (Brainerd, Reyna, & Ceci, 2008; Brainerd, Reyna, & Forrest, 2002; Howe, 2005, 2006; Zhang, Gross, & Hayne, 2017).

From a practical perspective, the present results should also make us cautious when we are asked to evaluate adults' memories of childhood events in the courtroom. One striking feature of many historical cases of abuse is the high level of detail with which the event is recounted (Howe, 2013a). We know that this level of detail is highly persuasive to a jury (Bell & Loftus, 1988, 1989; Klettke & Powell, 2011), but are these details actually real? The present data add to a growing body of research suggesting that adults' accounts of early childhood events are far richer than we would predict on the basis of the accounts of children taken at the time the event took place. By way of example, in both the present study and in Strange and Hayne (2013), 5-year-olds never reported information about the weather, the time of day, the date, the day of the week, or the duration of the event in question, yet some adults did report this information when they were recounting an event that took place when they were 5. These details reflect the kind of information that is required in Court to particularise a criminal charge and they are known to influence the decision-making of police, prosecutors, judges, and juries (Darwinkel, Powell, & Sharman, 2015; Howe, 2013a, 2013b). Although the details that the adults reported in the present experiment were largely accurate (or at least possible) based on their parents' evaluations, this may not always be the case. A high level of detail, although persuasive, should not be taken as a proxy for accuracy. In turn, accuracy should also not be taken as evidence of fidelity; the source of the information may not have come from the direct experience of the rememberer.

In summary, prior research with adults has often been used to draw conclusions about memory development. Although this work has helped us to understand some basic principles about the relation between memory and age, when it comes to the details, this same work has sometimes led us astray. In terms of the age of earliest memories, for example, studies with adults would lead us to overestimate the period of childhood amnesia (but see Wang et al., 2017); studies conducted with children clearly show that children encode and retain memories (at least for some period of time) from much earlier epochs in their lives (Jack et al., 2009; Peterson et al., 2011; Peterson, Noel, et al., 2009; Reese et al., 2010). Similarly, prior research with adults has shown that the content of our memories increases as a function of our age at the time of the experience, yet the current study and others (Gross et al., 2013; Strange & Hayne, 2013) also show that these studies with adults lead us to overestimate what children may have encoded in the first place. Taken together, these two lines of research underscore the importance of a developmental perspective; the only way to truly understand how memory develops is to examine memory during development.

Notes

1. All the children and adolescents were of European descent (one child also indicated Māori ethnicity) and all were native English speakers. This information was not collected for this sub-sample of adults, however, the socioeconomic profile of this area of New Zealand is relatively flat; all of the participants would have been classified as middle to upper-middle class.
2. Note that the children were also interviewed about more distant self- and parent-nominated events but those data are not reported here.
3. A series of paired t-tests were conducted to determine whether there were any differences in the total amount of information reported about self- and parent-nominated events at each target age by each group of participants. There were no differences in the amount of information reported about self- and parent-nominated events for the recent target age for any age group, largest $t(11) = -1.17$, $p = .27$. The adults reported the same amount of information for self- and parent-nominated events for target ages 5 and 13 years, largest $t(10) = -2.19$, $p = .053$, but reported more information about parent-nominated events at target age 10 ($M = 36.30$, $SD = 10.28$) than they did about self-nominated events at target age 10 ($M = 26.10$, $SD = 10.08$), $t(9) = -3.05$, $p = .01$, $d = 1.06$ (95% CI [−5.29, 3.18]).

Acknowledgements

We thank Julien Gross, Fiona Jack, Debbie McLachlan, Nicola Davis, Jenny Richmond, and Michelle Tustin for their help with data collection, interview transcription, inter-observer reliability, and data analysis. Special thanks to all of the families who participated in our study.

Disclosure statement

No potential conflict of interest was reported by the authors.

Funding

This research was supported by the Marsden Fund Council from Government funding, managed by Royal Society Te Apārangi.

References

Bachevalier, J. (2014). The development of memory from a neurocognitive and comparative perspective. In P. J. Bauer & R. Fivush (Eds.), *The Wiley handbook on the development of children's memory* (Vol. 1, pp. 109–125). West Sussex: John Wiley & Sons.

Bauer, P. J. (2007). *Remembering the times of our lives: Memory in infancy and beyond*. Mahwah, NJ: Erlbaum. doi:10.4324/9781315785226

Bauer, P. J. (2014). The development of forgetting: Childhood amnesia. In P. J. Bauer & R. Fivush (Eds.), *The Wiley handbook on the development of children's memory* (Vol. 2, pp. 519–544). West Sussex: John Wiley & Sons.

Bauer, P. J., & Larkina, M. (2014). The onset of childhood amnesia in childhood: A prospective investigation of the course and determinants of forgetting of early-life events. *Memory, 22*, 907–924. doi:10.1080/09658211.2013.854806

Bauer, P. J., Tasdemir-Ozdes, A., & Larkina, M. (2014). Adults' reports of their earliest memories: Consistency in events, ages, and narrative characteristics over time. *Consciousness and Cognition, 27*, 76–88. doi:10.1016/j.concog.2014.04.008

Bell, B. E., & Loftus, E. F. (1988). Degree of detail of eyewitness testimony and mock juror judgments. *Journal of Applied Social Psychology, 18*, 1172–1192. doi:10.1111/j.1559-1816.1988.tb01200.x

Bell, B. E., & Loftus, E. F. (1989). Trivial persuasion in the courtroom: The power of (a few) minor details. *Journal of Personality and Social Psychology, 56*, 669–679. doi:10.1037/0022-3514.56.5.669

Brainerd, C. J., Reyna, V. F., & Ceci, S. J. (2008). Developmental reversals in false memory: A review of data and theory. *Psychological Bulletin, 134*, 343–382. doi:10.1037/0033-2909.134.3.343

Brainerd, C. J., Reyna, V., & Forrest, T. (2002). Are young children susceptible to the false–memory illusion? *Child Development, 73*, 1363–1377. doi:10.1111/1467-8624.00477

Crovitz, H., & Harvey, M. (1979). Early childhood amnesia: A quantitative study with implications for the study of retrograde amnesia after brain injury. *Cortex, 15*, 331–335. doi:10.1016/S0010-9452(79)80037-4

Darwinkel, E., Powell, M., & Sharman, S. J. (2015). Police and prosecutors' perceptions of adult sexual assault evidence associated with case authorisation and conviction. *Journal of Police and Criminal Psychology, 30*, 213–220. doi:10.1007/s11896-015-9162-9

Dudycha, G., & Dudycha, M. (1933a). Adolescents' memories of preschool experiences. *Journal of Genetic Psychology, 42*, 468–480. doi:10.1080/08856559.1933.10532453

Dudycha, G., & Dudycha, M. (1933b). Some factors and characteristics of childhood memories. *Child Development, 4*, 265–278. doi:10.1111/j.1467-8624.1933.tb05873.x

Fivush, R. (1991). The social construction of personal narratives. *Merrill-Palmer Quarterly, 37*, 59–82.

Fivush, R., Gray, J., & Fromhoff, F. (1987). Two-year-old talk about the past. *Cognitive Development, 2*, 393–409. doi:10.1016/s0885-2014(87)80015-1

Fivush, R., Haden, C., & Reese, E. (1996). Remembering, recounting, and reminiscing: The development of autobiographical memory in social context. In D. Rubin (Ed.), *Reconstructing our past: An overview of autobiographical memory* (pp. 341–359). New York, NY: Cambridge University Press. doi:10.1017/cbo9780511527913.014

Fivush, R., Haden, C. A., & Reese, E. (2006). Elaborating on elaborations: Role of maternal reminiscing style in cognitive and socioemotional development. *Child Development, 77*, 1568–1588. doi:10.1111/j.1467-8624.2006.00960.x

Fivush, R., & Hamond, N. (1990). Autobiographical memory across the preschool years: Toward reconceptualizing childhood amnesia. In R. Fivush & J. Hudson (Eds.), *Knowing and remembering in young children* (pp. 223–248). New York, NY: Cambridge University Press.

Fivush, R., & Schwarzmueller, A. (1998). Children remember childhood: Implications for childhood amnesia. *Applied Cognitive Psychology, 12*, 455–473. doi:10.1002/(SICI)1099-0720(199810)12:5<455::AID-ACP534>3.0.CO;2-H

Freud, S. (1953). Three essays on the theory of sexuality. In J. Strachey (Ed.), *The standard edition of the complete psychological works of Sigmund Freud* (Vol. 7, pp. 125–248). London: Hogarth Press. (Original work published 1905)

Gross, J., & Hayne, H. (1998). Drawing facilitates children's verbal reports of emotionally laden events. *Journal of Experimental Psychology: Applied, 4*, 163–179. doi:10.1037/1076-898X.4.2.163

Gross, J., Jack, F., Davis, N., & Hayne, H. (2013). Do children recall the birth of a younger sibling? Implications for the study of childhood amnesia. *Memory, 21*, 336–346. doi:10.1080/09658211.2012.726628

Gryson, A., & Hudson, J. A. (2013). Gender differences in autobiographical memory: Developmental and methodological considerations. *Developmental Review, 33*, 239–272. doi:10.1016/j.dr.2013.07.004

Hayne, H., Gross, J., McNamee, S., Fitzgibbon, O., & Tustin, K. (2011). Episodic memory and episodic foresight in 3- and 5-year-old children. *Cognitive Development, 26*, 343–355. doi:10.1016/j.cogdev.2011.09.006

Hayne, H., & Jack, F. (2011). Childhood amnesia. *Wiley Interdisciplinary Reviews: Cognitive Science, 2*, 136–145. doi:10.1002/wcs.107

Henri, V., & Henri, C. (1898). Earliest recollections. *Popular Science Monthly, 21*, 108–115.

Howe, M. L. (2005). Children (but not adults) can inhibit false memories. *Psychological Science, 16*, 927–931. doi:10.1111/j.1467-9280.2005.01638.x

Howe, M. L. (2006). Developmentally invariant dissociations in children's true and false memories: Not all relatedness is created equal. *Child Development, 77*, 1112–1123. doi:10.1111/j.1467-8624.2006.00922.x

Howe, M. L. (2013a). Memory lessons from the courtroom: Reflections on being a memory expert on the witness stand. *Memory, 21*, 576–583. doi:10.1080/09658211.2012.725735

Howe, M. L. (2013b). Memory development: Implications for adults recalling childhood experiences in the courtroom. *Nature Reviews Neuroscience, 14*, 869–876. doi:10.1038/nrn3627

Howes, M., Siegel, M., & Brown, F. (1993). Early childhood memories: Accuracy and affect. *Cognition, 47*, 95–119. doi:10.1016/0010-0277(93)90001-C

Jack, F., & Hayne, H. (2010). Childhood amnesia: Empirical evidence for a two-stage phenomenon. *Memory, 18*, 831–844. doi:10.1080/09658211.2010.510476

Jack, F., MacDonald, S., Reese, E., & Hayne, H. (2009). Maternal reminiscing style during early childhood predicts the age of adolescents' earliest memories. *Child Development, 80*, 496–505. doi:10.1111/j.1467-8624.2009.01274.x

Johnson, M., Foley, M. A., Suengas, A. G., & Raye, C. L. (1988). Phenomenal characteristics of memories for perceived and imagined autobiographical events. *Journal of Experimental Psychology: General, 117*, 371–376. doi:10.1037/0096-3445.117.4.371

Johnson, M., Hashtroudi, S., & Lindsay, D. (1993). Source monitoring. *Psychological Bulletin, 114*, 3–28. doi:10.1037/0033-2909.114.1.3

Klettke, B., & Powell, M. (2011). The effects of evidence, coherence and credentials on jury decision-making in child sexual abuse trials. *Psychiatry, Psychology and Law, 18*, 263–269. doi:10.1080/13218719.2010.543400

MacDonald, S., Uesiliana, K., & Hayne, H. (2000). Cross-cultural and gender differences in childhood amnesia. *Memory, 8*, 365–376. doi:10.1080/09658210050156822

Mullen, M. K. (1994). Earliest recollections of childhood: A demographic analysis. *Cognition, 52*, 55–79. doi:10.1016/0010-0277(94)90004-3

Nelson, K. (1989). Monologue as representation of real-life experience. In K. Nelson (Ed.), *Narratives from the crib* (pp. 27–72). Cambridge, MA: Harvard University Press.

Nelson, K. (1993a). Explaining the emergence of autobiographical memory in early childhood. In A. Collins, S. Gathercole, M. Conway, & P. Morris (Eds.), *Theories of memory* (pp. 355–385). Hillsdale, NJ: Lawrence Erlbaum Associates.

Nelson, K. (1993b). The psychological and social origins of autobiographical memory. *Psychological Science, 4*, 7–14. doi:10.1111/j.1467-9280.1993.tb00548.x

Nelson, K., & Fivush, R. (2004). The emergence of autobiographical memory: A social cultural developmental theory. *Psychological Review, 111*, 486–511. doi:10.1037/0033-295X.111.2.486

Peterson, C., Grant, V., & Boland, L. (2005). Childhood amnesia in children and adolescents: Their earliest memories. *Memory, 13*, 622–637. doi:10.1080/09658210444000278

Peterson, C., Noel, M., Kippenhuck, L., Harmundal, L., & Vincent, C. D. (2009). Early memories of children and adults: Implications for infantile amnesia. *Cognitive Sciences, 4*, 65–89.

Peterson, C., Wang, Q., & Hou, Y. (2009). "When I was little": Childhood recollections in Chinese and European Canadian grade school children. *Child Development, 80*, 506–518. doi:10.1111/j.1467-8624.2009.01275.x

Peterson, C., Warren, K. L., & Short, M. M. (2011). Infantile amnesia across the years: A 2-year follow-up of children's earliest memories. *Child Development, 82*, 1092–1105. doi:10.1111/j.1467-8624.2011.01597.x

Reese, E. (2009). The development of autobiographical memory: Origins and consequences. *Advances in Child Development and Behavior, 37*, 145–200. doi:10.1016/S0065-2407(09)03704-5

Reese, E., Haden, C. A., & Fivush, R. (1993). Mother–child conversations about the past: Relationships of style and memory over time. *Cognitive Development, 8*, 403–430. doi:10.1016/S0885-2014(05)80002-4

Reese, E., Jack, F., & White, N. (2010). Origins of adolescents' autobiographical memories. *Cognitive Development, 25*, 352–367. doi:10.1016/j.cogdev.2010.08.006

Roberts, K. (2002). Children's ability to distinguish between memories from multiple sources: Implications for the quality and accuracy of eyewitness statements. *Developmental Review, 22*, 403–435. doi:10.1016/S0273-2297(02)00005-9

Robinson, E., & Whitcombe, E. (2003). Children's suggestibility in relation to their understanding about sources of knowledge. *Child Development, 74*, 48–62. doi:10.1111/1467-8624.t01-1-00520

Rubin, D. (1982). On the retention function for autobiographical memory. *Journal of Verbal Learning and Verbal Behavior, 21*, 21–38. doi:10.1016/S0022-5371(82)90423-6

Rubin, D. (2000). The distribution of early childhood memories. *Memory, 8*, 265–269. doi:10.1080/096582100406810

Rubin, D., & Wenzel, A. (1996). One hundred years of forgetting: A quantitative description of retention. *Psychological Review, 103*, 734–760. doi:10.1037/0033-295X.103.4.734

Rubin, D., Wetzler, S., & Nebes, R. (1986). Autobiographical memory across the lifespan. In D. Rubin (Ed.), *Autobiographical memory* (pp. 202–221). New York, NY: Cambridge University Press. doi:10.1002/0470018860.s00646

Ruffman, T., Rustin, C., Garnham, W., & Parkin, A. (2001). Source monitoring and false memories in children: Relation to certainty and executive functioning. *Journal of Experimental Child Psychology, 80*, 95–111. doi:10.1006/jecp.2001.2632

Strange, D., & Hayne, H. (2013). The devil is in the detail: Children's recollection of details about their prior experiences. *Memory, 21*, 431–443. doi:10.1080/09658211.2012.732722

Tessler, M., & Nelson, K. (1994). Making memories: The influence of joint encoding on later recall by young children. *Consciousness and Cognition, 3*, 307–326. doi:10.1006/ccog.1994.1018

Tustin, K., & Hayne, H. (2010). Defining the boundary: Age-related changes in childhood amnesia. *Developmental Psychology, 46*, 1049–1061. doi:10.1037/a0020105

Waldfogel, S. (1948). The frequency and affective character of childhood memories. *Psychological Monographs: General and Applied, 62*, i–39. doi:10.1037/h0093581

Wang, Q. (2001). Cultural effects on adults' earliest childhood recollection and self-description: Implications for the relation between memory and the self. *Journal of Personality and Social Psychology, 81*, 220–233. doi:10.1037/0022-3514.81.2.220

Wang, Q., Peterson, C., Khuu, A., Reid, C., Maxwell, K., & Vincent, J. (2017). Looking at the past through a telescope: Adults postdated their earliest childhood memories. *Memory*. doi:10.1080/09658211.2017.1414268

Wetzler, S., & Sweeney, J. (1986). Childhood amnesia: An empirical demonstration. In D. Rubin (Ed.), *Autobiographical memory* (pp. 191–201). New York, NY: Cambridge University Press.

White, K. G. (2001). Forgetting functions. *Animal Learning and Behavior, 29*, 193–207. doi:10.3758/BF03192887

Wickelgren, W. A. (1972). Trace resistance and the decay of long-term memory. *Journal of Mathematical Psychology, 9*, 418–455. doi:10.1016/0022-2496(72)90015-6

Wickelgren, W. A. (1974). Single-trace fragility theory of memory dynamics. *Memory and Cognition, 2*, 775–780. doi:10.3758/BF03198154

Wickelgren, W. A. (1975). Age and storage dynamics in continuous recognition memory. *Developmental Psychology, 11*, 165–169. doi:10.1037/h0076457

Zhang, W., Gross, J., & Hayne, H. (2017). If you're happy and you know it: Positive moods reduce age-related differences in false memory. *Child Development*. doi:10.1111/cdev.12890

The relationship between sociocultural factors and autobiographical memories from childhood: the role of formal schooling

Manuel L. de la Mata, Andrés Santamaría, Eva Mª Trigo, Mercedes Cubero, Samuel Arias-Sánchez, Radka Antalíková, Tia G.B. Hansen and Marcia L. Ruiz

ABSTRACT

Cross-cultural differences in autobiographical memory (AM) are associated with cultural variations. In models of the self and parental reminiscing style, but not many studies have analysed the relationship between AM and specific cultural practices such as formal schooling. Theoreticians like [Greenfield, P. M. (2009). Linking social change and developmental change: Shifting. pathways of human development. *Developmental Psychology, 45*, 401–418. doi:10.1037/a0014726; Kağıtçıbaşı, C. (2005). Autonomy and relatedness in cultural context. Implications for self and family. *Journal of Cross-Cultural Psychology, 36*, 403–422. doi:10.1177/0022022105275959] and [Keller, H. (2007). *Children development across cultures*. New York: Lawrence Erlbaum Associates] have considered formal schooling as an engine towards the model of independence; however, the empirical evidence in this regard is inconclusive: while some studies found evidence of a relation between formal schooling and characteristics of AM, others did not. To solve this inconsistency, the present study compared orally narrated childhood memories of Mexican adults with three different levels of education (from rudimentary literacy to university). Results support a relationship between formal schooling and AM in the predicted direction: More educated participants reported longer, more specific and more self-oriented memories than those with less schooling experience did. Some gender differences were also observed, with males generally reporting more individually and less socially oriented memories than females, except for university level participants. We conclude that these results support Greenfield's theory about formal schooling as a sociocultural factor that promotes the cultural pathway to independence, as well as complexity and context-boundedness of gender differences in AM.

Cross-cultural research has provided extensive evidence of cultural variations in autobiographical memory (AM). Several studies have found that memories of individuals from Western cultures (European Americans, Europeans, etc.) are typically earlier, longer, more elaborated and include more references to emotions and internal states than memories reported by individuals from Asia and other non-Western cultures (Fivush, 2011; Han, Leichtman, & Wang, 1998; MacDonald, Uesiliana, & Hayne, 2000; Mullen, 1994; Nelson & Fivush, 2004; Wang, 2001, 2004, 2006; Wang, Conway, & Hou, 2004; Wang, Hutt, Kulkofsky, McDermott, & Wei, 2006). Studies also found that memories of Western individuals include fewer characters and are more focused on the self than memories from non-Westerners (Fivush, 2011; Wang, 2006).

To account for the reported differences in AM, various cultural influences have been considered, notably self-construal and narrative environment (Leichtman, Wang, & Pillemer, 2003).

The notion of self-construal refers to the culturally influenced ways in which "*individuals define and make meaning of the self*" (Cross, Hardin, & Gercek-Swing, 2011, p. 143). The seminal study by Markus and Kitayama (1991) identified two distinct views of the self: the independent and the interdependent self-construal. While the independent self-construal represents the typical Western view of the self, the interdependent self-construal represents views of the self as always related to other selves.

The distinction between independent vs. interdependent self-construal may account for the above-mentioned differences in AM between individuals from Western and Eastern cultures. While the independent self-construal would facilitate emergence and development of an organised and elaborate memory system for events that happen to the self, conceived as the main protagonist of the memories, the interdependent self-construal's focus on communion (rather than agency) would de-emphasise individuality and promote social integration and interdependence (Wang et al., 2004).

Despite its great influence, Markus and Kitayama's distinction has received numerous criticisms. Recent research has challenged some of its basic assumptions, notably that culture determines self-construal and that individuals from different cultures have reliable differences in self-construal. From this perspective, independent and interdependent self-construals are not mutually exclusive. Rather, they can coexist at the individual level and, hence, could be conceptualised more as a trend than as culturally predetermined categories.

In support of this argument, authors such as Oyserman and colleagues (Oyserman & Lee, 2007; Oyserman, Coon, & Kemmelmeier, 2002), Kam, Xiaolin, Zhang, and Ho (2012) and Vignoles et al. (2016) have reformulated the classical distinction between individualism and collectivism (Hofstede, 2001; Triandis, 1995) at the cultural level, and independent and interdependent self (Markus & Kitayama, 1991) at the individual level. Instead of two poles of a single dimension, these conceptual pairs are considered as orthogonal and domain-specific constructs that can be elicited by different social and situational cues. Rather than assuming the existence of a homogeneous notion of the self in a given country, these authors see a need to establish how different dimensions of the self are combined in specific social, historical, and cultural contexts. From this perspective, individuals may be characterised by specific combinations of independent and interdependent trends modulated by social and cultural contexts and practices (Green, Deschamps, & Paez, 2005). Therefore, (cultural) self-construals would reflect the prevalent patterns in a specific cultural context, but not all members of a specific cultural context fit into this pattern due to individual differences. In this view, self-construals are dynamic and change across the diverse cultural practices and contexts that people are engaged in (Markus & Kitayama, 2010). A focus on the independent or interdependent type of self-construal would not deny the co-existence of its counterpart. So, the focuses on independence and interdependence in self-construal may vary across individuals and situations, influencing the content, style, and accessibility of autobiographical memories.

Another mechanism of cultural influence on AM is narrative environment (Leichtman et al., 2003). As a relatively extensive volume of research has demonstrated, the use of highly elaborative-evaluative parental reminiscing styles is associated with ways of remembering the personal past that are characterised by autonomy and self-centration (Fivush, 2011, 2014; Fivush, Haden, & Reese, 2006). A highly elaborative parental reminiscing style seems to be characteristic in middle-class mothers in Western societies (Fivush, 2007, 2011; but see also Leyva, Reese, Grolnick, & Price, 2009, for evidence of this relationship in low-income families in the US), and cross-cultural research has evidenced its links to cultural models that emphasise autonomy (Schröder et al., 2013). In contrast, a less elaborative parental reminiscing style is characteristic in cultural groups that emphasise relatedness and tend to promote ways of remembering that are consistent with the model of self as interdependent.

Research has also found gender differences in parental reminiscing style. In general, mothers (and fathers, too) make more references to emotions when conversing with their daughters than they do when conversing with their sons (Fivush, 2007). These differences in parental reminiscing style are consistent with gender differences in the memories of children and adults regarding aspects such as the age in the earliest memory (see Davis, 1999; Hayne & MacDonald, 2003; but see also Wang, 2001; Wang et al., 2004) and the form and content of the memories, with females' memories being longer, more detailed and more emotionally charged than males' memories (Fivush, 2007, 2014; Niedzwienska, 2003). Moreover, females' memories are characterised by a predominance of themes related to affiliation, in comparison with males whose memories, in turn, are more oriented towards autonomy and agency (Niedzwienska, 2003). However, it should be noted that gender differences may vary across cultures (Wang & Fivush, 2005), evidencing the complexity of the relationship between gender, culture and AM (Cala & de la Mata, 2010).

The studies reviewed above indicate some of the processes by which culture influences AM. However, we think that there is an important gap in cross-cultural research, with too sparse attention paid to the relationship between specific cultural practices and AM. Among these practices, we are going to focus on formal schooling (Rogoff, 1981, 1990; Scribner & Cole, 1981). The need to study this relationship has both theoretical and empirical foundations.

At a theoretical level, authors such as Kağitçibaşi and Greenfield consider formal schooling to be a factor that promotes the model of independence. For Kağitçibaşi (2005, 2007), an autonomous-related self is often found in traditional societies that used to emphasise relatedness between parents and children but are now beginning to value children's autonomy, too. She has also suggested that this shift is caused by vast and rapid urbanisation and socio-economic development in these countries. The extension of formal education in the population is an important factor in this development. In a similar vein, Greenfield (Greenfield, 2009; Greenfield, Keller, Fuligni, & Maynard, 2003) has proposed two opposing cultural pathways of development, one emphasising individuation and independence, the other promoting group membership and interdependence. For Greenfield (2009), particular socio-demographic changes in society, such as the movement from rural to urban residence, from informal education in the family to formal education, and from subsistence economy and low-technology environments to highly technological environments, have resulted in a general shift towards independence. Research carried out by Keller and colleagues (Keller, 2007) has supported this claim, showing that formal education and urbanisation promote qualitative changes that mitigate the model of interdependence and emphasise the model of independence in different settings, which has important implications for individuals' cognitive processes, including autobiographical memory (Demuth, Chaudary, & Keller, 2011; Keller, 2007).

With regard to empirical evidence, the picture is varied and complex. At least three sources of evidence, coming from different research fields and traditions, must be considered. One important set of contributions are from cross-cultural studies about the relationship between formal schooling and memory strategies (Cole 1990, 1996; Rogoff, 1981). These studies have documented the existence of differences between individuals associated with their level of schooling. It was found that children and adults with more school experience tended to employ memory strategies that enhanced their recall, while people who were not exposed to Western schooling did not use such strategies (Cole, 1996; Rogoff, 1981, 1990). Moreover, such differences only appeared after the schooled participants had received several years of formal schooling (Mistry, 1997). Although these studies did not focus on autobiographical memory, they have provided a first piece of evidence of a relationship between formal schooling and memory. Moreover, some of the proposed mechanisms of the relationship (e.g., the tendency of schooling activities to promote reflection) can be also involved in the relationship between schooling and AM. We shall return to this issue later.

More recently, studies by Lai (2004) with Taiwanese and by Küntay and Atham (2004) with Turkish mothers and their 2–3 years old children have related formal schooling and parental reminiscing style. In both cases, the authors found significant correlations between parental reminiscing style and the educational experience of the mothers. More specifically, the mothers with more years of education used a highly elaborative reminiscing style when conversing with their children about shared past events more frequently than mothers with less educational background did. These mothers, in contrast, adopted a low elaborative style in these conversations in most cases. Given the importance of parental reminiscing style in explaining differences in the ways children and adults remember their personal past (Fivush, 2011, 2014; Fivush et al., 2006), we think that analysis of the links between parental reminiscing style and educational background of the mothers (and, eventually, of the fathers) is particularly relevant and necessary.

The last set of empirical evidence comes from a few studies that have considered the relationship between formal schooling and AM. However, the findings of these studies are not easy to interpret. While some of them have found differences in AM characteristics associated with years of formal education (Heidenreich, Junghanns-Royack, & Stangier, 2007; Kingo, Berntsen, & Krøjgaard, 2013; Reid & Startup, 2010; Wessel, Meeren, Peeters, Arntz, & Merckelbach, 2001), others have not (Berna, Schönknecht, Seidl, Toro, & Schröder, 2012; Conway, Skitka, Hemmerich, & Hershaw, 2009; Janssen, Chessa, & Murre, 2005).

In support of the relationship, Kingo et al. (2013) reported a significant effect of educational level (that varied from basic school to university education) on the age at the earliest memory. Participants with 9–10 years of basic compulsory schooling reported later memories than those with higher levels of education. It is interesting to note that the age of the participants (ranging from 20 to 70 years old) had no significant effect on this variable.

In a related vein, a few studies have found significant differences in AM specificity associated with years of schooling (Heidenreich et al., 2007; Reid & Startup, 2010; Wessel et al., 2001). Although the focus of these studies was not assessment of the relationship between formal schooling and AM specificity, in all three cases the participants' schooling experience (measured in years of education) was considered a moderating or control factor and had a statistically significant effect on specificity.

Finally, other studies have found no evidence of a relationship between years of education and certain AM dimensions and characteristics. These dimensions include the age distribution of autobiographical memories (Janssen et al., 2005), the consistency of flashbulb memories about 911 (Conway et al., 2009), and certain phenomenological characteristics of the memories of healthy vs. cognitively impaired adults (Berna et al., 2012).

In concert, the studies summarised above have provided mixed and inconsistent evidence about the relationship between formal education experience and AM. How can we interpret these inconsistencies? It should be taken into account that these studies varied in many aspects, both conceptually (with diverse theoretical approaches to AM), and methodologically (design and techniques for data-collection and the specific characteristics of the autobiographical memories measured). However, a systematic analysis of these dimensions does not seem to account for the inconsistent results. Instead, we think that a promising aspect to be considered is the range of years of education of the participants. In this regard, some of the studies reporting positive effect of formal education included participants with a range that went from relatively low levels (basic school, 9 years in the case Heidenreich et al., 2007, and even less in other cases) to university education. In the three studies that did not find significant effect of the years of education, only Conway et al. (2009) reported the range of education experience (from less than high school to university degree). The other two studies did not specify the range of years of education of their participants.

The study by De la Mata, Santamaría, and Ruiz (2016) may support the previous interpretation. In this study, participants were Mexican adults aged from 30 to 55 years old, with three different levels of educational background (literacy only, primary school, and university degree). They were asked to give an oral narration of their earliest memory. The results indicated significant differences across educational level for several characteristics of the memories: reported age, content (social vs. individual) and self-focusing. The memories of participants with higher levels of education (especially those with a university degree) were earlier, more individually oriented and more focused on the self than the memories of less educated participants. The fact that some of the characteristics of the autobiographical memories observed in the university level participants were similar to those observed among individuals from cultures of independence supports the consideration of formal schooling as a factor that promotes the cultural pathway to independence (Greenfield, 2009; Greenfield et al., 2003).

The present study

Given that previous evidence about the relationship between formal schooling and AM is not conclusive, we have carried out a replication and extension of the study by De la Mata et al. (2016). As in the previous study, the sample consisted of Mexican adults with the three different levels of formal schooling (literacy only, primary school, and university degree). Besides practical reasons, the choice of Mexican participants was due to the ease of access to a sample of adults with a very low level of formal education (the literacy level). In the present study, we have introduced two main changes: we asked for three memories from childhood (instead of the earliest memory) and have extended the sample to 90 participants (instead of 60). This allowed us to also analyse gender differences and the interaction between educational background and gender.

In the present study, the participants were asked to orally narrate three memories from their childhood. The analysis used several characteristics of the memories as dependent measures: memory volume (measured as the number of words in the memory), specificity, content (social vs. individual), autonomous orientation, individual-social orientation (in terms of self-others ratio) and self-focusing. Most of these measures have been extensively used in previous research (see, for instance, De la Mata et al., 2016; Wang, 2001, 2004) and allowed us to analyse some aspects of autobiographical memories (e.g., autonomy and relatedness) which are also central to self-construal. Age and gender were controlled across educational levels.

Based on the aforementioned theoretical considerations and previous evidence, we hypothesised that the autobiographical memories of participants with more formal schooling experience would be more voluminous, more specific, more individually (with a higher level of autonomous orientation) and less socially oriented, and more self-focused than the memories of participants with less education background.

Besides the role of formal schooling, we also considered gender differences. Previous evidence about gender differences in AM, although not conclusive, led us to hypothesise that females' memories, relative to males' memories, would be longer, more socially oriented, and present lower levels of autonomous orientation and self-focusing.

Method

Participants

Ninety-six adults (48 males and 48 females) from Ciudad Victoria, Tamaulipas (Mexico), participated in the study. Ciudad Victoria is the capital city of the Mexican state of Tamaulipas. It is located in the north east of the country, at the border between Mexico and the United States. The population of Ciudad Victoria is around 350,000 inhabitants (Instituto Nacional de Estadística, 2010). The participants varied in formal schooling experience, and for this variable, three different levels were considered: *literacy level*, with participants that were learning to read and write; *basic level*, participants that had completed primary education, and *university level*, participants that had completed a university degree. Potential participants were contacted through municipal educational institutions, workplaces (private companies) and the local university (Autonomous University of Tamaulipas, UAT, in Spanish). Participation was entirely voluntary, unpaid and based on informed consent. Quota sampling was used to recruit 32 participants (16 females and 16 males) for each level. None of them reported any sensory handicap that may have affected their participation in the research. The mean age of the participants wase 42.32 years (SD = 10.31) for the literacy level (42.5, SD = 10.48 for women; 42.15, SD = 10.69 for men), 42.53 (SD = 10.20) years for the basic level (women, 42.52, SD = 10.18; men, 42.55, SD = 10.78) and 42.7 (SD = 10.87) for the university level (women, 42.75, SD = 10.76; men, 42.65, SD = 11.09). The socio-economic status (SES) of the participants varied, ranging from low or medium-low in the literacy level, medium-low in the basic level, and medium or medium-high in the university level.

Design

The independent variables of our study were educational level, (literacy, basic, and university) and gender (males and females).

The dependent measures concerned autobiographical memory (childhood memory) and were largely based on Wang (2001, 2004) and on De la Mata et al., 2016). The measures employed are presented below along with definitions of the categories.

Instruments and procedure

Literacy level participants could hardly read and write. Therefore, an oral interview ("*Personal Memories Interview*") was designed and applied to collect memories from different life periods.

The procedure had two phases. In the first phase, the purpose of the study and the interview was explained to participants. Procedures to ensure data confidentiality were also explained, and participants' informed consent was obtained. In the second phase, participants were asked to orally narrate their earliest memory and three memories from each of three life periods (childhood, adolescence/youth and adulthood).

All interviews were conducted in Spanish and transcribed by the last author. The total duration of the interview, including the questions about memories from different life-periods, ranged from 30 to 45 min. In this article, only the data of the three memories from childhood are reported. Interviews were videotaped and transcribed verbatim. The transcription was analysed according to the following coding system.

Coding

The categories employed were based on previous studies by Qi Wang (2001, 2004) and De la Mata et al. (2016), with some adjustments. To calculate inter-judges reliability, two collaborators that were unaware of the sociodemographic characteristics of the participants whose memories they were coding independently coded a sample of 20 memories. Kappa indexes (Cohen, 1960) were calculated for this subset of memories. Disagreements between coders were resolved through discussion. The remaining 76 narratives were coded by the same collaborators. The Kappa values for each category are included in the following.

Memory volume. The number of words was counted for each memory as an index of memory volume. The average volume of the three narratives was considered. Previous research indicates that the use of a word count provides a proximal index of volume in each language (Wang, 2001, 2004).

Memory specificity (specific vs. general). Each memory was coded as either "specific" (1) or "general" (0):

> *Specific*: refers to an event that happened one particular moment in time ("I only remember when my mom died. I was seven years old when she died. This is what I remember the most ... ").
>
> *General*: refers to events that took place regularly or on multiple occasions ("My mother helped me to do my homework every day").

The number of specific memories was counted and the Kappa value for this analysis was $K = .96$ *Memory content.* Each memory was coded as either "individual" (0) or "social" (1):

> Individual: focuses on purely personal experiences (e.g. success, frustration, fears, etc.).
>
> Social: centers on activities of a social group such as the family, neighbourhood, school, etc.

Memory content was categorised based on the central focus of the memory narrative rather than the contextual background of each event. For this analysis, the number of social memories was considered and the Kappa value was $K = .91$.

Autonomous orientation. Participants' tendency to express autonomy and self-determination in their memories was coded according to the narrative content analysis developed by Wang and Leichtman (2000). For that purpose, the number of occurrences of the following instances was counted and summed up to produce a general score for autonomous orientation:

(a) Reference to personal needs, desires or preferences ("I really wanted to open my birthday gift").
(b) Reference to personal dislikes or avoidance ("I didn't like that walk").
(c) Reference to personal judgements, opinions or evaluations of people, objects or events ("I loved my birthday gift").
(d) Reference to control over own actions, or to pressure of a social groups they belonged to "I wanted to be in the boy scouts group, but they asked me so many things".

For this analysis, the average score for each of the three memories was calculated and the Kappa value obtained was $K = .91$.

Individual-social orientation: self/others ratio. The number of times each participant mentioned him/herself and the number of times s/he mentioned other people was counted. The ratio of self/others was calculated by dividing the number of mentions of the self by the number of the mentions of others. We used the average of this ratio in the three memories analysed. The Kappa value obtained for this analysis was $K = .86$.

Self-descriptions. The way the participants described themselves in the memories was coded in two mutually exclusive and exhaustive categories in relation to the agency dimension of the self:

(a) Personal self-descriptions. Mentions of personal qualities, attributes, beliefs or behaviours, unrelated to other people, were included in this category ("I'm happy"; "I had a nice house").
(b) Social self-descriptions. Mentions of social categories, group memberships, interpersonal relations, and sensitivity to the viewpoints of others. ("I love my daddy"; "She is my friend").

For this analysis, Kappa value obtained was $K = .92$.

A *self-focusing* index was calculated for each participant by dividing the number of personal self-descriptions by the total number of self-descriptions (personal + social self-descriptions). This index was between 0 and 1, and higher scores indicated a greater degree of personal self-focusing.

Results

All the dependent variables involved in the hypotheses related to education level and gender (memory volume, specificity, content, individual/social orientation, autonomous orientation, and self-focusing) were analysed through a factorial ANOVA with educational level (literacy, basic education, and university) and gender (male, female) as between-group factors. First, the homoscedasticity assumption was tested using the Levene test. When the assumption was not met, we also calculated the heteroscedastic Welch F in a one-way design, with educational level as the unique factor, because the Welch F is not available for our factorial design. A Bonferroni adjustment was applied on 3 of the measures ($p * 3$), because Pearson correlations between them were above .30 (medium effect size). Post-hoc Tukey tests were employed for pairwise comparisons of educational levels when the general test found statistically significant differences with $\alpha = .05$. Finally, we calculated generalised η^2 as the effect size index (Bakeman, 2005; Olejnik & Algina, 2003; Trigo & Martínez Cervantes, 2016) for two non-experimental factors. This index was evaluated in accordance with the levels defined by Cohen (1988): small (.01), medium (.06) and high (.14).

Table 1 shows the statistics for all factorial ANOVAs. As can be seen in the table, the main effect of educational level was statistically significant for memory volume, with a medium effect size. Tukey tests revealed statistically significant differences between university level and the other two levels: literacy ($p = .001$) and basic level ($p = .029$). As hypothesised, the memories of university students had a higher volume than the memories from the other two levels did (see Table 2). Contrary to expectations, we found no gender difference in memory volume.

The same pattern was obtained for memory specificity. We found a significant main effect of educational level, with a high effect size in this case (see Table 1), and statistically significant differences in the pairwise comparisons university-literacy level ($p < .001$), and university-basic level ($p = .004$), with higher specificity in the university level group (see Table 2), as predicted.

With regard to the dependent variable content (social vs individual), although two main effects were statistically significant with the normal F, only gender had a significant effect with the heteroscedastic Welch F, with a medium effect size (see Table 1). In this case, women's autobiographical memories presented higher levels of social themes than those of men (see Table 2).

In the analysis of autonomous orientation, we found two statistically significant effects, a main effect of gender and an interaction between gender and educational level, which modulated the former (see Table 1). As Figure 1 shows, while the index of autonomous orientation was higher for men than women at the literacy and basic level, in the university levels the pattern was the opposite, with women presenting more autonomous orientation than men.

With regard to individual-social orientation (self/others ratio), the two main effects of educational level and gender were statistically significant (see Table 1). However, only the variable educational level reached a medium effect size. Tukey tests revealed that the difference between university and literacy level was statistically significant ($p = .001$), with a higher mean at university than literacy level (see Table 2). Differences between the other levels were not significant. The data were not conclusive regarding the hypothesis of women being more socially oriented than men, because of a small effect size.

The last dependent variable analysed was the self-focusing index. Statistically significant differences were obtained for this variable, with a high effect size for educational level, and medium effect size for gender (see Table 1). The Tukey test revealed statistically significant differences between

Table 1. Statistical results for each source of variability (SV) in the factorial ANOVAs for each dependent variables (DV).

DV	SV	F	df	p	η_g^2
Memory volume	Educational Level (EL)	7.45**	2,89	.001	.13
	Gender (G)	1.27	1,89	.263	.01
	EL * G	0.04	2,89	.964	< .01
Specificity	Educational Level (EL)	8.94**	2,89	< .001	.16
	Gender (G)	0.38	1,89	.539	< .01
	EL * G	1.52	2,89	.224	.03
Content	Educational Level (EL)	3.49	2,89	.105[a]	.07
		(2.62)	(2,59.71)	(1.000[a])	
	Gender (G)	6.33*	1,89	.042[a]	.07
		(6.07*)	(1,77.98)	(.048[a])	
	EL * G	0.33	2,89	1.000[a]	< .01
Individual/Social orientation	Educational Level (EL)	7.38**	2,89	.003[a]	.13
	Gender (G)	5.43	1,89	.066[a]	.05
	EL * G	2.91	2,89	.198[a]	.05
Autonomous orientation	Educational Level (EL)	0.84	2,89	.437	.01
	Gender (G)	6.12*	1,89	.015	.05
	EL * G	7.54**	2,89	.001	.13
Self-focusing index	Educational Level (EL)	11.93**	2,89	< .003[a]	.19
	Gender (G)	7.29*	1,89	.024[a]	.06
	EL * G	3.23	2,89	.132[a]	.05

* Significant at $\alpha = .05$; ** significant at $\alpha = .05$; Welch F data in the second row between brackets; [a] adjusted p ($p * 3$).

Table 2. Mean and standard deviations (between brackets) of all dependent variables (DV) with statistically significant main effects.

DV	Literacy	Basic	University	Men	Women
Memory volume	274.34	317.59	414.69	318.42	352.67
	(143.33)	(164.03)	(145.25)	(21.51)	(21.51)
Specificity	0.34	0.47	1.16	0.71	0.61
	(0.79)	(0.67)	(0.99)	(0.12)	(0.12)
Content	2.63	2.69	2.22	2.31	2.71
	(0.14)	(0.14)	(0.14)	(0.95)	(0.58)
Individual/Social orientation	0.86	1.08	1.28	1.17	0.97
	(0.44)	(0.44)	(0.48)	(0.50)	(0.45)
Autonomous orientation	0.52	−.55	.55	0.58	0.51
	(0.19)	(.17)	(.16)	(0.15)	(0.12)
Self-focusing index	0.44	0.27	0.44	0.38	0.30
	(0.15)	(0.16)	(0.15)	(0.18)	(0.14)

university level and the other two levels: literacy ($p = .002$) and basic level ($p < .001$). As predicted, university level participants had a higher self-focusing index than participants from the other two levels did, and the self-focusing index was higher in men than in women (see Table 2).

Discussion

The aim of this study was to provide evidence of a relationship between formal schooling and AM. An additional goal was to examine gender differences in AM and interaction between formal schooling and gender in this regard. For that purpose, we asked Mexican women and men to orally narrate a memory from their childhood. The level of education of the participants ranged from a very low level (the literacy level, with participants that were learning to read and write), to university background (participants with a university degree), and including an intermediate (basic) level (participants that had concluded the six years of compulsory primary education).

In support of our hypotheses, we found statistically significant relations between level of education and most dimensions of AM (volume, specificity, content, individual-social orientation and self-focusing index). In the case of autonomous orientation, we did not find the expected effect of education. Instead, we found a significant interaction between education and gender. Men at the literacy and basic level had higher levels of autonomous orientation than men did, whereas at the university level, women scored higher than men.

A further examination of the data revealed that the differences associated to education background were always between the university level and the other two levels, with no significant differences between basic and literacy level. In this regard, the memories of the more educated participants (university level) were more voluminous (including more words), more specific, and more focused on the self (rather than on others) than the memories of literacy and basic level participants. Moreover, the effect sizes for all these variables were medium or high.

These results confirm the findings of the study by De la Mata et al. (2016). In their study, the authors found significant differences between the same educational levels (from literacy to university level) in some characteristics of the earliest memory (age, social vs. individual content and self-focusing index). The present study represents a replication and extension of the previous one. Besides the differences in the sample size, the type of memory studied (three memories from childhood in the present study) and the AM characteristics analysed, the findings of both studies are consistent. They are also consistent with the results reported by Kingo et al. (2013), as well as with the evidence from studies showing a positive correlation between years of schooling and AM specificity (Heidenreich et al., 2007; Reid & Startup, 2010; Wessel et al., 2001). In a broader perspective, these results are also convergent with the findings of classical cross-cultural research about formal schooling and memory (Cole, 1990; Mistry, 1997; Rogoff, 1981; Scribner & Cole, 1981). Among all the cultural factors studied in this area (cultural group, urban

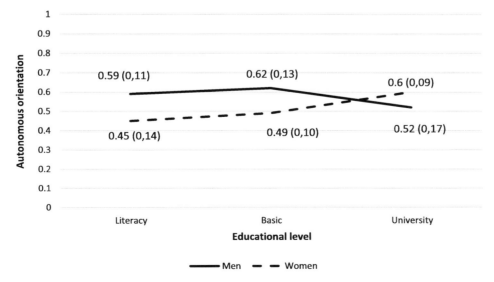

Figure 1. Mean and standard deviations (between brackets) of autonomous orientation depending on educational level and gender.

vs, rural residence, formal schooling and literacy), formal schooling experience seems to be the best predictor of differences in memory skills (Rogoff, 1981; Scribner & Cole, 1981). Although the memory skills assessed in those studies are quite different to AM, we think that our data may be considered as an extension of the findings of classical cross-cultural research about memory.

Some other studies, however, have not found a significant relation between education and AM (Berna et al., 2012; Conway et al., 2009; Janssen et al., 2005). To account for these inconsistent findings about the possible role of formal schooling in AM, we have considered the range of years of education of the participants. As stated above, the differences may only appear when groups with short experience in formal schooling are studied (e.g. literacy and basic level).

Other authors have advocated for alternative explanations, pointing to the possible influence of different factors that may co-vary with education, such as the number of siblings (see Bender & Chasiotis, 2011), or the socio-economic status (SES) of the families. In this regard, we must not forget that formal education experience cannot be experimentally controlled. Indeed, that goes for all cultural factors such as educational background, SES and urban vs. rural residence. Moreover, and from a more theoretical perspective, they all comprise a large set of experiences that are difficult (and very often impossible) to disentangle. We therefore need to be cautious when interpreting differences and cannot establish causal relationships.

Nevertheless, we think that formal schooling is a cultural activity that needs to be considered to account for at least part of the observed differences. There are several reasons to do so. With regard to other variables, such as the number of siblings, we have argued elsewhere (De la Mata et al., 2016) that unlike Bender and Chasiotis (2011), our study included participants with almost no schooling experience and this may increase the relative importance of this factor in explaining the differences. At the same time, there is extensive evidence that educational background of individuals and families are prevailing factors in explanations of both cognitive achievement of children (Dubow, Boxer, & Huesmann, 2009) and cognitive functioning in the elderly (Jefferson et al., 2011). Finally, as we have discussed above, cross-cultural research about formal schooling and memory has demonstrated that among the cultural factors and experiences studied in this field, formal schooling seems to be the one most clearly associated with memory (Cole, 1990; Rogoff, 1981; Scribner & Cole, 1981). All in all, we think that this evidence supports the consideration of the relationship between formal schooling and AM.

The analysis of our data showed that when a statistically significant effect of education was found, the difference was always between the university level and the other two levels (literacy and basic level). How can we interpret this finding? To answer that question some theoretical and methodological issues must be taken into account. First, our methodology was based on the analysis of narratives reported by the participants. These narratives were reported orally (the participants from the literacy level could hardly read and write) and it seems very likely that university graduates would possess better narrative skills than participants from the other two levels. Therefore, whether the differences should be attributed to the autobiographical narratives or to the autobiographical memories of the participants remains an open question. Further studies might examine this issue by investigating differences in non-verbal or non-narrative aspects of autobiographical memories as a function of educational background.

Second, our analysis of the autobiographical narratives focused on dimensions related to autonomy and self-orientation versus relatedness and other-orientation. According to Greenfield (2009) and Kağitçibaşi (2007) formal schooling can be considered a cultural factor, which promotes a model of the self that emphasises autonomy and self-determination. From this theoretical perspective, it is not surprising that autobiographical memories of people with high levels of formal education are individually oriented and focused on the self.

A second independent variable in our study was gender. As discussed in the introduction, previous evidence about gender differences in AM is rather complex and sometimes unclear. While some studies have reported gender differences in AM characteristics such as the age at the earliest memory, themes and social orientation, other studies have not found such differences (see Fivush, 2011; Grysman & Hudson, 2013; Niedzwienska, 2003, for a review of these studies). In still other cases, the differences were not as expected, including culture by gender interactions (Wang, 2004). In our study, we found gender differences in some AM dimensions (themes, autonomous orientation, individual-social orientation and self-focusing index). In all cases, the differences observed supported our hypotheses. The memories reported by female participants were more socially oriented than those reported by males, while the memories reported by the males were more oriented towards autonomy and more focused on the self than were those reported by the females. However, as in most previous studies, the effect sizes were small. In the specific case of autonomous orientation, the main effect of gender was modulated by the educational background of the participants. While men from the literacy and basic level scored higher than women in this variable, the pattern observed in the university level participants was the opposite, with women presenting higher values of autonomous orientation than men. It is interesting to note that in this case, the size effect was medium.

From our perspective, these results show the complexity and contextual nature of gender differences in AM. According to Grysman and Hudson (2013), factors such as the specific instructions given to the participants, various aspects of the context (including the researcher's gender), gender salience, and the measures of AM used can affect and in many cases mitigate or even eliminate gender differences. Besides these factors, it is also necessary to consider the relationship between gender identity and AM as well as developmental changes in these relations. In this vein, Grysman and Fivush (2016) argue that the relatively inconsistent findings in the literature about AM and gender may be due to the focus of these studies on categorical gender, rather than on gender identity (the fit with gender stereotypes). Moreover, most studies have examined gender differences in emerging adults and, especially, in university students, Since issues of professional identity may become central in this period, it is expectable to find a lesser degree of endorsement of gender-typical dimensions (such as relatedness for women). The results obtained by Grysman and Fivush (2016) and by Grysman, Merril, and Fivush (2017) support this view. In these studies, the authors found that gender identity (not least the fit with feminine gender stereotypes), rather than categorical gender, predicted AM phenomenology and the use of emotion expressions in autobiographical memories. Moreover, in both studies the effect sizes were large. For the authors, these findings confirm the need to focus on gender identity and the complexity of the relationship between gender, identity and AM.

The results of our study are consistent with a contextual and identity-focused conception of the relationship between gender and AM. More specifically, they call for the consideration of the role of education as a mediating factor in that relationship. The interaction between gender and educational level observed for autonomous orientation can be interpreted as an example of that complexit and may not be unique to AM. In this regard, we have found a similar pattern of interaction between gender and education in argumentation (Cala & de la Mata, 2004). In the same way as the present study, Cala and de la Mata found that gender differences were modulated by educational background, with fewer differences in the university level group than in the others.

At a general theoretical level, our study provides additional support to the consideration of formal education as a sociocultural activity that promotes the model of independence (Greenfield, 2009; Greenfield et al., 2003; Kağıtçıbaşi, 2005, 2007; Keller (2007). The fact that the memories of participants with a higher level of education (university level) was characterised by more self-focusing and less orientation towards others, in comparison with those of the literacy and primary school-level participants, seems to support this interpretation.

However, accepting the relationship between formal schooling and AM does not answer the question of *how* this sociocultural practice may promote forms of autobiographical remembering that are characterised by an emphasis on individuality and self-focusing. The study reported in this paper does not provide evidence in this regard. We can only speculate about the possible processes by which formal schooling activities may influence AM. One possible avenue is likely to be parental reminiscing style. As we have argued above, there is extensive evidence of the links between highly elaborative styles in parent-child conversation about past events and children's ways of remembering. Western middle-class mothers and fathers typically use a more elaborative reminiscing style than non-Western parents (Fivush, 2011; Schröder et al., 2013) and, consequently, their children tend to recall earlier and more elaborative autobiographical memories. Moreover, these narratives are usually characterised by a greater emphasis on autonomy, with the self as the central protagonist. In contrast, autobiographical memories of non-Western children are typically dated later, are less elaborated (including less references to child's mental states), more socially oriented (Fivush, 2007, 2011; Fivush et al., 2006; Reese, Haden, & Fivush, 1993) and more didactic, placing the child's individual experiences in the context of the group and moral behaviour (Fivush, 2011). These studies are based on comparisons of mother-child dyads from different cultures (Western and Easter cultures, typically). The studies developed by Keller and colleagues (see Schröder et al., 2013, for a review) that analyse reminiscing situations and memories of parent-child dyads, which represent the cultural models of autonomy, relatedness and autonomy-relatedness, mark a significant advancement in disentangling how culture modulates AM. In our view, it is necessary to also analyse how cultural practices like formal schooling may relate to AM via reminiscing situations. In this vein, results of the studies by Lai (2004) and Küntay and Atham (2004) demonstrating a positive relationship between mothers' education and highly elaborative reminiscing style, provide one step further in this direction and support the idea of parental reminiscing style as a privileged link between formal education and AM.

Besides parental reminiscing style, we have speculated elsewhere (De la Mata et al., 2016) that another possible mechanism, by which formal schooling can influence AM, is the tendency of schooling activities to promote metacognitive reflection. Authors such as Scribner and Cole (1981), Rogoff (1981) and Olson (1994, 2016) have proposed that Western schools (and universities) encourage students to verbally explain the ways that tasks are solved and to express autonomy and self-determination. From our perspective, more research on the proximal processes by which formal education activities may promote the model of independence, would be very relevant.

While the evidence reported in this article is promising, it also has a number of limitations. As mentioned above, formal schooling background co-varies with other cultural factors and experiences such as SES, number of siblings (Bender & Chasiotis, 2011) and rural vs. urban residence (Nourkova & Dnestrovskaya, 2013).

The present study cannot disentangle influence from these factors. Although there are cases in which such disentanglement may be possible, formal schooling, SES or rural-urban residence are cultural factors that comprise a set of experiences of individuals and groups and disentanglement is not the only fruitful avenue of further research. We think that cultural and cross-cultural research must also delve deeper into the ways that formal education (and the other cultural factors and experiences) promotes forms of remembering personal experiences that characterise the cultural model of independence. To do so, we think that it is necessary to conduct in-depth analyses of cultural practices that may promote these ways of remembering (and, hence, of constructing the self).

We have indicated two of the specific ways of relating formal schooling an AM. The first is parent-child reminiscing situations. In this regard, we believe it is necessary to identify the characteristics of parent-child conversation in parents with different levels of formal schooling, and analyse how these characteristics may eventually relate to children's autobiographical memories.

Additionally, we would advocate studies with more in-depth analyses of the specific features and elements involved in formal schooling activities, and in their relation to forms of personal remembering that are characterised by emphasis on autonomy and self-centredness. The theoretical ideas of authors such as Scribner and Cole (1981) and Olson (1994, 2016), which include the role of school literacy activities in promotion of autonomy and self-reflection, may guide future research in this area.

Acknowledgements

The research reported in this manuscript was supported by the Autonomous University of Tamaulipas (UAT), Mexico to Marcia L. Ruiz. The writing of the manuscript was supported by the *Programa Estatal de Fomento de la Investigación, Científica y Técnica de Excelencia, Subprograma Estatal de Generación de Conocimiento, en el marco del Plan Estatal de Investigación Científica y Técnica y de Innovación 2013–2016* [National Programme for the Promotion of Scientific and Technical Research of Excellence, within the National Plan for the Promotion of Scientific and Technical Research and Innovation 2013-2016] to Manuel de la Mata, Andrés Santamaría, Mercedes Cubero and Samuel Arias. The authors express their deep and abiding gratitude to the participants in the study, data from which are reported in this manuscript.

Disclosure statement

No potential conflict of interest was reported by the authors.

Funding

This work was supported by the Autonomous University of Tamaulipas (UAT), Mexico to Marcia L. Ruiz. Subsecretariat of Higher Education. General Directorate of Higher Education University. Program for Higher Teaching Professional Development. Secretary of Public Education. Mexico.

References

Bakeman, R. (2005). Recommended effect size statistics for repeated measures designs. *Behavior Research Methods*, *37*(3), 379–384. doi:10.3758/BF03192707

Bender, M., & Chasiotis, A. (2011). Number of siblings in childhood explains cultural variance in autobiographical memory in Cameroon, people's republic of China, and Germany. *Journal of Cross-Cultural Psychology*, *42*, 998–1017. doi:10.1177/0022022110381127

Berna, F., Schönknecht, P., Seidl, U., Toro, P., & Schröder, J. (2012). Episodic autobiographical memory in normal aging and mild cognitive impairment: A population-based study. *Psychiatry Research*, *200*, 807–812. doi:10.1016/j.psychres.2012.03.022

Cala, M. J., & de la Mata, M. L. (2004). Educational background, modes of discourse and argumentation: Comparing women and men. *Argumentation*, *18*, 403–426. doi:10.1007/s10503-004-4906-1

Cala, M. J., & de la Mata, M. L. (2010). Género, identidad y memoria autobiográfica. *Estudios de Psicología*, *31*(1), 3–20. doi:10.1174/021093910790744653

Cohen, J. A. (1960). Coefficient for agreement for nominal scales. *Educational and Psychological Measurement*, *20*, 37–46. doi:10.1177/001316446002000104

Cohen, J. A. (1988). *Statistical power analysis for the behavioral sciences* (Second). Hillsdale, NJ: Lawrence Erlbaum Associates. Retrieved from http://books.google.com/books?id=TI0N2IRAO9oC&pgis=1

Cole, M. (1990). Cognitive development and formal schooling: The evidence from cross-cultural research. In L. Moll (Ed.), *Vygotsky and education: Instructional implications and applications of sociohistorical psychology* (pp. 89–110). Cambridge: Cambridge University Press.

Cole, M. (1996). *Cultural psychology. A once and future discipline*. Cambridge, MA: Harvard University Press.

Conway, A. R. A., Skitka, L. J., Hemmerich, J. A., & Hershaw, T. C. (2009). Flashbulb memory for 11 September 2001. *Applied Cognitive Psychology*, *23*, 605–623. doi:10.1002/acp.1497

Cross, S. E., Hardin, E. E., & Gercek-Swing, B. (2011). The what, how, why, and where of self-construal. *Personality and Social Psychology Review*, *15*, 142–179. doi:10.1177/1088868310373752

Davis, P. (1999). Gender *differences* in autobiographical memory for childhood emotional experiences. *Journal of Personality and Social Psychology*, *76*, 498–510. doi:10.1037/0022-3514.76.3.498

De la Mata, M. L., Santamaría, A., & Ruiz, M. (2016). Toward the model of independence: The influence of formal schooling experience on earliest autobiographical memories and self-construals: A preliminary study. *Journal of Cross-Cultural Psychology*, *47*, 670–679. doi:10.1177/0022022116635745

Demuth, C., Chaudary, N., & Keller, H. (2011). Memories of me: Comparisons from Osnabrueck (Germany) and Delhi (India) students and their mothers. *Integrative Psychological and Behavioral Science*, *45*, 48–67. doi:10.1007/s12124-010-9136-5

Dubow, E. F., Boxer, P., & Huesmann, R. (2009). Long-term effects of parents' education on children's educational and occupational success: Mediation by family interactions, child aggression, and teenage aspirations. *Merrill-Palmer Quarterly*, *55*, 224–249. doi:10.1353/mpq.0.0030

Fivush, R. (2007). Maternal reminiscing style and children's developing under-standing of self and emotion. *Clinical Social Work Journal*, *35*, 37–46. doi:10.1007/s10615-006-0065-1

Fivush, R. (2011). The development of autobiographical memory. *Annual Review of Psychology*, *62*, 559–582. doi:10.1146/annurev.psych.121208.131702

Fivush, R. (2014). Maternal reminiscing style: The sociocultural construction of autobiographical memory across childhood and adolescence. In P. J. Bauer, & R. Fivush (Eds.), *The Wiley handbook on the development of children's memory, volume I/II* (pp. 568–585). New York, NY: Wiley-Blackwell.

Fivush, R., Haden, C. A., & Reese, E. (2006). Elaborating on elaborations: Role of maternal reminiscing style on cognitive and socioemotional development. *Child Development, 77*, 1568–1588. doi:10.1111/j.1467-8624.2006.00960.x

Green, E. G. T., Deschamps, J-C., & Páez, D. (2005). Variation of Individualism and Collectivism within and between 20 Countries. *Journal of Cross-Cultural Psychology, 36*(3), 321–339. doi: 10.1177/0022022104273654

Greenfield, P. M. (2009). Linking social change and developmental change: Shifting. pathways of human development. *Developmental Psychology, 45*, 401–418. doi:10.1037/a0014726

Greenfield, P. M., Keller, H., Fuligni, A., & Maynard, A. (2003). Cultural pathways through universal development. *Annual Review of Psychology, 54*, 461–490. doi:10.1146/annurev.psych.54.101601.145221

Grysman, A., & Fivush, R. (2016). Gender identity predicts autobiographical memory phenomenology. *Applied Cognitive Psychology, 30*, 613–621. doi:10.1002/acp.3235

Grysman, A., & Hudson, J. A. (2013). Gender differences in autobiographical memory: Developmental and methodological considerations. *Developmental Review, 33*(3), 239–272. doi:10.1016/j.dr.2013.07.004

Grysman, A., Merril, N., & Fivush, R. (2017). Emotion, gender and gender typical identity in autobiographical memory. *Memory (Hove, England), 25*(3), 289–297. doi:10.1080/09658211.2016.1168847

Han, J. J., Leichtman, M. D., & Wang, Q. (1998). Autobiographical memory in Korean, Chinese and American children. *Developmental Psychology, 34*(701), 713. doi:10.1037/0012-1649.34.4.701.

Hayne, H., & MacDonald, S. (2003). The socialization of autobiographical memory in children and adults: The roles of culture and gender. In R. Fivush, & C. A. Haden (Eds.), *Autobiographical memory and the construction of a narrative self* (pp. 99–119). Mahwah, NJ: Lawrence Erlbaum Associates.

Heidenreich, T., Junghanns-Royack, K., & Stangier, U. (2007). Specificity of autobiographical memory in social phobia and major depression. *British Journal of Clinical Psychology, 46*, 19–33. doi:10.1348/014466506X106218

Hofstede, G. (2001). *Culturés consequences: Comparing values, behaviors, institutions, and organizations across nations.* Thousand Oaks, CA: Sage.

Instituto Nacional de Estadística. (2010). *Censo de población y vivienda. Principales resultados por localidad* (September 2017). Retrieved from http://www.inegi.org.mx/est/contenidos/proyectos/ccpv/cpv2010/iter_2010.aspx

Janssen, S. M. J., Chessa, A. G., & Murre, J. J. (2005). The reminiscence bump in autobiographical memory: Effects of age, gender, education and culture. *Memory, 13*(6), 658–668. doi:10.1080/09658210444000322

Jefferson, A. L., Gibbons, L. E., Rentz, D. M., Carvalho, J. O., Manly, J., Bennett, D. M., & Jones, R. N. (2011). A life course model of cognitive activities, socioeconomic status, education, reading ability, and cognition. *Journal of the American Geriatric Society, 59*, 1403–1411. doi:10.1111/j.1532-5415.2011.03499.x

Kağitçibaşi, C. (2005). Autonomy and relatedness in cultural context. Implications for self and family. *Journal of Cross-Cultural Psychology, 36*, 403–422. doi:10.1177/0022022105275959

Kağitçibaşi, C. (2007). *Family, self and human development across cultures. Theory and applications.* Mahwah, NJ: Lawrence Erlbaum Associates.

Kam, C., Xiaolin, Z., Zhang, X., & Ho, M. Y. (2012). Examining the dimensionality of self-construals and individualistic–collectivistic values with random intercept item factor analysis. *Personality and Individual Differences, 53*, 727–733. doi:10.1016/j.paid.2012.05.023

Keller, H. (2007). *Children development across cultures.* New York: Lawrence Erlbaum Associates.

Kingo, O. S., Berntsen, D., & Krøjgaard, P. (2013). Adults' earliest memories as a function of age, gender, and education in a large stratified sample. *Psychology and Aging, 28*, 646–653. doi:10.1037/a0031356

Küntay, A., & Atham, B. (2004). Annelerin Cocuklariyla Geçmis Hakkindaki Konusmalarinin Anne Egitim Düzeyiyle Iliskisi. *Türk Psikoloji Dergisi*, [Effect of maternal education on Turkish mothers' styles of reminiscing with their children. *Turkish Journal of Psychology*], *19*, 19–31.

Lai, W. F. (2004). *Co-constructing narratives with young children: A study of the relationships between Taiwanese mothers' discourse styles and mothers' education, family income, and children's age* (Unpublished doctoral dissertation). Boston University.

Leichtman, M. D., Wang, Q., & Pillemer, D. B. (2003). Cultural variations in interdependence and autobiographical memory: Lessons from Korea, China, India and the United States. In R. Fivush, & C. A. Haden (Eds.), *Autobiographical memory and the construction of a narrative self. Developmental and cultural perspectives* (pp. 73–97). Mahwah, NJ: Lawrence Erlbaum Associates.

Leyva, D., Reese, E., Grolnick, W., & Price, C. (2009). Elaboration and autonomy support in Low-income mothers' reminiscing: Links to children's autobiographical narratives. *Journal of Cognition and Development, 9*(4), 363–389. doi:10.1080/15248370802678158

MacDonald, S., Uesiliana, K., & Hayne, H. (2000). Cross-cultural and gender differences in childhood amnesia. *Memory, 8*(6), 365–376. doi:10.1080/09658210050156822

Markus, H. R., & Kitayama, S. (1991). Culture and the self: Implications for cognition, emotion, and motivation. *Psychological Review, 98*(2), 224–253. doi:10.1037/0033-295X.98.2.224

Markus, H. R., & Kitayama, S. (2010). Cultures and selves: A cycle of mutual constitution. *Perspectives on Psychological Science, 5*(4), 420–430. doi:10.1177/1745691610375557

Mistry, J. (1997). The development of remembering in cultural contexts. In N. Cowan, & Ch. Hulme (Eds.), *The development of memory in children* (pp. 343–367). Hove: Psychology Press.

Mullen, M. K. (1994). Earliest recollections of childhood: A demographic analysis. *Cognition, 52*(1), 55–79. doi:10.1016/0010-0277(94)90004-3

Nelson, K., & Fivush, R. (2004). The emergence of autobiographical memory: A social cultural developmental theory. *Psychological Review, 111*(2), 486–511. doi:10.1037/0033-295X.111.2.486

Niedzwienska, A. (2003). Gender differences in Vivid memories. *Sex Roles, 49*(7-8), 321–331. doi:10.1023/A:1025156019547

Nourkova, V., & Dnestrovskaya, M. (2013). Dynamics of autonomy and relatedness across lifespan in autobiographical narratives: Semantic and susceptibility. *Procedia Social and Behavioral Sciences, 86*, 475–481. doi:10.1016/j.sbspro.2013.08.600

Olejnik, S., & Algina, J. (2003). Generalized eta and omega squared statistics: Measures of effect size for some common research designs. *Psychological Methods, 8*(4), 434–447. doi:10.1037/1082-989X.8.4.434

Olson, D. R. (1994). *The world on paper.* New York: Cambridge University Press.

Olson, D. R. (2016). *The mind on paper: Reading, consciousness and rationality.* New York: Cambridge University Press.

Oyserman, D., Coon, H. M., & Kemmelmeier, M. (2002). Rethinking individualism and collectivism: Evaluation of theoretical assumptions and meta-analyses. *Psychological Bulletin, 128*(1), 3–72. doi:10.1037/0033-2909.128.1.3

Oyserman, D., & Lee, W. S. (2007). Priming "culture": Culture as situated cognition. In S. Kitayama, & D. Cohen (Eds.), *Handbook of cultural psychology* (pp. 255–275). New York: Guilford.

Reese, E., Haden, C. A., & Fivush, R. (1993). Mother-child conversations about the past: Relationships of styles and memory over time. *Cognitive Development, 8*(4), 403–430.

Reid, T., & Startup, M. (2010). Autobiographical memory specificity in borderline personality disorder: Associations with co-morbid depression and intellectual ability. *British Journal of Clinical Psychology, 49*(3), 413–420. doi:10.1348/014466510X487059

Rogoff, B. (1981). Schooling and the development of cognitive skills. In H. C. Triandis, & A. Heron (Eds.), *Handbook cross-cultural psychology, Vol. 4* (pp. 233–294). Boston: Allyn and Bacon.

Rogoff, B. (1990). *Apprenticeship in thinking. Cognitive development in social context*. Oxford: Oxford University Press.

Schröder, L., Keller, H., Kärtner, J., Kleis, A., Abels, M., Yovsi, R. D., ... Papaligoura, Z. (2013). Early reminiscing in cultural contexts: Cultural models, maternal reminiscing styles, and children's memories. *Journal of Cognition and Development*, 14(1), 10–34. doi:10.1080/15248372.2011.638690

Scribner, S., & Cole, M. (1981). *The psychology of literacy*. Cambridge, MA: Harvard University Press.

Triandis, H. C. (1995). *Individualism and collectivism*. San Francisco, CA: Westview Press.

Trigo, M. E., & Martínez Cervantes, R. J. (2016). Generalized eta squared for multiple comparisons on between-groups designs. *Psicothema*, 28(3), 340–345. doi:org/10.7334/psicothema2015.124

Vignoles, V., Owe, E., Becker, M., Smith, P. B., Easterbrook, M. J., Brown, R., ... Lay, S. (2016). Beyond the 'east–west' dichotomy: Global variation in cultural models of selfhood. *Journal of Experimental Psychology: General*, 145(8), 966–1000. doi:10.1037/xge0000175

Wang, Q. (2001). Culture *effects* on adult's earliest childhood recollection and self-description: Implications for the relation between memory and the self. *Journal of Personality and Social Psychology*, 81(2), 220–233. doi:10.1037/0022-3514.81.2.220

Wang, Q. (2004). The emergence of cultural self-construct: Autobiographical memory and self-description in American and Chinese children. *Developmental Psychology*, 40(1), 3–15. doi:10.1037/0012-1649.40.1.3

Wang, Q. (2006). Earliest recollections of self and others in European American and Taiwanese young adults. *Psychological Science*, 17(8), 708–714. doi:10.1111/j.1467-9280.2006.01770.x

Wang, Q., Conway, M. A., & Hou, Y. (2004). Infantile amnesia: A cross-cultural investigation. *Cognitive Science*, 1, 123–135.

Wang, Q., & Fivush, R. (2005). Mother-child conversations of emotionally salient events: Exploring the functions of emotional reminiscing in European-American and Chinese families. *Social Development*, 14(3), 473–495. doi:10.1111/j.1467-9507.2005.00312.x

Wang, Q., Hutt, R., Kulkofsky, S., McDermott, M., & Wei, R. (2006). Emotion situation knowledge and autobiographical memory in Chinese, immigrant Chinese, and European American 3-year-olds. *Journal of Cognition and Development*, 7(1), 95–118. doi:10.1207/s15327647jcd0701_5

Wang, Q., & Leichtman, M. D. (2000). Same beginnings, different stories: A comparison of American and Chinese children's narratives. *Child Development*, 71(5), 1329–1346. doi:10.1111/1467-8624.00231

Wessel, L., Meeren, M., Peeters, F., Arntz, A., & Merckelbach, H. (2001). Correlates of autobiographical memory specificity: The role of depression, anxiety and childhood trauma. *Behaviour Research and Therapy*, 39(4), 409–421. doi:10.1016/S0005-7967(00)00011-5

Unravelling the nature of early (autobiographical) memory

Mark L. Howe

ABSTRACT
In this article, I provide an overview of the problems associated with understanding the nature of early autobiographical memory and discuss issues concerning the forgetting of these memories (infantile/childhood amnesia). Specifically, I provide a brief exegesis as to whether such memories are stored in a fragile manner to begin with, become difficult to retrieve over time, or both. In order to answer this and other related questions, I review the contribution of the articles in this special issue to understanding the enigma that is infantile/childhood amnesia. I then outline some of the issues that remain and suggest a functional approach to understanding why the forgetting of early experiences may be more adaptive than remembering them. I conclude by suggesting that infantile amnesia may actually begin during infancy itself.

For at least three centuries (Henri & Henri, 1895; Miles, 1895), and probably much longer, students of memory have puzzled over the enigma of early childhood memory. More specifically, although it is clear that young children can exhibit various rudimentary forms of memory very early in life (see Bauer, 2015; Howe, 2011), researchers have wondered when memory for events themselves becomes part of a child's recollective armamentum. Of course, children can remember events but with the advent of the cognitive self at around 18–24 months of age, they now begin to remember these events as experiences that happened to "me" – in other words, these memories are now autobiographical (e.g., Howe & Courage, 1993, 1997).

The importance of the self in autobiographical memory is not limited to its genesis and early development, but is also key throughout the lifespan of an individual (e.g., Bluck & Alea, 2008; Conway, 2005; Prebble, Addis, & Tippett, 2013). In fact, the mnemonic benefits of self-referencing and self-generation (e.g., Cunningham, Brebner, Quinn, & Turk, 2014; Mulligan & Lozito, 2004) have been well established in both the child and adult memory literatures for some time. Indeed, for some (Humphreys & Sui, 2016; Sui & Humphreys, 2015), the self is the very "glue" that binds encoded elements together to create a strong and durable trace for personal (autobiographical) experiences.

Importantly, the advent of the cognitive self creates a necessary although not sufficient condition for the creation and retention of autobiographical memories. Indeed, not only are scientists concerned about the emergence of autobiographical memory, but also what happens to those memories over time. Although some have dated earliest memories back to around the age of two years, the same time as the emergence of the cognitive self, most of our early memories become irretrievable later in childhood or by early adulthood (see various articles in this special issue for examples). In fact, some prefer to think of two periods of forgetting childhood events: a particularly dense amnesia for memories up to the age of approximately two years (infantile amnesia) and another period of not-so-dense amnesia lasting up to about five to seven years of age (childhood amnesia) (e.g., see Jack & Hayne, 2010; Newcombe, Lloyd, & Ratliff, 2007).

A key question concerns whether these amnesias are brought about by failures in retrieval, failures in storage, or failures in both storage and retrieval. Concerning retrieval, the basic argument goes like this: memories that are formed early in life are constrained by the context in which they are encoded and although vestiges of these memories remain in storage, they are difficult to retrieve unless one can reinstate the original (infant) context in which they were stored (basically, an encoding specificity argument). Thus, although these memories remain retrievable as long as the context can be reinstated, as the child is developing rapidly, this context changes and the memories are no longer accessible (for reviews, see Bauer, 2015; Howe, 2011). Concerning storage, the argument is that memories that are formed early in life are fragile and hence, tend to be forgotten rapidly. The amnesia problem emerges because memories that were formed early in life dissipate rapidly, perhaps being replaced by newer memories. That is, early memories are no longer in storage and thus, are not available for retrieval (e.g., Alberini & Travaglia, 2017).

Of course, there are a number of other weighty matters concerning how or even if we remember early experiences. These include whether children and adults have rehearsed and elaborated these experiences through conversations with others, something that raises additional questions concerning whether what is being remember later on are the memories themselves or the discussions that ensued about those memories for early experiences. Another critical question is exactly when does infantile and childhood amnesia begin? Does it suddenly appear abruptly in late adolescence or early adulthood, or is it a more continuous process that emerges in childhood and continues to develop into adulthood? Finally, there are a number of individual and group differences questions including whether variation in the ability to remember early experiences across cultures, as a function of education, gender, or language skills contribute to one's ability to remember early experiences. The articles in this special issue all address various aspects of these problems in early memory and in what follows, I provide a brief synopsis of these papers. I then turn to a discussion of what we have learned from these (and other recent studies) and suggest a number of questions that require further research in order to help resolve the enigma that is infantile/childhood amnesia.

Adults' recall and dating of early memories

Some of the articles in this special issue focus on the question of how accurately adults date their early (or first) memories. For example, Wang et al. (2018) found in two experiments that North American college students' earliest memories could be dated as far back as 2.5 years of age (consistent with the time the cognitive self emerges). Of course, this age was calculated in part by removing what are known as telescoping errors, errors that arise when dating early memories. Specifically, earlier memories tend to be postdated because they are thought to have happened more recently than they actually have.

Ece, Demiray, and Gülgöz (2018) conducted an online survey where participants reported their earliest memories twice with an intervening two-year interval. Interestingly, they found a remarkable consistency in content, dating, and qualities of earliest memories being reported across this two-year interval. However, such consistency was not observed uniformly across all memories. Indeed, this consistency was seen primarily for the earliest of childhood memories (those dated before 48 months of age). Perhaps the extent to which early memories exhibit such consistency depends on how the data from adult recollection is analysed.

Using a similar line of thought, Wessel, Schweig, and Huntjens (2018) investigated the malleability of dating earliest memories. Specifically, these researchers examined undergraduate students' ability to date earliest memories by manipulating the instructions prior to recall. Here, one type of instruction informed students that early memories might be sketchy and fragmented and they were provided with some examples of such memories. Instructions also included vignettes that referred either to events that happened around the age of two years or events that happened later at age six years. As predicted, age of the event memories mentioned in the instructions affected the age of the earliest memories being recalled. As well, just thinking about events (self-relevant or public) that happened during their preschool years, also resulted in memories that were dated earlier than when no such instruction is given. Thus, age information introduced in the instructions to remember one's earliest memories can affect the age estimates provided for the memories that are retrieved.

These studies raise the issue as to how reliable age estimates are for early memories? Indeed, what these studies suggest is that the search for the dating, or the "when", of early memory is fraught with problems, particular ones to do with measurement. Of course, one of the most persnickety problems arises from the fact that the "when" of a memory is not necessarily encoded at the time of the event. What this means is that dating them at some later time amounts to a guestimate, one that may other faulty time estimates when we try to date related memories in order to date a target memory (i.e., when we estimate the date of our earliest memory based on memory for other events). So in essence, the dating of earliest memories relies on processes that are outside the realm of simple retrieval processes related to what is stored in memory – that is, we are asking for judgements about things we have never stored in the first place.

To put a finer point on this, consider a recent study by Akhtar, Justice, Morrison, and Conway (2018). They conducted a large-scale online survey of people's (6641 respondents) first memories, age-at-encoding, as well as a number of other memory judgements. Consistent with most previous research, as well as the studies published in this special issue, they found that age-at-encoding of earliest memories was 3.2 years of age on average (uncorrected for telescoping errors). However, unlike many previous studies in which there are few or no memories from the preverbal period (i.e., prior to two years of age), Akhtar et al. found that nearly 40% of the sample (or 2487 people) had first memories that were dated to an age of two years and earlier, with 893 (almost 14%) dating their first memories to the age of one year and younger.

So, if elaborate autobiographical memories from this period are theoretically impossible (as most researchers would agree), what accounts for this unusual frequency of very early (and improbable) memories? Akhtar et al. (2018) examined a number of hypotheses (errors in dating memories, potentially self-selective nature of the respondents, and the narrative and fictional nature of the "life story") and found all of them to be wanting. Instead, they proposed that given that memories are constructive in nature, these recollections come from a class of what they term, fictional memories. Specifically, because all memories are time-compressed and do not literally represent the experience from which they derive, these very early memories, like other memories, contain details that are either consciously or non-consciously inferred. In other words, fictional memories derive not from the reality that was experienced, but rather from how well it corresponds with, and is coherent with, other parts of autobiographical memory (also see Conway, 2005 and Conway, Loveday, & Cole, 2016 for a discussion of coherence and correspondence). The important point here is that because memory is (re)constructive and can rely on many different sources (e.g., remnants of the experience itself, conversations about those experiences, accrued [semantic-autobiographical] knowledge about how the world works, coherence pressures in autobiographical memory) when one is trying to retrieve a specific memory, the "when" of such memories may be as impenetrable and unreliable as the very content of the memory itself.

Children's recall and dating of early memories

Another strategy used by researchers to investigate questions about early childhood memories in this special issue is that of examining early memories in children themselves. Indeed, it has been known for some time now that amnesia for childhood events actually begins in childhood not adulthood (e.g., Bauer & Larkina, 2014; Cleveland & Reese, 2008; Peterson, Grant, & Boland, 2005; Tustin & Hayne, 2010; Wang & Peterson, 2014). Adding to this line of inquiry in the current issue, Bauer and Larkina (2018) examined the development of autobiographical memory (rather than its absence) in 4- to 10-year-olds children. Using a cohort-sequential design, they examined children's autobiographical narratives of events that had happened in the preceding four months. Each cohort (4-, 6-, and 8-year-olds) was tested twice, separated by a one-year interval between tests. For some events, the child was interviewed by the experimenter and for others, interviews involved both the mother and the child. These latter interviews were conducted in order to evaluate the influence of maternal narrative style, a variable thought to be important in the development of older children's ability to produce autobiographical narratives (e.g., Fivush, 2014).

The results showed that the length of children's autobiographical narratives increased with age, a finding that is fairly typical in this area (e.g., Fivush & Schwarzmueller, 1998). Of course, an increase in narrative length does not necessarily mean that the memories themselves are any better, simply that there may be a growth in narrative competence, something that affords an increase in verbal elaboration of what is in memory (Howe, 1998). Indeed, their results also showed that one of the better predictors of children's autobiographical narrative reports was change in children's language ability. Interestingly, maternal narrative style contributed little if anything to changes in children's autobiographical narratives. Perhaps most importantly, although narrative length increased with age, the slowest variable to change was the thematic coherence of those narratives. Thus, although children across the age range studied improved dramatically in narrative competence, autobiographical narratives were neither as complete not thematically coherent as those found for adults (similar outcomes have been obtained in cross-sectional studies as well; e.g., Reese et al., 2011).

In a related prospective study in this special issue, Reese and Robertson (2018) examined childhood memories in adolescents (16-year-olds) that have been followed since they were very young (1½ years of age). In addition to assessing measures of early memory at ages 12 and 16 years, they examined measures thought to be important in the preservation of earliest memories. These included self-awareness, attachment security, nonverbal and verbal memory, language, theory of mind, narrative, and mothers' elaborative reminiscing which were measured during the early childhood phase of this research (ages 1½ to 5½ years).

There were two key findings that emerged from this study. The first was that the age of earliest memory was still changing during adolescence. That is, the majority of 16-year-olds' (73%) earliest memory was significantly later than their earliest memory when measured at 12 years of age. Second, the link between the various measures taken between the ages 1½ to 5½ years and earliest memories recalled at 12 and 16 years of age showed that elaborative maternal reminiscing was critical to the ability to remember earlier memories. However, by the age of 16 years, mothers' elaborative reminiscing was important only for those children whose level of self-awareness was lower at the age of 19 months.

Although this research does not distinguish between forgetting and retrieval explanations of infantile and childhood amnesia, it does tell us that one's earliest memory does tend to become later and later as we develop into our teenage years. These findings from a longitudinal study dovetail nicely with other findings from similar studies (e.g., Peterson, Warren, & Short, 2011) as well as with cross-sectional research (e.g., Tustin & Hayne, 2010). This work also confirms that one's ability to remember early life events involves a confluence of factors, including maternal elaborative reminiscing and self-awareness.

Another paper examined the role of mother–child conversations in remembering what happened in Kindergarten (Leichtman, Steiner, Pillemer, Camilleri, & Thomsen, 2018). Here, mothers recorded their conversations with their 5- to 6-year-old children (Study 1) and 6- to 7-year-old children (Study 2) about the child's Kindergarten year and another specific episode of their own choosing. Like other studies in 2018 (and elsewhere in the literature), mothers' elaborative conversational style predicted children's memory contributions about all of the events being remembered. Of course, as the studies just reviewed indicate, when other variables are measured simultaneously, parental conversational style is not the only factor predicting children's autobiographical memory for their experiences.

Using a slightly different tact, Sonne, Kingo, Berntsen, and Krøjgaard (2018) also examined early memories in children and attempted to specifically address the question of encoding specificity of those memories. Here, 3½-year-old children were presented with one of two unique events (i.e., a "Teddy" event or a "Game" event) that were associated with a one of two unique boxes (i.e., a red metal box or a grey plastic box). Children experienced an event in one room and then returned a week later and were tested for their memory of the event either in the same room or a different one. The results showed that changing the spatial context for retrieval (at least as implemented by changing rooms) did not alter children's ability to spontaneously retrieve the earlier experienced event. Of course, this change was one of external context and perhaps amnesia for earlier experienced events is more a matter of change in the internal (cognitive) context.

Interestingly, Tustin and Hayne (2010) have argued that differences in the dating of early memories may arise due to correlated differences in what a person (child or adult) considers to be the criteria for a memory, with these differences varying as a function of culture, gender, and a number of other individual differences variables. In the current issue, Tustin and Hayne (2018) extend this line of argument and note that what we remember from our earliest years may not actually reflect what was originally encoded about that event as a child. Indeed, as adults, we may end up embellishing these memories when asked to recall such information. In their experiment, they asked children, adolescents, and adults to remember events from different points in their lives. In this way, they could vary both the age of the rememberer and the retention interval while keeping constant the age at the time the event occurred. What they found was that adults not only provided the same amount of information about past events regardless of when it happened, but they also reported either the same amount or more information about memories from age 5, 10, and 13 than did children of those same ages. Thus, in order to truly understand what early memories are like, there may be some folly in asking adults to remember the past when it is not tempered by examining what children encode and remember about those events in the first place.

Individual differences in recalling early memories

One individual difference factor that contributes to how far back one can remember into one's childhood, formal schooling, was examined by De la Mata et al. (2018). These authors examined the role of three levels of schooling (from rudimentary literacy to primary school to formal university education) in the narration of childhood memories in Mexican adults. They asked participants to provide oral narratives of three childhood memories (not necessarily their earliest memory) and then analysed a number of factors related to these narratives. As predicted, they found a positive correlation between extent of formal education and the length, specificity, and self-orientation of childhood memories. Clearly these results show that sociocultural factors (in this case level of education) can play a critical role in one's ability to provide complex narratives about childhood memories.

Old memories in new bottles: what have we learned?

So how far have we advanced over the last several centuries? It is clear from this special issue that myriad developments contribute to a mature autobiographical memory system. These include fundamental changes in cognitive (the self, language), social (e.g., conversations about the past with others), cultural, and formal educational components in a child's development. It is laudable that many current models of autobiographical memory development incorporate multivariate theories that include self-awareness, elaborate reminiscence (with parents as well as peers), language and general memory development, attachment factors, culture, and gender, among a number of others. Additional research on other, related factors would be welcome as well. For example, examining the impact of changes in self-awareness throughout childhood, adolescence, and adulthood would contribute greatly to our understanding of the dynamic link between the self and autobiographical memory throughout the lifespan. Similarly, new research on the role that stress and trauma can play on autobiographical memory would also be worthwhile as it might dispel certain myths that early childhood stress and trauma make memories either more or less susceptible to the effects of infantile amnesia.

We have also learned that infantile and childhood amnesia do not represent abrupt transitions in memory, at least not at the behavioural level (but see later discussion concerning neuroscience evidence). As reviewed here, and as seen in other recent articles, evidence has accumulated that infantile amnesia begins early in childhood and continues through adolescence and into adulthood. But now that we know this, why would early memories be forgotten during childhood? Is it because they are no longer adaptive and have been supplanted (modified, overwritten; also see Richardson & Hayne, 2007) by newer experiences that are more germane to our current needs? After all, what good is it to keep memories of the past when they are no longer functional, either in terms of our current or future survival requirements, especially when memories of more recent experiences serve us better?

More questions: where do we go from here?

Despite all of these advances in our understanding of the development of autobiographical memory, we have still not answered the basic question as to what happens to our early memories and do they still affect our psychological development across the lifespan even if we cannot consciously remember them? Moreover, are traumatic experiences immune to infantile and childhood amnesia or do these memories also succumb to the ravages of forgetting (whether storage-based or retrieval-based)? Finally, are early memories simply poorly encoded in the first place, leading to more rapid forgetting, or are they encoded just fine but become "trapped" and irretrievable due to internal changes in one's cognitive context?

First, concerning the latter storage-retrieval issue, the evidence provided by longitudinal studies, showing that with increasing age early memories appear to become irretrievable, augers well for a retrieval interpretation of infantile and childhood amnesia. However, such data do not completely rule out the idea that early memories are poorly and incompletely encoded and stored and then simply fade into the background. Indeed, evidence from adults recalling early memories suggests that these recollections are sparse and fragmented (e.g., Akhtar et al., 2018). Moreover, often what children remember of early experiences is similarly sparse and fragmented, although, unlike adults, such findings are constrained by relatively immature language and narrative skills.

Second, concerning stress and trauma, although these issues were not dealt with specifically in this special issue, there is evidence that the majority of early memory reports do not involve emotional or traumatic events (e.g., Akhtar et al., 2018; Bruce et al., 2005). Indeed, painful and traumatic experiences early in life (e.g., circumcision without anesthetic) often do not translate into declarative memories for those experiences and behavioural evidence of their persistence often dissipating within a relatively short period of time (e.g., see Taddio, Katz, Ilersich, & Koren, 1997). Although there will no doubt be exceptions to this pattern, depending perhaps on age at the time of the experience, it would seem that for early-life (before the age of two years) experiences, such memories, like other early memories, are either very poorly encoded, forgotten rapidly, or both (for a review, see Howe, 2011).

Third, whether early experiences, consciously remembered or not, can still have an impact on subsequent psychological development is still a matter for debate. Some have argued that adverse early-life experiences are associated with the development of depression and anxiety-related illnesses in adulthood in both humans (e.g., Struber, Struber, & Roth, 2014) and non-human primates (e.g., Conti et al., 2012). It might seem from studies such as these that regardless of whether one does or does not form a conscious, autobiographical memory for these early experiences, adverse early events affect our subsequent psychosocial development. However, interpretation of these outcomes must be tempered by the fact that, at least in studies with humans, these conclusions are primarily based on correlational not causal data. Although studies with non-human animals can involve experimental (potentially causal) manipulations, it is not always clear what the link is between these various animals (primates, rats, mice) and humans.

In what follows, I summarise some crucial recent findings that shed some additional light on these questions and that suggest additional avenues of investigation. I begin with some recent neuroscience research that addresses the storage-retrieval question. I then turn to a potentially new approach to asking questions about infantile and childhood amnesia, namely, a functional/adaptive analysis of memory and forgetting.

Recent neuroscientific evidence

To be blunt, the battle still rages on as to whether memories are still there but just cannot be retrieved (Travaglia, Bisaz, Sweet, Blitzer, & Alberini, 2016) or whether they fail to store/consolidate in the first place (neurogenesis; Akers et al., 2014; Josselyn & Frankland, 2012). For example, one recently examined neuroscientific mechanism (increased neurogenesis during early infancy) has been suggested as a source of storage-based amnesia for early events. Here, given rapid neurogenesis (thought to be critical in the formation of memories) that occurs during the infantile amnesia period, memories that are formed during this time are subsequently erased or at least modified by additional experiences so that they can no longer be retrieved. This explanation squares well with a recently proposed cognitive, adaptive approach to memory whereby early memories are blended with more recent experiences in order to form schemas that better represent the world in which the young organism finds itself (for an overview, see Howe, 2011). Although these schemas provide for better organisation of experiences of the past, allowing the infant to interpret the present and anticipate the future, it comes at the expense of remembering specific, individual experiences that took place early in life.

The idea of neurogenesis as a factor in both adult forgetting and infantile amnesia certainly makes physiological sense. That is, new neurons overwrite old ones at memory sites and although this overwriting still preserves some of the structural features corresponding to the original memory, it also substantially changes its contents (particularly memory context). Importantly, however, although neurogenesis is high during the infantile amnesia period, the fact that forgetting is also high may simply be correlational. I would argue that there exists a preference to rewrite memories stored early in life with new, more representative contemporaneous information as experience accrues. What the neurogenesis data show is that while meaning may be preserved in traces that undergo rapid change, the context of what is being learned is overwritten. These findings are consistent with what we know at a cognitive level about how infant memory develops. Once these early memories are better organised, perhaps through the development of binding processes (e.g., Olson & Newcombe, 2014) that link the various features of events (including with reference to an emerging self-consciousness), they become more durable and stable, and infantile amnesia wanes.

Infantile and childhood amnesia as adaptive forgetting

There are myriad advantages to forgetting, both in childhood and adulthood. These include emotional regulation, knowledge restructuring, automatisation, and memory updating, to name but a few (for a recent review, see Nørby, 2015). Indeed, oftentimes we may sacrifice specific episodic details of experiences in order to form semantic memories about how things work in the world. For example, it is not necessary to remember every time we tried to learn how to ride a bicycle to then ride a bicycle once learning has been accomplished.

The theory just espoused concerning the forgetting of early memories is in line with the recently advanced adaptive memory view in which early memories are particularly fragile as they are being reworked across multiple experiences to generate reliable information structures that guide future behaviours. That is, earlier representations are reshaped by new experiences, iterating toward a more viable worldview that promotes accurate models that can be used to anticipate and deal with the current needs and future demands (for an overview, see Howe, 2011, 2014, 2015). After all, what would be the purpose to remembering outdated information once it has been replaced by newer, more recent (and ostensibly accurate) information? As Rovee-Collier and Cuevas (2009, p. 168) noted,

> … at each point in development, infants of all species epitomize
> a successful evolutionary adaptation … [where] they
> rapidly learn the relationships that define their niche and confer
> survival and reproductive advantage …. To meet each new set of ecological demands, infants select aspects of episodes to learn and remember until their niche changes again.

Therefore, from a more functional perspective, rapid forgetting of early experiences in light of more recent and diagnostic information may be a very adaptive mechanism. This is particularly true during early infancy where one is learning about the world and trying to form schemas (or other semantic devices) that allow the infant to survive in the environment they find themselves. Indeed, more rapid forgetting early in life may promote better adaptation to one's surroundings. That is, early infant experiences may no longer be relevant even in later infancy – knowing how to interact with objects when one can crawl may no longer be relevant once one has learned to walk. Thus, infantile amnesia may start during infancy itself!

Disclosure statement

No potential conflict of interest was reported by the author.

References

Akers, K. G., Martinez-Canabal, A., Restivo, L., Yiu, A. P., De Cristofaro, A., Hsiang, H.-L., … Frankland, P. W. (2014). Hippocampal neurogenesis regulates forgetting during adulthood and infancy. *Science, 344*, 598–602.

Akhtar, S., Justice, L. V., Morrison, C. M., & Conway, M. A. (2018). Fictional first memories. *Psychological Science, 29*, 1612–1619.

Alberini, C. M., & Travaglia, A. (2017). Infantile amnesia: A critical period of learning to learn and remember. *The Journal of Neuroscience, 37*, 5783–5795.

Bauer, P. J. (2015). A complementary processes account of the development of childhood amnesia and a personal past. *Psychological Review, 122*, 204–231.

Bauer, P. J., & Larkina, M. (2014). The onset of childhood amnesia in childhood: A prospective investigation of the course and determinants of forgetting of early-life events. *Memory, 22*, 907–924.

Bauer, P. J., & Larkina, M. (2018). Predictors of age-related and individual variability in autobiographical memory in childhood. *Memory*.

Bluck, S., & Alea, N. (2008). Remembering being me: The self-continuity function of autobiographical memory in younger and older adults. In F. Sani (Ed.), *Self-continuity: Individual and collective perspectives* (pp. 55–70). New York: Psychology Press.

Bruce, D., Wilcox-O'Hearn, L. A., Robinson, J. A., Phillips-Grant, K., Francis, L., & Smith, M. C. (2005). Fragment memories mark the end of childhood amnesia. *Memory & Cognition, 33*, 567–576.

Cleveland, E. S., & Reese, E. (2008). Children remember early childhood: Long-term recall across the offset of childhood amnesia. *Applied Cognitive Psychology, 22*, 127–142.

Conti, G., Hansman, C., Heckman, J. J., Novak, M. F., Ruggiero, A., & Suomi, S. J. (2012). Primate evidence on the late health effects of early-life adversity. *Proceedings of the National Academy of Sciences, 109*, 8866–8871.

Conway, M. A. (2005). Memory and the self. *Journal of Memory and Language, 53*, 594–628.

Conway, M. A., Loveday, C., & Cole, S. N. (2016). The remembering-imagining system. *Memory Studies, 9*, 256–265.

Cunningham, S. J., Brebner, J. L., Quinn, F., & Turk, D. J. (2014). The self-reference effect on memory in early childhood. *Child Development, 85*, 808–823.

De la Mata, M. L., Santamaría, A., Trigo, E. M., Cubero, M., Aria, S., Antalíková, R., … Ruiz, M. L. (2018). The relationship between sociocultural factors and autobiographical memories from childhood: The role of formal schooling. *Memory*.

Ece, B., Demiray, B., & Gülgöz, S. (2018). Consistency of adults' earliest memories across two years. *Memory*.

Fivush, R. (2014). Maternal reminiscing style: The sociocultural construction of autobiographical memory across childhood and adolescence. In P. J. Bauer & R. Fivush (Eds.), *The Wiley-Blackwell handbook on the development of children's memory* (pp. 568–585). West Sussex, UK: Wiley-Blackwell.

Fivush, R., & Schwarzmueller, A. (1998). Children remember childhood: Implications for childhood amnesia. *Applied Cognitive Psychology, 12*, 455–473.

Henri, V., & Henri, C. (1895). On earliest recollections of childhood. *Psychological Review, 2*, 215–216.

Howe, M. L. (1998). Language is never enough: Memories are more than words reveal. *Applied Cognitive Psychology, 12*, 475–481.

Howe, M. L. (2011). *The nature of early memory: An adaptive theory of the genesis and development of memory*. New York: Oxford University Press.

Howe, M. L. (2014). The co-emergence of the self and autobiographical memory: An adaptive view of early memory. In P. J. Bauer & R. Fivush (Eds.), *The Wiley-Blackwell handbook on the development of children's memory* (pp. 545–567). West Sussex, UK: Wiley-Blackwell.

Howe, M. L. (2015). Memory development. In R. M. Lerner (Ed.), *Handbook of child psychology and developmental science*, L. S. Liben & U. Müller (Vol. Eds.), *Vol. 2: Cognitive processes* (7th ed., pp. 203–249). Hoboken, NJ: Wiley.

Howe, M. L., & Courage, M. L. (1993). On resolving the enigma of infantile amnesia. *Psychological Bulletin, 113*, 305–326.

Howe, M. L., & Courage, M. L. (1997). The emergence and early development of autobiographical memory. *Psychological Review, 104*, 499–523.

Humphreys, G. W., & Sui, J. (2016). Attentional control and the self: The self-attention network. *Cognitive Neuroscience, 7*, 5–17.

Jack, F., & Hayne, H. (2010). Childhood amnesia: Empirical evidence for a two-stage phenomenon. *Memory, 18*, 831–844.

Josselyn, S. A., & Frankland, P. W. (2012). Infantile amnesia: A neurogenic hypothesis. *Learning & Memory, 19*, 423–433.

Leichtman, M. D., Steiner, K. L., Pillemer, D. B., Camilleri, K. A., & Thomsen, D. K. (2018). What happened in kindergarten? Mother-child conversations about life story chapters. *Memory*.

Miles, C. (1895). A study of individual psychology. *The American Journal of Psychology, 6*, 534–558.

Mulligan, N. W., & Lozito, J. P. (2004). Self-generation and memory. *Psychology of Learning and Motivation, 45*, 175–214.

Newcombe, N., Lloyd, M. E., & Ratliff, K. R. (2007). Development of episodic and autobiographical memory: A cognitive neuroscience perspective. *Advances in Child Development and Behavior, 21*, 297–340.

Nørby, S. (2015). Why forget? On the adaptive value of memory loss. *Perspectives on Psychological Science, 10*, 551–578.

Olson, I. R., & Newcombe, N. S. (2014). Binding together the elements of episodes: Relational memory and the developmental trajectory of the hippocampus. In P. J. Bauer & R. Fivush (Eds.), *The Wiley-Blackwell handbook on the development of children's memory* (pp. 285–308). West Sussex, UK: Wiley-Blackwell.

Peterson, C., Grant, V., & Boland, L. (2005). Childhood amnesia in children and adolescents: Their earliest memories. *Memory, 13*, 622–637.

Peterson, C., Warren, K. L., & Short, M. M. (2011). Infantile amnesia across the years: A 2-year follow-up of children's earliest memories. *Child Development, 82*, 1092–1105.

Prebble, S. C., Addis, D. R., & Tippett, L. J. (2013). Autobiographical memory and sense of self. *Psychological Bulletin, 139*, 815–840.

Reese, E., Haden, C. A., Baker-Ward, L., Bauer, P. J., Fivush, R., & Ornstein, P. A. (2011). Coherence of personal narratives across the lifespan: A multidimensional model and coding method. *Journal of Cognition and Development, 12*, 424–462.

Reese, E., & Robertson, S.-J. (2018). Origins of adolescents' earliest memories. *Memory*.

Richardson, R., & Hayne, H. (2007). You can't take it with you: The translation of memory across development. *Current Directions in Psychological Science, 16*, 223–227.

Rovee-Collier, C., & Cuevas, K. (2009). Multiple memory systems are unnecessary to account for infant memory development: An ecological model. *Developmental Psychology, 45*, 160–174.

Sonne, T., Kingo, O. S., Berntsen, D., & Krøjgaard, P. (2018). Thirty-five-month-old children have spontaneous memories despite change of context for retrieval. *Memory*.

Struber, N., Struber, D., & Roth, G. (2014). Impact of early adversity on glucocorticoid regulation and later mental disorders. *Neuroscience Biobehavioral Review, 38*, 17–37.

Sui, J., & Humphreys, G. W. (2015). The integrative self: How self-reference integrates perception and memory. *Trends in Cognitive Sciences, 19*, 719–728.

Taddio, A., Katz, J., Ilersich, A. L., & Koren, G. (1997). Effect of neonatal circumcision on pain response during subsequent routine vaccination. *The Lancet, 349*, 599–603.

Travaglia, A., Bisaz, R., Sweet, E. S., Blitzer, R. D., & Alberini, C. M. (2016). Infantile amnesia reflects a developmental critical period for hippocampal learning. *Nature Neuroscience, 19*, 1225–1233.

Tustin, K., & Hayne, H. (2010). Defining the boundary: Age-related changes in childhood amnesia. *Developmental Psychology, 46*, 1049–1061.

Tustin, K., & Hayne, H. (2018). Recollection improves with age: Children's and adults' accounts of their childhood experiences. *Memory*.

Wang, Q., & Peterson, C. (2014). Your earliest memory may be earlier than you think: Prospective studies of children's dating of earliest childhood memories. *Developmental Psychology, 50*, 1680–1686.

Wang, Q., Peterson, C., Khuu, A., Reid, C. P., Maxwell, K. L., & Vincent, J. M. (2018). Looking at the past through a telescope: Adults postdated their earliest childhood memories. *Memory*.

Wessel, I., Schweig, T., & Huntjens, R. J. C. (2018). Manipulating the reported age in earliest memories. *Memory*.

Index

Note: Page numbers in *italics* refer to Figures, and in **bold** refer to Tables.

accuracy of memory recall: age of earliest memories 1–2, 19–24, 26, 80, 83–84, **84**, 87, 95, 96; episodic memories 1, 95, 96; location memories 64

adaptive memory theory 120

adolescents: consistency of memories 29, 30, 33, 81, 85, 86–87; dating memories 7, 81, 82–88; earliest memory recall 2, 7, 29, 81, 82–88; episodic memories 93–100, **96**, *97*; life-chapter memories, coherence of 51; *see also* children

adults: consistency of earliest memories 29–35, **34**, 81; contextual cues and recall 46; dating memories 7, 32–33, 34–35, 92, 116–117; earliest memory recall 7, 29, 30–35; episodic memories, supplementary details 93, 115–116, 118; *see also* young adults

age (estimates) of earliest memories: accuracy 1–2, 19–24, 26, 80, 83–84, **84**, 87, 95, 96; adolescents 7, 81, 82–88; adults 7, 32–33, 105–112, 116–117; and autobiographical knowledge use 10, 14; and belief in memory below age 2 (research study) 6, 9, **9**, 10, 11, **13**, 14; children 6, 81, 92; confidence (of study participants) in estimates **9**, 10, **13**, 14; consistency 32–33, 34–35, 81; contextual cues and factors 1–2, 6, 7, 8–17; cultural/ethnic differences 16–17, 26, 80, 111, 118; and education levels 105–106; fragment memories 7; gender differences 80, 87; malleability 2, 6–7, 15–17; and maternal narrative style 86; and parental verification 2, 19–24, 26, 80, 83–84, **84**, 87, 95, 96; in previously reported studies 4, 6, 7, 19, 26, 28, 35, 63, 79, 92, 116; strategies for estimates **9**, 10–11; telescoping errors *see* telescoping errors in dating memories; young adults 2, 8–17, **9**, **13**, 20–26, 32–33; *see also* childhood amnesia

autobiographical memories: age of onset 79–80, 93, 115; as constructive 115–116; cultural contexts and differences 103–105; defined 50; and education levels 104–112, **108–109**, 118; emergence and development, factors influencing 26, 28, 49, 50, 51, 60, 63–64, 66, **67**, 68–75, **71**, **72**, **73–75**, 79–81, 87, 104–112, 118; and "fictional" early memories 116–117; importance of cognitive self 28, 38, 115, 118; and language skills 3, 28, 38, 50, 63, 64, 72, **73–75**, 80–81, 86, 98–99; life-chapters *see* life-chapter/repetitive memories; narrative coherence 50–51, 64, 66–77, **73–75**; narrative production, age-related changes 66–77, *69*, *70*; narrative production, and non-autobiographical story recall 64, 70, **72**, 76; theories of 11, 79–81, 87; *see also* episodic memories

autonoetic theory of autobiographical memory 79–80

autonomous orientation of memories 107, 108, **108–109**, *109*, 110

Bachevalier, J. 92

Bauer, P. J. 1, 2, 3, 6, 19, 22, 23, 26, 29, 31, 33, 34, 35, 46, 50, 63, 64, 65, 66, 75, 76, 79, 80, 87, 88, 92, 93, 115

Bender, M. 110

Berna, F. 105, 110

Berntsen, D. 46

Bohn, A. 51

Boyacioglu, I. 12

Bruce, D. 1, 7, 8, 11, 15, 16, 19, 22, 23, 26

Cala, M. J. 111

Cavanaugh, J. C. 66

Centrality of Event Scale (CES) 13

characteristics of memories 8, 11, **11**, 13, **15**, 98; autonomous orientation 107, 108, **108–109**, *109*, 110; consistency 30, 31, 33, **34**, 35; cultural differences 103; emotional intensity 8, **11**, 13, **15**, **34**; emotional valence 8, **11**, **15**, 26, **34**; gender differences 109, 110–111; questionnaires 8, **11**, 13, **15**; self-focusing index 107, **108–109**, *109*; self/others ratio 107–110, **108–109**; sensory details 8, **11**, 13; specificity 107, 108, **108–109**; vividness **11**, 13, **34**; volume 107, 108, **108–109**

Chen, Y. 51

childhood amnesia: age of onset 19, 79, 116, 117, 120; gender differences 28; vs. infantile amnesia 115; offset *see* age (estimates) of earliest memories; possible influencing factors and mechanisms 28, 38, 46, 50, 79–81, 115–116, 119–120; and telescoping errors 20, 26; theories of 79–80, 87, 92, 120; *see also* infantile amnesia

children: consistency of earliest memories 29, 33, 81; contextual cues and recall 39; dating memories 6, 9, 19–20, 29, 80, 81, 92, 117–118; episodic memories 57–59, 93–100, **96**, *97*, 98; episodic memories, age of encoding 93; episodic memories, coding 66–68, **67**; episodic memories, narrative coherence 64, 65–77, 81, 98–99; life-chapter memories 50–57, 58–61; location memories, accuracy of 64; non-autobiographical story recall 64; parent-child conversations *see* parent-child conversations; *see also* adolescents

Cleveland, E. S. 82, 83

cognitive self, development of 28, 38, 115, 118

Cole, M. 105, 109

consistency of earliest memories 28–29; adolescents 29, 30, 33, 81, 85, 86–87; adults 29–35, **34**, 81; children 29, 33, 81; measurement methods 30, 31, 34; young adults 29–35, **34**; *see also* earliest memory recall

consistency of later memories 29, 105

contextual cues and factors: and adults' memory recall 46; and age estimates of earliest memories 1–2, 6, 7, 8–17; and childhood amnesia 46; and children's memory recall 39; and earliest memory recall 7, 8–17; encoding specificity principle 39; environmental cues 39–47, *40*, **45**; and spontaneous memory recall 39, 40–44, *40*, **44**, **45**, 46–47; and strategic recall 44–45, **45**, 46; Timeline procedure

94–95, *94*; and young adult's memory recall 8–17; and young children's memory recall 3, 39, 40–44, *40*, **44**, 45, 46–47, 48; *see also* parent-child conversations
Conti, G. 119
Conway, A. R. A. 105
Conway, M. A. 11, 16, 50, 110, 117
courtroom evidence 99–100
Cross, S. E. 103
cultural/ethnic contexts and differences: age of earliest memories 16–17, 26, 80, 111, 118; autobiographical memories 103–105; characteristics of memories 103; parent-child conversations 60, 104, 111; self-construals 103–104; telescoping errors 26

dating memories: adolescents 7, 81, 82–88; children 6, 9, 19–20, 29, 80, 81, 92, 117–118; earliest memories *see* age (estimates) of earliest memories; as reconstructive activity 6–7, 20; telescoping errors *see* telescoping errors in dating memories; young adults 2, 8–17, **9**, **13**, 20–26, *22*, *23*, *24–25*, 32–33, 34–35
Davis, P. 104
De la Mata, M. L. 105–106, 107, 109, 110, 111
Deese-Roediger-McDermott paradigm 99

Eacott, M. J. 19, 22, 23, 30
earliest memory recall: adolescents 2, 7, 29, 81, 82–88; adults 7, 29, 30–35; consistency *see* consistency of earliest memories; and early childhood variables 85–86, **85–86**, 87; fragment memories 7; memory characteristics 11, **11**, 13; young adults 8–17, **9**, **13**, 20–26, 29, 30–35
education levels: and autobiographical memories 104–112, **108–109**, 118; parental, and reminiscing style 105, 112
elaborative parental conversational style: and age of earliest memories 86, 87; characteristics of 51, **54**, **55**, **57**, **58**; coding 53, **53**, 68; and episodic memory recall 57–58, **58**; and life-chapter memory recall 51, 54–57, **55**, **58**, 59–60; and memory detail and quality (earlier studies) 49, 51; and older children's autobiographical narratives 76; and parental education levels 105; and socio-cultural model of memory 51; and volume of early memories (earlier studies) 80–81; *see also* parent-child conversations
Emerging Life Story Interview 82
emotional intensity of memories 8, **11**, 13, **15**, **34**
emotional valence of memories 8, **11**, **15**, 26, **34**
encoding specificity principle 39
episodic memories 3, 7; accuracy 1, 95, 96; adolescents 93–100, **96**, *97*; adults, supplementary details 93, 115–116, 118; children *see under* children; coding 95–96; level of detail 93, 96–98, **96**, *97*, **98**, 99–100; parent-child conversations 49–50, 51, 62, 66, 68; recall, and cues 7; supplementing with additional detail 93, 99–100, 115–116, 118; young adults 93–100, **96**, *97*, **98**; *see also* autobiographical memories
event memories: characteristics 11, **11**; defined 9; as earliest memory 10–11, 14; *see also* non-autobiographical story recall

false memories 99
family narrative practices 3; *see also* parent-child conversations
Farrant, K. 82, 83
"fictional" early memories 116–117
Field, A. 88
Fivush, R. 49, 51, 53, 59, 60, 66, 80, 87, 88, 104, 110, 117
fragment memories: defined 9; encouraging reporting of 8; vs. snapshot memories 16; subjective measurement of fragmentation 8–9, **9**, 13, **13**; underreporting 7, 10, 16, 118
Freud, S. 63, 79, 88, 92
Frued, S. 1, 50

gender differences: age of earliest memories 80, 87; autonomous orientation of memories 110; childhood amnesia 28; consistency of later memories 29; level of detail in reporting memories 93, 97–98; memory characteristics 109, 110–111; parent-child conversations 104
Ghetti, S. 64
Greenfield, P. M. 104, 106, 110
Gross, J. 93, 99, 100
Grysman, A. 110–111
Gryson, A. 93
Güler, O. E. 64

Habermas, T. 50–51, 88
Haden, C. A. 60, 63
Han, J. J. 64
Harley, K. 63, 87
Harley, K. 82, 83
Hayne, H. 3, 46, 79, 81, 92, 104
Heidenreich, T. 105, 109
Henri, V. 28, 92, 93
Herschkowitz, N. 81
Hershkowitz, I. 39
Howe, M. L. 79, 87, 115, 119, 120
Howes, M. 1, 19, 93

image memories 7; *see also* fragment memories
infantile amnesia 115, 118, 119–120; *see also* childhood amnesia
involuntary memories *see* spontaneous memories and recall

Jack, F. 1, 3, 7, 17, 19, 20, 25, 29, 33, 34, 80, 81, 82, 83, 87, 100, 115
Janssen, S. J. 26
Janssen, S. M. J. 105, 110
Johnson, M. 93
Josselyn, S. A. 80

Kağıtçıbaşı, C. 104, 110
Kam, C. 104
Keller, H. 104–105
Kihlstrom, J. 81, 86
Kihlstrom, J. F. 29, 30, 31, 33, 34, 35
Kingo, O. S. 6, 7, 8, 15, 105, 109
Krøjgaard, P. 39, 45, 46
Küntay, A. 105, 111

La Rooy, D. 39, 45
Lai, W. F. 105, 111
language skills: and autobiographical memory 3, 28, 38, 50, 63, 64, 72, **73–75**, 80–81, 86, 98–99; and earliest memory recall 85, **85–86**, 86; and maternal narrative style 72, **72**; measuring 66, **67**
Larkina, M. 29, 64, 66, 76
Leichtman, M. D. 39, 53, 60
Levya, D. 104
life-chapter/repetitive memories: defined 9, 50; as earliest memory 14; emergence of 50–51; parent-child conversations 3, 51–57, 58–61, 62; and self-conceptions 50; young children 3, 51–57, 58–61
literacy levels *see* education levels
location memories: accuracy 64; in life-chapter memories 50, 51, 52, 54, 55, 56, 58, 59; and Memory Characteristics Questionnaire 13
Loftus, E. F. 26

MacDonald, S. 79, 93
Malinoski, P. T. 6
Markus, H. R. 103–104

memory characteristics *see* characteristics of memories
Memory Characteristics Questionnaire (MCQ) 13, **15**; AMCQ 8, **11**
metamemory 64, 66, **67**, 69–70, **71**, 72, **72**, 75–77
Miles, C. 28, 63
Mistry, J. 105
Morris, G. 67, 81, 87
mother-child conversations *see* parent-child conversations
Mullen, M. K. 7, 16, 93

Narrative Coherence Coding Scheme (NaCCs) 66–67
narrative organisation of memories 7
Neisser, U. 49, 80
Nelson, K. 3, 39, 50, 51, 87
neurogenesis and childhood amnesia 80, 119–120
Newcombe, N. 115
Newcombe, R. 82, 83
Niedzwienska, A. 110
non-autobiographical story recall: and autobiographical story narrative production 64, 70, **72**, 76; children 64
Nørby, S. 120

Olson, I. R. 80, 111, 112, 120
Orbach, Y. 39
Ornstein, P. A. 80, 81
Oyserman, D. 104

parental verification of childhood memories: age estimates 2, 19–24, 26, 80, 83–84, **84**, 87, 95, 96; content accuracy 95, 96; parental telescoping errors 26
parent-child conversations: coding 52–53, **53**, 68; conversation instructions 62; cultural differences 60, 104, 111; elaborative style *see* elaborative parental conversational style; episodic memory conversations 49–50, 51, 62, 66, 68; gender differences 104; life-chapter conversations 3, 51–57, 58–61, 62; and parental education levels 105, 112; samples 62
Perner, J. 79–80
Peterson, C. 1, 20, 22, 23, 25, 26, 29, 30, 33, 34, 64, 76, 81, 86, 87, 100, 117
Peterson, T. 6, 8, 15
Pillemer, D. B. 6, 26, 50, 53, 60, 79
Prebble, S. C. 81, 88

qualities of memories *see* characteristics of memories

Reese, E. 3, 40, 50, 53, 63, 64, 66, 76, 79, 80–81, 82, 83, 87, 88, 100, 117
Reid, T. 105, 109
reminiscing style, parental *see* elaborative parental conversational style
repetitive memories *see* life-chapter/repetitive memories
Richardson, R. 118
Riggins, T. 76
Roebers, C. 64
Rogoff, B. 105, 109–110, 111
Rovee-Collier, C. 120
Rubin, D. C. 6, 26, 87

Sahin-Acar, B. 60
Schaefer, A. 12
schooling, and autobiographical memories 104–112, **108–109**, 118
Schröder, L. 111
Scribner, S. 109–110, 111, 112
self-construals, cultural contexts 103–104

self-focusing index of memories 107, **108–109**, 109
self/others ratio of memories 107–110, **108–109**
self-recognition theory of autobiographical memory 11, 79, 80–81
semantic memory 7
sensory details of memories 8, **11**, 13
Simcock, G. 81
sketchy memories *see* fragment memories
Smith, S. M. 39, 45
snapshot memories 8, 11; characteristics **11**, 16; defined 9; as earliest memory **9**, 10–11, **13**, 14, 15 vs. fragment memories 16; *see also* fragment memories
specificity of memories 107, 108, **108–109**
spontaneous memories and recall: coding 42–43, **44**, 48; and contextual cues 39, 40–44, *40*, **44**, 45, 46–47; defined 38; vs. voluntary/strategic recall 38–39; young children 39, 40–44, *40*, **44**, 45, 46–47, 48
Steiner, K. L. 50, 51
Strange, D. 93, 98, 99–100
stress and trauma, and early memories 118, 119
Struber, N. 119
Suggate, S. P. 83

Taddio, A. 119
telescoping errors in dating memories 20; adolescents 84–85, 87; adults 32–33, 34–35, 92; children 6, 19, 20, 29, 80, 81; cultural/ethnic differences 26; parents 26; postdating bias 6, 19–20, 22, *22*, 24, *24*, 25–26, 29, 34, 35, 80, 81, 84–85, 92; predating bias 19, 20, 22, *22*, 24, *24*, 34; young adults 20–26, *22*, *23*, *24–25*, 34–35
Thompson, C. P. 26
Thomsen, D. K. 50, 59
Timeline procedure 94–95, *94*
Todd, C. M. 39
Tõugu, P. 88
trauma and stress, and early memories 118, 119
Tulving, E. 39
Tustin, K. 6, 7, 15, 20, 25, 80, 87, 95, 117, 118

Usher, J. A. 88

vicarious memory 3
Vignoles, V. 104
vividness of memories **11**, 13, **34**
volume of memories 107, 108, **108–109**

Wang, Q. 2, 3, 4, 6, 16, 19–20, 21, 24–25, 26, 29–30, 31, 33, 34, 35, 50, 59–60, 63, 79, 80, 86, 88, 93, 100, 104, 106, 107
Watkins, O. C. 45
Welch-Ross, M. K. 81
Wessel, L. 105, 109
West, T. A. 16
White, S. H. 50
Woodock, R. W. 66

young adults 20–26; consistency of earliest memories 29–35, **34**; consistency of later memories 29; contextual cues and recall 8–17; dating memories 2, 8–17, **9**, **13**, 20–26, *22*, *23*, *24–25*, 32–33, 34–35; earliest memory recall 8–17, **9**, **13**, 20–26, 29, 30–35; episodic memories 93–100, **96**, *97*, **98**; *see also* adults
young children: contextual cues and recall 3, 39, 40–44, *40*, **44**, 45, 46–47, 48; life-chapter memory 3, 51–57, 58–61; and memory recall 2, 3; parent-child conversations *see* parent-child conversations; spontaneous memories and retrieval 39, 40–44, *40*, **44**, 45, 46–47, 48; *see also* children